Policy-Making in EU Security and Defense

European Administrative Governance Series

Series Editors: **Thomas Christiansen**, Professor of European Institutional Politics, Department of Political Science, Maastricht University, The Netherlands

Sophie Vanhoonacker, Professor of Administrative Governance, Department of Political Science, Maastricht University, The Netherlands.

The series maps the range of disciplines addressing the study of European public administration. In particular, contributions to the series will engage with the role and nature of the evolving bureaucratic processes of the European Union, including the study of the EU's civil service, of organization aspects of individual institutions such as the European Commission, the Council of Ministers, the External Action Service, the European Parliament, the European Court and the European Central Bank and of inter-institutional relations among these and other actors. The series also welcomes contributions on the growing role of EU agencies, networks of technical experts and national officials, and of the administrative dimension of multilevel governance including international organizations. Of particular interest in this respect will be the emergence of a European diplomatic service and the management of the EU's expanding commercial, foreign, development, security and defence policies, as well as the role of institutions in a range of other policy areas of the Union.

Beyond this strong focus of EU administrative governance, the series will also include texts on the development and practice of administrative governance within European states. This may include contributions to the administrative history of Europe, which is not just about rules and regulations governing bureaucracies, or about formal criteria for measuring the growth of bureaucracies, but rather about the concrete workings of public administration, both in its executive functions as in its involvement in policy-making. Furthermore the series will include studies on the interaction between the national and European level, with particular attention for the impact of the EU on domestic administrative systems.

European Administrative Governance Series
Series standing order ISBN 978–1137–29475–3 (paperback) and 978–0230–35976–5 (cased)

You can receive future titles in this series as they are published by placing a standing order. Please contact your bookseller or, in case of difficulty, write to us at the address below with your name and address, the title of the series and the ISBNs quoted above.

Customer Services Department, Macmillan Distribution Ltd, Houndmills, Basingstoke, Hampshire RG21 6XS, England

Policy-Making in EU Security and Defense

An Institutional Perspective

Hylke Dijkstra
University of Oxford

© Hylke Dijkstra 2013

All rights reserved. No reproduction, copy or transmission of this publication may be made without written permission.

No portion of this publication may be reproduced, copied or transmitted save with written permission or in accordance with the provisions of the Copyright, Designs and Patents Act 1988, or under the terms of any licence permitting limited copying issued by the Copyright Licensing Agency, Saffron House, 6–10 Kirby Street, London EC1N 8TS.

Any person who does any unauthorized act in relation to this publication may be liable to criminal prosecution and civil claims for damages.

The author has asserted his right to be identified as the author of this work in accordance with the Copyright, Designs and Patents Act 1988.

First published 2013 by
PALGRAVE MACMILLAN

Palgrave Macmillan in the UK is an imprint of Macmillan Publishers Limited, registered in England, company number 785998, of Houndmills, Basingstoke, Hampshire RG21 6XS.

Palgrave Macmillan in the US is a division of St Martin's Press LLC, 175 Fifth Avenue, New York, NY 10010.

Palgrave Macmillan is the global academic imprint of the above companies and has companies and representatives throughout the world.

Palgrave® and Macmillan® are registered trademarks in the United States, the United Kingdom, Europe and other countries.

ISBN 978–1–137–35786–1

This book is printed on paper suitable for recycling and made from fully managed and sustained forest sources. Logging, pulping and manufacturing processes are expected to conform to the environmental regulations of the country of origin.

A catalogue record for this book is available from the British Library.

A catalog record for this book is available from the Library of Congress.

Typeset by MPS Limited, Chennai, India.

Contents

List of Tables and Figures	vi
Acknowledgements	vii
List of Abbreviations	ix
1 Introduction	1
2 Delegation and Agency in International Relations	20
3 Institutional Development in EU Security and Defense	46
4 Policy-Making in EU Security and Defense	78
5 Military Operation in Bosnia	100
6 Monitoring Mission in Aceh	124
7 Military Operation in Chad	145
8 Rule of Law Mission in Kosovo	167
9 Conclusion	190
Notes	205
References	208
Index	223

List of Tables and Figures

Tables

1.1	Indicators of influence of EU officials	15
4.1	Overview of the planning documents	83
5.1	Chronology of Operation Althea	104
5.2	Influence of EU officials in Operation Althea	123
6.1	Chronology of the AMM	128
6.2	Commission's accompanying measures for AMM	139
6.3	Influence of EU officials in the AMM	143
7.1	Chronology of EUFOR Tchad/RCA	149
7.2	Commission's accompanying measures for EUFOR Tchad/RCA	162
7.3	Influence of EU officials in EUFOR Tchad/RCA	166
8.1	Chronology of EULEX Kosovo	171
8.2	Projects under the Instrument for Pre-Accession	186
8.3	Influence of EU officials in EULEX Kosovo	189
9.1	Influence of EU officials in the CSDP	196

Figure

4.1	Organizational chart of the EEAS	81

Acknowledgements

One of the most enjoyable things about life in academia is without doubt the exchange of ideas and collaboration with others. This social dimension of research has not only made my life more durable while writing this book, it has also significantly improved my thinking about the Common Security and Defence Policy. This is my turn to acknowledge all support.

It is always tricky to single out individuals, but I think it is fair to say that I owe – like many others – most gratitude to Sophie Vanhoonacker. Our relations date back to 2004, and two years later we started collaborating on a small research project dealing with an obscure body in the European Union called the General Secretariat of the Council. That this would be the start of this book and a career in academia I did not realize then. Equally, I need to thank Tannelie Blom, who was always ready and available for intellectual debate.

My book is, however, not completely a Maastricht product. The foundations were laid at the University of Cambridge. Christopher Hill's continual support was important in this respect. Moreover, whenever my views became a bit intergovernmental, Geoffrey Edwards was there to set me straight. I also spent a month at Stockholm University. Jonas Tallberg and his colleagues were most generous in hosting me. The final revisions were made at the University of Oxford, where I am currently an EU Marie Curie fellow. The University and Nuffield College continue to inspire.

I want to mention furthermore Bram Akkermans, Patrick Bijsmans, Thomas Christiansen, Thomas Conzelmann, Christine Neuhold, Gergana Noutcheva, Petar Petrov, Karolina Pomorska, Paul Stephenson, Esther Versluis, and Maarten Vink at Maastricht University. With so much EU expertise within one department, there is hardly any need to look elsewhere. In addition, I have greatly benefited from my discussions with David Allen, Doreen Allerkamp, Derek Beach, Sven Biscop, Gijs Jan Brandsma, Tom Casier, Mai'a Cross, Simon Duke, An Jacobs, Ana Juncos, Stephan Keukeleire, Nadia Klein, Alexander Mattelaer, Benjamin Pohl, Michael H. Smith, and Wolfgang Wagner.

Credit is also due to the great many interviewees who kindly took their time to receive me and patiently answered my undoubtedly ignorant questions. I recall in particular a very senior EU official, who invited me to his private home on a Saturday morning to spend four hours explaining to me the details of EU foreign policy. This was a rewarding experience. In academic terms, it is worth noting that several journal articles have served as stepping stones for this book. These articles benefit from countless referees' reports and suggestions by editors. Similarly, in preparing this manuscript, I have had the pleasure of working with Amber Stone-Galilee and I cannot speak highly enough of the review process.

During the final phase of writing this book, I received funding from the People Programme (Marie Curie Actions) of the European Union's Seventh Framework Programme (FP7/2007–2013) under REA grant agreement No. [298081].

Finally, I need to thank my parents and sister for their continuous support. They were the first to show me Europe and they promoted a notion of internationalism along the way. The last word of thanks is for my wife, Karine, whom I met at about the same time that I started doing my very first interviews in Brussels. She has been with me since.

List of Abbreviations

AEI	Archive of European Integration
AFP	Agence France-Presse
AFSOUTH	Allied Forces Southern Europe (NATO)
AMIS	African Union Mission in Sudan
AMM	Aceh Monitoring Mission
ASEAN	Association of Southeast Asian Nations
CARDS	Community Assistance for Reconstruction, Development and Stabilisation
CFSP	Common Foreign and Security Policy
CIVCOM	Committee for Civilian Aspects of Crisis Management
CMPD	Crisis Management Planning Directorate
CMI	Crisis Management Initiative
CONOPS	Concept of Operations
COREPER	Committee of Permanent Representatives
COREU	*Correspondance européenne*
COSA	Commission on Security Arrangements
CPCC	Civilian Planning and Conduct Capability
CPCO	*Centre de planification et de conduite des opérations*
CRCT	Crisis Response Coordination Team
CSDP	Common Security and Defence Policy
CVCE	*Centre virtuel de la connaissance sur l'Europe*
DG	Directorate-General
DG AGRI	Directorate-General for Agriculture and Rural Development
DG DEVCO	Directorate-General for Development and Cooperation
DG E	Directorate-General External Relations (Council)
DG E VIII	Directorate for Defence Issues
DG E IX	Directorate for Civilian Crisis Management

DG ELARG	Directorate-General for Enlargement
DG RELEX	Directorate-General External Relations (Commission)
DG SANCO	Directorate-General for Health and Consumers
DPKO	Department of Peacekeeping Operations (UN)
DSACEUR	Deputy Supreme Allied Commander Europe (NATO)
ECHO	Directorate-General for Humanitarian Aid and Civil Protection
EEAS	European External Action Service
EPC	European Political Cooperation
ESDP	European Security and Defence Policy
EU	European Union
EUCE	European Union Command Element
EUFOR	European Union Force
EULEX	European Union Rule of Law Mission in Kosovo
EUMC	European Union Military Committee
EUMS	European Union Military Staff
EUPM	European Union Police Mission in Bosnia-Herzegovina
EUSR	European Union Special Representative
FOC	Full Operational Capability
FT	*Financial Times*
GAM	*Gerakan Aceh Merdeka* (Free Aceh Movement)
GDP	Gross Domestic Product
HOMs	Heads of Mission
ICR	International Civilian Representative in Kosovo
ICTY	International Criminal Tribunal for the former Yugoslavia
IFOR	Implementation Force (NATO)
IHT	*International Herald Tribune*
IMD	Initiating Military Directive
IMP	Interim Monitoring Presence
INTCEN	Intelligence Centre
IOC	Initial Operational Capability

ISAF	International Security Assistance Force (NATO)
KFOR	Kosovo Force (NATO)
LOTs	Liaison and Observation Teams
MINURCAT	United Nations Mission in the Central African Republic and Chad
NATO	North Atlantic Treaty Organization
NGO	Non-governmental Organization
OHQ	Operations Headquarters
OHR	Office of the High Representative in Bosnia
OPLAN	Operations Plan
OSCE	Organization for Security and Cooperation in Europe
PIFWCs	Persons Indicted for War Crimes
PMG	Political-Military Group
POLAD	Political Advisor
PSC	Political and Security Committee
PSOR	Provisional Statement of Requirements
RELEX group	Group of External Relations Counselors
SAP	Stabilization and Association Process
SEA	Single European Act
SFOR	Stabilization Force (NATO)
SHAPE	Supreme Headquarters Allied Powers Europe (NATO)
SITCEN	Joint Situation Centre
SOFA	Status of Forces Agreement
SRSG	Special Representative of the Security-General (UN)
TEC	Treaty establishing the European Community
TEU	Treaty on European Union
TFEU	Treaty on the Functioning of the European Union
UK	United Kingdom
UN	United Nations
UNAMID	African Union/United Nations Hybrid operation in Darfur
UNHCR	United Nations High Commissioner for Refugees

UNIFIL	United Nations Interim Force in Lebanon
UNMIBH	United Nations Mission in Bosnia-Herzegovina
UNMIK	United Nations Mission in Kosovo
UNOSEK	Office of the Special Representative for Kosovo (UN)
UNPROFOR	United Nations Protection Force
UNSC	United Nations Security Council
UNSCR	United Nations Security Council Resolution
US	United States
WEU	Western European Union

1
Introduction

In 2005 and 2006 the European Union (EU) sent a monitoring mission to the Province of Aceh in Indonesia. Its mandate was to observe the implementation of the Memorandum of Understanding between the Government of Indonesia and the Free Aceh Movement. This peace agreement, which had been negotiated in the wake of the devastating tsunami of 2004, brought a decades-long civil conflict to an end. For 16 months, EU monitors oversaw the disarmament of the rebels and verified the withdrawal of government troops. The former belligerents had specifically asked for the EU's involvement as a result of its credibility and perceived neutrality. The Aceh Monitoring Mission is still considered as a major success story. While the EU monitors concluded their mission seven years ago, the Province of Aceh has remained relatively peaceful ever since. The EU was a force for good and delivered added value.

The Aceh Monitoring Mission is just one example of the 27 crisis management missions that the EU has carried out in the last 10 years. Through its Common Security and Defence Policy (CSDP), it has sent soldiers, monitors, policemen, judges, prosecutors, penitentiary officers and customs guards to many of the world's trouble spots. They carry out a whole range of functions from conflict prevention to peace-making and post-conflict stabilization (TEU, Article 43). Some CSDP operations are small-scale in character, but the EU often makes a considerable effort. In addition to Aceh, its contribution in places such as Afghanistan, Bosnia, Chad, Congo, Kosovo, Georgia, and Somalia is significant. As a result of all this activity, the CSDP has become one of the most dynamic fields of European integration. The CSDP has helped the EU develop into a more serious security actor in international relations.

Looking at the plethora of different missions across three continents, it is sometimes hard to believe that the CSDP is barely a decade old.

Envisioned at a bilateral summit of France and the United Kingdom (UK) in St Malo in 1998, it is one of the most recent additions to the process of European integration. Historically, issues of security and defense were not within the realm of the EU. It was indeed only in 2003 – with the launch of the Police Mission in Bosnia – that the EU started autonomously to send uniformed personnel on missions abroad. In spite of the fact that the CSDP is such a recent phenomenon, the EU has hardly had the time to learn the ropes of effective crisis management. Shortly after some of the first operations were concluded, it launched missions of substantial size, significant intensity and with serious mandates.

The various CSDP operations have perhaps received most visibility. Yet as they increased in number, so did the supportive bureaucratic services in Brussels. Behind the scenes, a complete machinery was put in place. The Crisis Management Planning Directorate (CMPD), for instance, carries out initial fact-finding missions and is in charge of strategic planning after a crisis situation presents itself. The Military Staff (EUMS) and the Civilian Planning and Conduct Capability (CPCC) prepare detailed operational documents. The Operations Centre serves as a civil–military headquarters. The Regional Departments provide the CSDP officials with background expertise about the political processes on the ground. Finally, the Intelligence Centre (INTCEN) carries out risk assessments and collects intelligence. These bureaucracies have all been created as a result of the CSDP. They were originally part of the Council Secretariat, but have since been transferred to the European External Action Service (EEAS).

The sight of uniforms near the Schuman roundabout in Brussels came as a shock to many observers. Not only had the EU generally been regarded as a civilian organization, the involvement of EU officials in the formulation and implementation of foreign policy also marked a clear break with past practice. After all, EU foreign policy – of which the CSDP is an integral part – was traditionally known for its "intergovernmental method" of policy-making. Contrary to much of the rest of European integration, this implied that decisions were predominantly made in the national capitals and that the EU bureaucracies were kept at arm's length. Most of the foreign policy activity in the EU was traditionally for consultation and information only. In other words, EU foreign policy was regarded as the *domaine réservé* of the member states. It was best seen, as Simon Nuttall (1992: 11) once noted, as a "private club operated by diplomats for diplomats."

In reality, of course, EU foreign policy had never been completely intergovernmental. Since its foundation in 1970, it had gradually become institutionalized (Smith 2004). Yet time and again, the member states preferred to rely on their own resources. Rather than delegating foreign policy tasks to the EU bureaucracies, which was the practice in other parts of European integration, the six-monthly rotating Presidency was given responsibility for convening meetings, issuing declarations and speaking on behalf of the Union. By keeping such tasks "in-house," the member states benefited from consultation and cooperation in foreign policy, while avoiding excessive sovereignty loss. When France and the UK held their bilateral summit in St Malo, there were only two dozen EU officials working on foreign policy in Brussels. Half of them were seconded from the member states.

The rapid institutionalization and the creation of a plethora of EU bureaucracies in security policy, which took place in the period 1999–2009, therefore presents an important empirical puzzle. Whereas the member states had previously made the explicit choice not to involve EU officials in their foreign policy deliberations, they now decided otherwise and empowered the Brussels-based bureaucracies in the area of security and defense.[1] This change of heart is particularly surprising given the importance that states typically attach to sovereignty in these areas. Indeed, the CSDP is arguably a "least likely" case for the delegation of functions to EU officials. Moreover, the speed with which the member states have established the CSDP machinery in Brussels remains puzzling. After years of limited delegation in EU foreign policy, the member states created a professional CSDP machinery in less than a decade.

The involvement of Brussels bureaucracies in the CSDP also presents a theoretical puzzle. Scholars have repeatedly claimed that international cooperation between states in security issues and economic affairs takes different paths. Stanley Hoffmann (1966), for example, made a famous distinction between "high" and "low" politics. High politics, he argued, follows the logic of diversity, which makes cooperation problematic and the involvement of EU officials undesirable. As a matter of fact, the whole International Political Economy research agenda followed from the observation that international economic relations were more cooperative than international relations theory suggested. Several scholars have furthermore tried to show, by means of game theory and formal reasoning, that the nature of international security results in different degrees of institutionalization (Jervis 1982; Lipson 1984; Haftendorn, Keohane and Wallander 1999; Wagner 2003). Theoretically, the creation of EU bureaucracies in Brussels for the purpose of the CSDP was not expected.

These empirical and theoretical puzzles therefore demand a closer look at the establishment of the EU bureaucracies in Brussels. They merit an institutional perspective on policy-making in EU security and defense. Now that the Treaty of Lisbon (2009) has come into force, it is a good moment to study the rapid creation of the CSDP machinery following the turn of the twenty-first century. This book first takes a step back and asks *why do the EU member states delegate functions in the area of security and defense?* As noted before, delegation is by no means automatic. States tend to jealously guard their sovereignty. Delegation is therefore never the default option. This holds particularly true in the areas where sovereignty really matters, such as security and defense. Studying the very rationale of delegation and the considerations of the EU member states will thus provide important insights.

Analyzing delegation in the CSDP constitutes, however, only a first step. Institutional design is, after all, not only a dependent variable, but also affects the way policy is made. Indeed, the very reason why member states have long preferred to keep EU bureaucracies away from security and defense is that they knew that bureaucratic involvement inevitably alters policy outcomes. To put it slightly differently, the consequences of delegation are arguably the real topic of interest here. CSDP officials in the External Action Service (and previously the Council) carry out important functions such as fact finding, preparing risk assessments, and drafting military options. It is on the basis of their work that the member states make crucial decisions concerning force deployments and the conduct of the CSDP operations. Despite the fact that security and defense remains one of the least likely areas for EU officials to exert influence, it is clear that the contribution of the CSDP officials will not be completely impartial.

The role of international bureaucracies and their officials in policy-making is increasingly a topic of interest in within international relations (Barnett and Finnemore 2004; Biermann and Siebenhuener 2009; Oestreich 2012). Following the delegation of certain competences, functions or resources, international civil servants are in a position to affect policy-making in international organizations. Indeed, any act of delegation implies, almost by definition, a certain loss of control over policy outcomes. The member states cannot have it all. They cannot benefit from outsourcing functions to Brussels while at the same time keeping full control. As David Lake and Matthew McCubbins (2006: 343) succinctly state "no pain, no gain."

The influence of international bureaucrats is, however, more than a necessary by-product of delegation. It is a topic that demands academic attention in its own right. Particularly in the realm of international security, where states are regarded as the main actors and the importance of self-help and sovereignty is stressed (e.g. Waltz 1979), the study of the work of several hundred CSDP officials is potentially important. Indeed, the role of member states in the CSDP is well explored (e.g. Miskimmon 2007; Mérand 2008; Matlary 2009; Gross 2009a; Peters 2010; Cross 2011; Weiss 2011), while the EU bureaucracies remain mostly ignored. To get a clearer understanding of what instances of delegation allow the CSDP officials to affect policy, the second question of this book is *under which conditions do the EU officials exercise influence (i.e. agency) in the area of security and defense?* By answering this question, the book provides an institutionalist perspective of day-to-day policy-making and offers unique views from behind the scenes.

These two research questions constitute subsequent steps in the research design of this book. The book first addresses delegation and then studies agency. Both questions are nonetheless related. The rationale for delegation, as noted, affects the bureaucratic resources – and thus the agency – of EU officials (Pollack 2003; Majone 2001). Moreover, when EU officials exert excessive agency, states may take tasks back in future delegation rounds (Pratt and Zeckhauser 1985; Tallberg 2002a). Keeping this interactive nature in mind, both research questions are addressed as analytically distinct *loci*. This is the normal practice in the study of principal–agent relations in the EU and international organizations (Pollack 2003; Hawkins et al. 2006; Tallberg 2006; Milner and Moravcsik 2009). It has considerable conceptual and empirical advantages.

The literature

EU bureaucracies and other supranational institutions have been the subject of academic debate since the beginning of European integration.[2] In the *Uniting of Europe*, Ernst Haas (1958) put them at the heart of further unification, as they could help to cultivate spillover. By delegating authority to the EU bureaucracies, Haas argued, the member states introduced new actors in their game. These actors would have an interest in further integration and the ability to exert entrepreneurship in the negotiations, trigger functional spillover across sectors, and act as focal points for like-minded societal actors. His ideas – known as neofunctionalism – were shared by contemporaries. Leon Lindberg (1963), for example, outlined several scope conditions, under which delegation to supranational bureaucracies could result in further integration. The idea that the EU bureaucracies play an important role was thus present in academia from the start.

The theory of neofunctionalism has largely been discredited in academia – not least by Haas himself (1975). Despite several qualifications, spillover and the process of European integration were described by proponents of neofunctionalism as automatic. The actions of French President Charles de Gaulle quickly proved otherwise (Hoffmann 1966). The empirical record of neofunctionalism is frequently used as a critique. At a theoretical level, however, it also has several weaknesses. First, the theory does not explain why states delegate tasks. Haas (1964) noted functional pressures to move beyond the nation-state, but the voluntary nature of delegation was not addressed. Second, it remained unclear why EU officials exclusively held the key to entrepreneurship and further integration (Moravcsik 1993, 2005). Third, neofunctionalism failed to account for control mechanisms of the member states (Taylor 1990). Neofunctionalism has nevertheless made a significant revival since the Single European Act of 1987 (Sandholtz and Zysman 1989; Tranholm-Mikkelsen 1991; Burley and Mattli 1993, but also Niemann 2006).

Intergovernmentalism became, as time passed by, the main rival theory to neofunctionalism. It emphasizes the centrality of the member states in the process of European integration (Hoffmann 1966; Milward 1984, 1992; Moravcsik 1991, 1993, 1998). Intergovernmentalism has significantly contributed to our understanding of European integration, but it has preciously little to say about the role of the EU bureaucracies. According to Andrew Moravcsik (1998), they only played a marginal role in treaty negotiations, as they did not possess better negotiating means than the member states. Member states delegate functions, because the EU bureaucracies can make the agreements between the member states more credible. By delegating "the right to propose, legislate, implement, interpret, and enforce agreements," Moravcsik notes, "governments restructure future domestic incentives, encouraging future cooperation by raising the cost of nondecision or noncompliance" (ibid.: 73). Credible commitments between the member states are necessary, as the future is inherently uncertain and complex agreements tend to be incomplete (Williamson 1985).

While neofunctionalism was thus expecting too much from the EU bureaucracies, the theory of intergovernmentalism neglected their role. Intergovernmentalism could be conveniently used, for decades, in the area of foreign and security policy to explain non-delegation and non-cooperation. Moravcsik, in particular, has made a powerful argument that due to a lack of domestic pressures for cooperating in the area of high policies (cf. economic lobby groups), the member states never had an incentive to pool and delegate sovereignty. The trouble is, of course, that the sovereign member states eventually decided to create the above-mentioned EU bureaucracies. This significant change cannot

Introduction 7

be explained convincingly by developments in domestic preference formation. As a result, the explanatory and predictive power of (liberal) intergovernmentalism is limited in the case of EU foreign and security policy.

This black-and-white debate over the role of the EU bureaucracies between the theories of neofunctionalism and intergovernmentalism reached a stalemate by the mid-1990s. To "move on," a number of "middle-range" theories were developed. These do not aim to explain the whole process of European integration, but focus on specific instances. With a view to the role of the EU bureaucracies, rational choice institutionalism – and the use of the principal–agent model – stands out (e.g. Pollack 1997, 2003; Meunier and Nicolaïdes 1999; Majone 2001; Tallberg 2000, 2002a, 2006; Keleman 2002; Elgie 2002; Beach 2005; Franchino 2007; Alter 2009). By analyzing under which conditions the EU bureaucracies matter rather than whether they matter, this approach tries to come to "a series of hypotheses about supranational autonomy... more precise than those generated by either neofunctionalist or intergovernmentalist theory" (Pollack 1997: 101). The great merit of rational choice institutionalism is that it takes the preferences of the member states and their sovereignty concerns as the starting point, but it also accepts that delegation inevitably involves a loss of agency.

Rational choice institutionalism argues that delegation results from intentional cost–benefit analyzes by the member states. Member states have a demand for certain functions, which can be met by the EU bureaucracies. Jonas Tallberg (2002a: 25) notes that member states "face the choice of whether to perform the desired functions 'in-house', or to 'out-source' them." In line with the theory of intergovernmentalism, credible commitments are a prominent explanation for delegation. By monitoring and enforcing agreements, the Commission and the Court of Justice can improve domestic compliance (Pollack 2003). EU agents can also provide a (partial) solution to the problem of incomplete contracting: one of the main functions of the Court is to interpret agreements in case of a lack of clarity among the member states. Rational choice institutionalism, however, goes beyond intergovernmentalism in that it also studies many other reasons for delegation (Pollack 2003; Tallberg 2002a; Kassim and Menon 2003). In particular, the efficiency of policy-making is important (Majone 2001; Beach 2005; Tallberg 2006). EU bureaucracies can facilitate the process between the member states.

Rational choice institutionalism stresses that delegation leads, almost by definition, to a loss of agency on the side of the member states (Kiewiet and McCubbins 1991). The member states take these sovereignty costs into account when making their initial delegation decisions. Uncertainty may result in non-delegation or less delegation than is functionally optimal (Stone 2009; Miller 2005). The member states are also likely to establish control mechanisms to avoid excessive influence by the EU officials. These range from strict mandates to agent selection, institutional checks and balances, re-contracting, appointment procedures, limited budgets, regular reporting requirements, and sending seconded national experts (e.g. Hawkins et al. 2006). Such mechanisms, however, are costly and inhibit the EU bureaucracies from effectively carrying out their work. Apart from formal competences, EU officials have other resources that they can use to exert agency. They may have a better insight than the individual member states into the state-of-play of policy-making. They may also have informational surpluses resulting from their process and content expertise (e.g. Wall and Lynn 1993; Beach 2005; Tallberg 2006).

While neofunctionalism, intergovernmentalism and rational choice institutionalism have their distinctive features, they are essentially based on the same actor-centered, intentional, and utilitarian ontology.[3] It is therefore worthwhile to contrast them with constructivist approaches. A word of warning is appropriate. Despite recent advances in constructivist literature, scholars have still to develop a comprehensive and internally consistent theory of delegation and agency that can compete with the rational choice approaches outlined above. This has partially to do with actor-centered intentionality, which is to some extent implicit in delegation and agency. The constructivist literature is more interested other concepts, such as institutional adaptation, development and isomorphism (Goodin 1996; Offe 2006). It prefers to study preference formation of actors, resulting from the context in which they are operating, rather than to analyze their struggles for power (Checkel 2005). It is nonetheless possible to think of competing non-utilitarian explanations concerning delegation and agency.

Constructivist approaches, for example, suggest that while the member states may intentionally delegate tasks, their reasons for doing so are structure-related and not necessarily calculative (e.g. March and Olsen 1984, 1998). In their delegation decisions, member states create bureaucracies that they consider as "appropriate" or legitimate. Their preferences are endogenous. They take into account best practices and they avoid structures that in their opinion have not worked. Such action is only rational, Kathleen McNamara (2002: 48) notes, if "placed within a very specific cultural and historical context that legitimises delegation." Learning is important in this respect (Checkel 2001). Through their experiences, member states internalize notions of what is considered as appropriate. The creation and empowerments of the European Parliament are a prime example of delegation resulting from such legitimacy concerns (e.g. Rittberger 2003). Even the rationalist Mark Pollack (2003) notes that there are no functionalist reasons to get the Parliament involved. In addition to the logic of appropriateness, sociological and historical institutionalists point at the difficulty of changing institutions to the needs of the time. Increasing returns lead to path dependence and inefficiency (March and Olsen 1998; Pierson 2004).

Constructivism also has things to say about agency. In particular, it argues that EU officials are not necessarily competence-maximizers. Similarly, the diplomats of the member states do not act as control mechanisms. Instead, the EU officials and diplomats try to come to mutually acceptable decisions as a result of deliberate problem-solving (e.g. Joerges and Neyer 1997a, b; Lewis 1998, 2005). In this process, it is not the relative size of the member states, their veto-power, or the formal rules that matter. It is about the claim of different actors to authority and their ability to put forward persuasive arguments on the basis of better information and expertise (e.g. Kratochwil 1989; Hall 1997; Barnett and Finnemore 1999, 2004; Risse 2000). Constructivists are conscious of the fact that having a good argument is not always sufficient in international relations (Risse 2000). This alternative explanation is nonetheless distinct from the rationalist argument, which is essentially based on the ability of the EU officials to intentionally manipulate the member states.

To conclude, rational choice and constructivism both have important things to say about delegation and agency in the EU. They provide competing explanations of why the member states empower the Brussels-based bureaucracies and why EU officials exert influence in day-to-day policy-making. The rationalist argument stresses the efficiency gains and sovereignty costs of delegation, while constructivists are concerned with legitimacy, learning and the historical context of decisions. Rationalists furthermore focus on the asymmetries of information and control mechanisms in everyday policy processes, while the constructivist explanation is essentially about authority, problem-solving, and the better argument.

The argument

After this overview of the literature on the role of EU bureaucracies, it is now time to turn to the field of the CSDP. The argument presented below is based on rational choice institutionalism and uses the principal–agent model. In the sensitive field of security and defense – it is argued – delegation is intentional and based on utilitarian calculations by the member states. It takes place because the EU bureaucracies make CSDP policy-making more efficient. The member states balance such efficiency gains with their anticipated loss of sovereignty. After the delegation of functions, EU officials try to exert influence in order to maximize their competences. They do so through their privileged position in the policy process and their superior expertise. While the principal–agent model is thus applicable in the field of EU security and defense, the CSDP also has its distinctive features. These are reflected in the argument.

The starting point of this book is that delegation is best seen as a process rather than a one-off affair (Tallberg 2002a). In order to better understand contemporary developments, one has to go back to the start of foreign policy coordination under European Political Cooperation (EPC). Since the 1970s, the member states have gradually established, through subsequent delegation rounds, EU bureaucracies in the area of "high politics." Their means were initially a series of informal reports outside the legal structure of European integration. When EPC became more prominent, the member states made use of formal treaty change and subsequent implementing decisions. More recently, in establishing the CSDP institutional framework, the member states have avoided extensive treaty revisions and have instead preferred lower level joint actions and Council decisions. Delegation in the area of foreign and security policy was a process of subsequent decisions, in which member states used feedback from previous rounds to better appreciate the effects of delegation.

This process of delegating functions to EU bureaucracies was by no means automatic. The member states constantly balanced the costs and benefits of delegation. The initial focus of the member states was to make foreign policy cooperation run more efficiently by addressing the negotiation, coordination, and representation costs. They sometimes delegated tasks to EU agents, but their strong preference was to keep tasks in-house by delegating them to the six-monthly rotating Presidency. Delegation to the EU bureaucracies only seriously started with the Amsterdam Treaty, which significantly strengthened the capability for information analysis and representation. With the creation of the CSDP, delegation was on top of the agenda. To efficiently plan civilian and military operations, the member states established the relevant planning bureaucracies in Brussels. In the area of implementation – command and control – the member states also debated, time and again, the empowerment of the EU bureaucracies. The recent Treaty of Lisbon seeks to strengthen the information, coordination, and representation functions.

While the member states thus lowered their transaction costs of cooperation by delegating negotiation, information, coordination, and implementation functions to the EU bureaucracies, they were also very conscious of the loss of sovereignty that is intimately connected to the delegation process. As a matter of fact, the member states often did not delegate functions at all. To give an example: for the first 17 years of foreign policy cooperation (1970–1987), there was no standing secretariat. Moreover, while the demand for a military headquarters and efficient command and control in the CSDP is crystal clear, some of the member states have so far prevented the creation of such facilities in Brussels. They have also, time and again, delegated functions to agents, over which they have most control. Foreign policy tasks were initially given to the Presidency, then to the EPC Secretariat, the Council Secretariat and currently the EEAS. Member states avoided at all costs equipping the formally autonomous and resource-rich Commission in the area of foreign policy. Arguably, however, the Commission remains the best agent to provide executive functions in the EU.

There exists thus a clear trade-off between the anticipated efficiency gains of delegation and the anticipated sovereignty costs. As a result, the member states almost always delegated fewer tasks to the EU bureaucracies than was functionally optimal. In addition to instances where sovereignty trumped efficiency, one also has to account for the uncertainty connected with delegation and the potential for unintended effects. Such uncertainty naturally made the member states even more reluctant to delegate. The UK, for example, is not afraid of a small-scale command element in Brussels. It is worried, however, that this will be the first step and will lead to a sizeable military headquarters. Moreover, when member states anticipated that the re-contracting of functions would be difficult as a result of their own divisiveness, they avoided delegation as well. While the rationale for delegation in foreign and security policy was thus one of efficiency, the outcomes were typically sub-optimal, with risk-averse member states being wary of the future.

Given the subsequent delegation of tasks, under which conditions do EU officials exercise influence in the CSDP? Since they facilitate policy-making, their formal competences are limited (Majone 2001). Their influence thus has to come from other bureaucratic resources. In the specific field of security and defense, EU officials have accumulated two kinds of resources. First, they are at the heart of the machinery, which gives them informational advantages over the member states in terms of process expertise, knowledge about the state-of-play of policy-making, and the preferences of all actors. Second, EU officials have relatively strong content expertise in civilian crisis management (i.e. police, monitors, rule of law) compared to the member states. The diplomats of the member states, who control the EU officials during civilian missions, are at a particular disadvantage compared to their military counterparts. They are thus less capable of keeping Brussels on a tight rein. As a result of their position and content expertise, EU officials exert substantial influence in the shaping of the agenda. They have more influence in civilian than in military operations.

In shaping the agenda of the CSDP, EU officials have not been at the forefront of generating ideas. Many ideas for operations have been around (Kingdon 1984). These included the EU's responsibility in the Western Balkans or the need to "do something" about Darfur. Other ideas come from the United Nations (UN) or non-governmental organizations. EU officials have, however, been very effective in using some of these ideas to further their private interests by putting them on the European agenda. In all four case studies of this book, they were involved much earlier in these dossiers and in the planning of the missions than the large majority of the member states. They sometimes worked in collaboration with one or two member states, but also as actors in their own right. The head start of EU officials was in all four cases at least four months, but in some cases it was more than a year. Given that the CSDP is marked by rapid response, this is substantial. In all cases, the involvement of EU officials at an early stage led to an advantageous position and to a *fait accompli* for most of the member states.

As regards content expertise, there is a difference in the planning of military and civilian missions. While states have improved their military art to perfection, they still have very limited experience in sending police officers, monitors, or even prosecutors and judges abroad. Civilian doctrine thus remains underdeveloped. For this reason, member states have been more reluctant to delegate tasks in civilian than in military crisis management. However, given challenging civilian operations in Afghanistan, Georgia, and Kosovo, the member states eventually had to delegate for functional reasons. EU officials have conducted no fewer than 18 civilian missions in the last 10 years. They have accumulated significant content expertise. Yet while the member states have delegated additional tasks in civilian crisis management, they have not strengthened their main control mechanism: the Committee for the Civilian Aspect of Crisis Management (CIVCOM). Compared to the Military Committee (EUMC), CIVCOM remains a junior body. It lacks expertise, high-quality instructions from the capitals, and is overloaded.

EU officials can therefore exert more influence in civilian than military operations.

When looking at delegation and agency in EU security and defense, the principal–agent model thus presents a useful analytical framework. It gives a rather precise picture of the cost–benefit analyzes of the member states in their delegation decisions. The efficiency gains of delegation are weighed against anticipated sovereignty costs. In case of uncertainty about the costs or benefits, the member states are likely to be wary of delegation. This can lead to non-delegation or too little delegation. The model also allows for a nuanced analysis of the influence of EU officials. It identifies the conditions under which agency takes place, such as a privileged position and superior information. In some instances (agenda-setting; civilian crisis management), the influence of EU officials can be described as excessive. In most instances, however, the member states have their agents under control.

Methodology

This argument can only be sustained by empirical evidence. Yet before we can embark on a tour of the CSDP in the remainder of this book, which covers about 40 years and civilian and military crisis management activities across three continents, some words on methodology are required. As mentioned above, this book addresses the two research questions separately in empirical terms. Chapter 3 discusses the delegation of functions in EU security and defense. Chapters 5–8 focus on the influence of EU officials.

Delegation is extensively analyzed in European integration and in international relations more broadly. This book takes a qualitative approach and studies empirically the most important instances of delegation and non-delegation in the field of the CSDP. These include the delegation decisions taking place in the context of the various Treaties, but also lower level Council Decisions. Studying instances of non-delegation is important, since those are the moments where sovereignty concerns trumped functional considerations. Through detailed process-tracing (George and Bennett 2005), the book tries to uncover the precise reasons of the member states for empowering the EU bureaucracies. In terms of sources, preparatory documents and the negotiation positions of the member states are the starting point. Such official documents are, however, not always available. This book therefore complements them with other empirical sources – newspaper articles and, where necessary, semi-structured elite interviews. The use of secondary literature and the *mémoires* of the leading actors is important as well. By bringing all these sources comprehensively together, this book tries to paint a rich picture of the various instances of (non-)delegation.

Researching the second question is less straightforward. Influence, after all, is a notoriously difficult concept to measure. In terms of the definition of influence, the ontological choices of this book are an important starting point. Given the assumption of actor intentionality, various structure-related forms of influence are not analyzed (e.g. Bachrach and Baratz 1962; Lukes 1974). Influence therefore takes place when EU officials get the member states to do something that they would not otherwise do (cf. Dahl 1957: 203). The member states are conceptualized as a collective principal (Nielson and Tierney 2003). While some of the member states may join forces with EU officials as a result of converging interests, at the end of the day the member states collectively hold decision-making power. This is particularly the case in the CSDP, where there is a unanimity requirement. In the most extreme case – that only one member state has a goal conflict with the EU officials – the latter thus exert influence when *they* get the member state in question to do something it would not otherwise do. If the member state joins the consensus due to peer pressure of the other member states, it is of course not an instance of influence.

An important method to measure influence is by means of process-tracing through in-depth case study analysis. This allows us to get a "reasonably good knowledge of nearly all factors influencing a political decision" (Dür 2008: 563). It also allows for counterfactual reasoning. One can, for example, ask whether the member states collectively would have done the same had it not been for the actions of the EU officials. Case study research, needless to say, has several drawbacks (ibid.). This book consciously addresses them. First, it studies *four* CSDP operations instead of just one or two cases to allow for better comparison. This remains exceptional in single-authored studies on the CSDP. Second, the number of observations within the case studies is increased (King, Keohane and Verba 1994) by looking at *three distinct phases* of the policy process: agenda-setting, decision-making, and implementation. Third, this book uses explicit indicators to measure influence (see Table 1.1). As such, it provides a yardstick that allows for cross-case comparisons.

External validity does not come at the expense of internal validity. Despite the fact that most official documents dealing with the CSDP remain restricted, this book is based on rigorous empirical research. For the case studies, it analyzes publicly available official documents

Introduction 15

Table 1.1 Indicators of influence of EU officials

High	EU officials played (with one/two member states) a *leadership role* during a phase of the policy process.
	Indicators: (a) active participation in discussions; (b) pursuing and achieving major distinctive ideas/policies; (c) having exclusive contacts with third parties; (d) acting on the basis of own resources (e.g. budget and personnel).
Medium	EU officials were a *necessary condition* in explaining the outcome of a phase of the policy process.
	Indicators: (a) active participation in discussions; (b) pursuing and partially achieving distinctive ideas/policies; (c) having contacts with third parties; (d) partially acting on the basis of own resources (e.g. budget and personnel).
Low	EU officials *actively participated* in the phase of the policy process, but their input was not indispensable.
	Indicators: (a) active participation in discussions.
None	EU officials were *not involved* in the phase of the policy process or at most only participated at the margins.
	Indicators: (a) no/limited of participation in discussions.

and it studies newspaper articles and secondary literature. Most importantly, however, it relies on data from 106 semi-structured elite interviews, which have been conducted with 98 officials from the Council Secretariat, the Commission, the permanent representations, ministries, embassies, international organizations, operations headquarters, the CSDP operations, and non-governmental organizations. Interviewees were selected on the basis of their functions. In all cases, interviews were conducted with at least one desk officer of the Council Secretariat and one of the Commission, one diplomat and/or military officer of the Presidency or leading member states, and one senior official in the operations ((deputy) Operations/Force Commander or Head of Mission). Most of the interviews lasted around one hour.

Various words on case selection are also apposite. Four CSDP missions have been selected on the basis of two main criteria: civilian and military missions/missions taking place in and outside Europe. These choices are theoretically informed. Civilian and military missions differ in terms of the planning process, command and control structure, recruitment of personnel, and operational doctrine. This logically leads to different resource asymmetries between the member states and the EU officials, control mechanisms, and opportunities for influence. The second criterion is whether the missions are taking place inside or outside Europe. Within Europe, the EU as a whole is actively engaged through pre-accession policies and financial instruments. It is interesting to see whether this makes a difference for the CSDP. In addition, the interests of the members states differ toward the neighborhood and toward areas further afield. Most member states, for example, have a clear Western Balkan strategy; few have truly global foreign policies.

The EU has carried out 27 CSDP operations to date. The question therefore remains how to select case studies within the four defined categories. This book has selected the most salient cases – defined in terms of (a) executive mandate, (b) size, and (c) duration. As smaller and less salient missions can more easily be dismissed as exceptional outliers, the choice for salient operations makes the evidence stronger. The security sector reform mission in Guinea-Bissau, which employed a few dozen EU officials, is less important than the monitoring mission in Georgia consisting of some 300 European personnel. Finally, it is important to note that this book does not include non-cases (where an operation was discussed but did not take place). This has to do with the lack of empirical sources, since non-cases are often not extensively discussed by the member states and they do not make it far in terms of planning documents. The selected CSDP operations in this book are the military operation in Bosnia-Herzegovina, the monitoring mission in Aceh, the military operation in Chad, and the rule of law mission in Kosovo.

Organization of the book

This book deals with delegation and agency in the CSDP. Both processes are, of course, intimately connected. As noted above, however, this book treats them as analytically distinct. In other words, the first part of the book deals with the question of why member states delegate, while the second part studies the agency of EU officials in the CSDP. The book consists of seven substantive chapters.

Chapter 2 provides the theoretical framework for analysis. First, it employs rational choice institutionalism to better understand why the member states delegate tasks to the Brussels-based bureaucracies in the CSDP. It argues that member states face transaction costs of cooperation, which can be lowered through delegation. Such efficiency gains come, however, at a sovereignty cost. In their delegation decisions, the member states thus carefully balance anticipated gains with losses. As a result, member states delegate fewer functions than would have been optimal. The use of feedback loops may, however, lead to new delegation rounds.

Second, this chapter discusses why EU officials can exert influence in the CSDP. It establishes four conditions. For a start, EU civil servants need to have goal conflicts with the member states. They also require superior bureaucratic resources. Their influence furthermore depends on the control mechanisms of the member states and the opportunities for influence in the policy process.

Chapter 3 presents an empirical-historical analysis of why the member states have (not) delegated tasks at various moments in time in the CSDP. It starts by giving a short overview of the various delegation rounds in EU foreign policy proper starting with the Luxembourg Report from 1970. It continues with the Treaty of Amsterdam (1999), which delegated many foreign policy tasks to the Council Secretariat. This made the Council Secretariat the logical home as well for the CSDP services. The chapter then turns to the delegation of functions in the CSDP. It shows that while the relevant bureaucracies were quickly established, the member states kept a number of functions "in-house," such as the Operations Headquarters. Finally, the chapter deals with the Treaty of Lisbon of 2009 and the decisions that have been made during its implementation. The conclusion gives an overview of the important moments of delegation and discusses how the rationalist theories help us to better understand these key episodes of European integration.

Chapter 4 is descriptive in nature. It provides a comprehensive description of the CSDP policy process. It starts with the process of agenda-setting, continues with decision-making, and concludes with implementation. In these three sections, it discusses from an informal institutional perspective the role of all the actors involved in a particular part of the process. In this respect the chapter goes beyond a number of publications that list the formal roles of actors and processes in CSDP policy-making. As such, it provides the basis for the case study Chapters 5–8. The chapter makes use of examples from the case studies to illustrate the points.

Chapter 5 presents the first case study. It deals with the European Union Force (EUFOR) Althea in Bosnia. This is the largest and longest EU military operation (2004–date). The chapter starts by describing how Javier Solana pushed the member states to take over the ongoing military operation from the North Atlantic Treaty Organization (NATO). All the crisis management procedures had just been established, so he argued that it was a good idea to try them in practice. Solana teamed up with France and the UK and they withstood the pressure of the United States (US) during the height of transatlantic tensions. The chapter continues with the decision-making phase, during which Solana tried to make the mission "new and distinct" from the NATO effort. He failed miserably, as the member states preferred continuity. During the actual implementation of the mission, however, the Force Commander (on the suggestion of Solana) tried through innovative means to make the operation "new and distinct" by fighting organized crime. This led to conflict with the member states, after which Althea was downsized. The termination of the operation, however, has taken a very long time and continues to date. The chapter concludes by giving an overview of the influence of the EU officials during the policy-making process.

Chapter 6 analyzes the Aceh Monitoring Mission in Indonesia (2005–2006). It commences with the Helsinki negotiations under the leadership of the former Finnish President Martti Ahtisaari, which led to a peace agreement between the Government of Indonesia and the Aceh rebels. It shows how EU officials were involved in the process from the very beginning and how they planned the monitoring mission. It then discusses the decision-making process in Brussels, during which Solana and his civil servants presented the member states with a *fait accompli* and found an innovative way of financing the operation. It subsequently moves on to the implementation phase, in which the EU officials held leadership positions in the mission. As with the previous chapter, this chapter ends by giving an overview of the influence of EU officials.

Chapter 7 is about the military operation of the EU in Chad and the Central African Republic (2008–2009). While this was a French-inspired operation, the chapter pays attention to the role of EU officials in early strategic planning. It highlights a number of bureaucratic tricks that France and the EU bureaucracies employed to convince the other member states of the merits of this operation. The chapter, however, subsequently discusses how EU officials were not able to affect the force generation process and the start of the operation. Major delays, in fact, took place due to the reluctance of many member states to send forces. Similarly, EU officials had very little impact on the implementation of the operation. The Operation and Force Commanders actually changed the initial plans in accordance with the changing circumstances on the ground. Finally, EU officials played a marginal role in getting the UN to agree to the takeover of the mission after the one-year mandate had expired.

Chapter 8 deals with the final case study: the rule of law mission of the EU in Kosovo (2008–date). The starting point is the 2004 riots, which set in motion a transition process from the UN Mission in Kosovo (UNMIK) to the European Union Rule of Law Mission in Kosovo (EULEX) operation. This chapter points at the involvement of Solana and his civil servants at the early moments of the process. It goes further into the status negotiations between Serbia and Kosovo and the parallel planning of the mission. It shows that the EU officials made a planning assumption that there would be a final settlement on status in order to be able to continue to plan the mission. The disagreement between the member states on the future status of Kosovo allowed the EU officials leeway. The chapter also pays substantial attention to the unilateral declaration of independence and the period in the run up to the mission. The extensive contact between UN and EU officials particularly stands out. The chapter finally describes the first two years of implementation. It concludes with an overview of the findings.

The conclusion of this book (Chapter 9) brings all the different findings together. It discusses why the member states delegated tasks in light of the alternative explanations. It shows that the rationalist account, as established above, provides good explanatory value in many instances of delegation. The chapter then compares the findings from the different case study chapters and explains the variation in influence of EU officials. It shows that EU officials have been particularly prominent in agenda-setting due to their favorable position in the policy process. It also shows that EU officials exerted more influence in the civilian than the military operations. This can be explained by the lack of control mechanisms in civilian crisis management.

2
Delegation and Agency in International Relations

This chapter presents the theoretical argument for delegation and agency in the CSDP. It explains why the member states delegate functions in this sensitive area and under which conditions EU officials exert agency. In addressing these research questions, it uses rational choice institutionalism and the principal–agent model. The chapter starts with delegation. It argues that delegation is best seen as a process in which member states at subsequent moments make cost–benefit calculations on whether to provide the EU bureaucracies with new functions or not. Delegation can be beneficial, as it potentially lowers the transaction costs of cooperation. However, it also involves a number of sovereignty costs, which limit delegation. The second section discusses the agency of EU officials. It starts with the goal conflicts between member states and EU officials. It then provides an overview of the resources of EU officials and the control mechanisms of the member states. It concludes by identifying opportunities for agency in the different phases of the policy process.

Delegation in the European Union

Rational choice institutionalism – and the principal–agent model – sees the delegation of functions to EU bureaucracies as a cost–benefit analysis by the member states (Keohane 1984; Pollack 1997; Thatcher and Stone Sweet 2002). Delegation takes place, because EU bureaucracies can carry out particular functions better and/or cheaper than the member states. Member states, in this respect, "face the choice of whether to perform the desired functions 'in-house,' or to 'outsource' them" (Tallberg 2002a: 25). The benefits of delegation must be sought in the ability of EU bureaucracies to lower the transaction costs of cooperation, while delegation at the same time inevitably results in some sovereignty costs. Studying the delegation process is critical, as it tells us something about the institutional setting in which EU bureaucracies operate, and the strategic resources that they have at their disposal. After identifying the initial rationale for delegation, more precise propositions can be formulated concerning institutional design and the opportunities for agency (e.g. Pollack 1997, 2003; Majone 2001; Tallberg 2000, 2002a).

In much of the rationalist literature, delegation is simplified to a one-shot game: at a certain moment in time, principals decide to delegate tasks to an agent because the benefits outweigh the costs. In reality, of course, the EU bureaucracies were not created all at once. This book therefore conceptualizes delegation as a "dynamic and interactive [process] subject to bargaining and revision by the parties" (Tallberg 2002a: 37). Over time, the member states make a number of subsequent delegation decisions, which in turn inform future delegation decisions. Apart from the fact that such conceptualization better reflects the empirical reality, it has two important theoretical consequences. First, by analyzing delegation as a process it becomes possible to account for a more incremental approach to institutional development. Given the uncertainty about the unintended effects of delegation, member states are likely to prefer delegation in smaller steps. Second, and related, the member states will be conscious of (the limits to) their ability to re-contract in future moments of delegation. This will inform their choices.

Under the assumption of "bounded rationality," which is typically a necessary condition for delegation, actors cannot completely oversee the long-term effects of their actions (e.g. Pierson 1996, 2004). Risk-averse actors, however, tend to know that their foresight is limited. They anticipate unintended consequences and they take them into account in their decisions (Abbott and Snidal 2000; Koremenos 2005). If there is uncertainty on the anticipated costs and benefits – which there generally is – actors are likely to be wary of delegation. Taking an incremental approach to delegation constitutes a functional solution to this problem. Through feedback loops, actors can better understand the consequences of delegation. Oliver Williamson notes, in this regard, that "once the unanticipated consequences are understood, those effects will thereafter be anticipated and the ramifications can be folded back into the organisational design. Unwanted costs will then be mitigated and unanticipated benefits will be enhanced" (quoted in Tallberg 2002a: 37).

While an incremental approach can have its benefits, delegation is not a teleological process leading automatically to strong and massive EU bureaucracies. The second consequence of conceptualizing delegation as a process is the "shadow of the future." In their delegation decisions, actors will take the possibility of future re-contracting into account. If actors anticipate that re-contracting will be difficult due to multiple "veto players" and a "joint decision trap" (e.g. Scharpf 1988; Tsebelis 1995, 2002), they are likely to be more reluctant to delegate in the first place. They may also insist on sunset clauses, unanimity in budget and personnel decisions, and strict appointment procedures for agents. The idea that the member states anticipate unintended consequences and problems with re-contracting makes this rationalist explanation of delegation quite distinct from incrementalism, which is so prominent in historical institutionalism.

Why delegate: efficiency gains

So what are the benefits from delegation? The rationalist answer is that delegation helps the member states to reduce their transaction costs of cooperation. The idea of transaction costs originated in the discipline of economics and a short recap is instructive. They have been defined by Kenneth Arrow as the "costs of running the system" (quoted in Williamson 1985: 18). Transaction costs differ from production costs, which are the main supply-side costs. They include search costs, contracting costs, monitoring costs, and enforcement costs (Dyer 1997). Oliver Williamson (1985) makes a useful analytical distinction between *ex ante* and *ex post* transaction costs. The former are costs involved in "drafting, negotiating and safeguarding an agreement" (ibid.: 20). The latter result from the fact that – under bounded rationality – a contract is inherently incomplete and there is a risk of non-compliance. *Ex post* costs need to be taken into account during the negotiating phase. Often the anticipation of non-compliance prevents an agreement in the first place.

The creation of institutions, and delegation in particular, can lower the costs of transactions between two or more actors. The establishment of a marketplace is a typical example. It lowers the search costs, because it brings sellers and buyers together. Moreover, if there is a choice of products in a marketplace, it becomes cheaper for potential buyers to compare products on quality, leading to more efficient transactions. Another, yet related, example is the delegation of tasks to arbitration courts (Abbott et al. 2000). This constitutes a credible solution to the problem of non-compliance and incomplete contracting. As a relatively neutral third party, courts can interpret agreements in case of *ex post* disagreement. This may give a buyer in a marketplace, for instance, more guarantee of reimbursement in case the product eventually turns out of inferior quality. By having such guarantees, actors will be more likely to buy the product. It therefore decreases the transaction costs of cooperation and benefits all actors involved.

The transaction cost approach is also highly relevant in the study of political science and EU bureaucracies. Agreements between *political* actors can be conceptualized as transactions as well and their formulation and implementation involve several costs. Transaction costs are indeed particularly visible in the EU, where negotiations are permanent, linked and continuous (Elgström and Smith 2000). The member states thus have strong incentives to reduce their negotiation costs. Delegation is one possibility. Moreover, the prospect of non-compliance and incomplete contracting are key issues in European integration, where the member states need to abolish trade barriers and adopt EU legislation. Needless to say, the use of economic concepts in the discipline of political science is not automatic (e.g. Moe 1984, 1990; Miller 2005). The *political* context needs to be accounted for, as it does not necessarily follow the economic logic of efficiency. Political power and sovereignty are, in this respect, important variables that put limits on delegation (Knight 1992; Abbott and Snidal 2000).

Ex ante transaction costs

The member states incur a number of *ex ante* transaction costs of cooperation. Three categories are usefully distinguished: negotiation, information, and coordination costs. They can be addressed by delegating functions to the EU bureaucracies. *Negotiation costs* in the EU are undoubtedly amongst the highest of any international organization. On a daily basis, thousands of diplomats and civil servants meet in different committees to discuss the details of all sorts of policies. If this process is sub-optimal, it becomes a very expensive affair. The member states thus have strong incentives to keep these costs as low as possible. Given the magnitude of EU negotiations, their complexity, the multinational environment, and the bounded rationality of actors, there is a functional demand for agenda and procedural management, brokerage and administrative support (e.g. Beach 2004, 2005; Tallberg 2004, 2006). These demands are major rationales for the delegation of functions to EU agents, whether they are rotating chairmanships and/or bureaucracies.

Agenda and procedural management is important, because of the risk of the endless cycling of proposals when all actors involved in policy-making have an equal right of initiative (e.g. Riker 1980; Shepsle and Weingast 1984, 1995). In the area of foreign and security policy, this certainly holds true given the volatile nature of the international system and the fact that all member states have their own interests and pet projects. Multilateral negotiations are also complex, as they "are not only multi-party, but also multi-issue and multi-level" (Tallberg 2006: 22). This increases the prospect of negotiation failure resulting from unstable, overcrowded or underdeveloped agendas. These agenda costs can be reduced by providing a single actor with the responsible for agenda and procedural management. There are different functional alternatives in this respect. Agenda as well as procedural management can be carried out by a rotating, elected or even permanent chairmanship (ibid.). In their delegation decisions, the member states thus have a choice. They can also choose the degree of delegation: for example, whether they delegate the exclusive or shared right of initiative (Pollack 2003).

Neutral brokerage is often a necessary condition as well to successfully conclude complex multilateral negotiations. Actors involved in negotiations have strong incentives not to reveal their bottom lines. Yet if none of the actors is willing to signal room for compromise, negotiations can ultimately fail in spite of the fact that an agreement was theoretically possible given the preferences of the various parties (Luce and Raiffa 1957; Lax and Sebenius 1986; Tallberg 2006). The functionalist solution to this problem is the use of an honest broker. This does not necessarily have to be formalized, though in international organizations the chairmanship and the supranational bureaucracies (e.g. the secretariat) are natural brokers due to their central position in the negotiations. Through bilateral contacts with the broker, individual member states can signal room to maneuver without openly committing themselves. Based on such information, the honest broker can put forward compromise proposals. One condition for brokerage is the perceived reputation of the potential broker. If the reputation is compromised, other actors have no problem stepping in (Moravcsik 1998, 1999). Given the need to act quickly in the area of foreign and security policy, neutral brokerage is in demand.

Finally, there are a number of administrative costs involved in the negotiation processes in the EU. Conference rooms need to be booked, millions of documents have to be translated and distributed, and the minutes need to be written and have to be kept. Those conference services are typically institutionalized in international organizations in the form of a standing secretariat. Needless to say, there are functional alternatives.[1] In many *ad hoc* international negotiations, the host country provides secretarial services. All member states can, of course, also bring their own translators and fax machines. Despite the fact that the delegation of administrative tasks seems relatively apolitical at first sight, this is certainly not the case. Scholars have, for example, noted that centralization in international organizations may turn out controversial (Abbott and Snidal 1998; Koremenos et al. 2001). Having a permanent standing secretariat clearly gives more prominence to an international organization, which may not be in the interest of all states.

If negotiation costs are a reason for delegation, *information costs* are another. The demand for information and expertise in the EU policymaking is high. Compared to other international organizations, the level of detail and complexity is striking, because decisions and actions often have an actual impact. For the EU to adopt binding targets on climate change, for example, requires the ability to process scientific data, analyze the effective reductions that member states can make, and make impact assessments of the economic consequences for particular industries in individual countries. Similarly, before a candidate country can accede to the EU, the member states have to decide whether the state in question has aligned itself with the thousands of pages of the *acquis* and whether it is fulfilling the Copenhagen criteria. To send military personnel on a peace operation to Africa requires adequate risk assessments and appropriate intelligence. Whatever decision the EU takes, information is likely to be a requirement.

The member states themselves are major sources of information during the negotiations. They have many resources and they know better than other actors which policies are in their best interest (Moravcsik 1998; Pollack 2003). Yet information is also highly political. It is questionable, in this respect, to what extent biased information provided by the member states can be used in the process of EU policy-making. In other words, there is a demand for independent verification of information provided by individual member states (Abbott and Snidal 1998). Without a commonly agreed pool of information, the negotiating parties are likely first to quarrel about whether the information is unbiased rather than to negotiate mutual beneficial agreements. The unavailability of "neutral" information could thus prevent them from concluding an agreement. In addition, the process of national information production may not be the most efficient. It implies that 27 national bureaucracies are being kept in place, which perform more or less the same functions for the purpose of coming to one single EU agreement.

The functional solution to reduce these information costs is to create an expert bureaucracy, which provides member states with relatively impartial information during the negotiations and with specialization gains (Hawkins et al. 2006). It is important to distinguish here between the tasks of information gathering and information analysis (Dijkstra and Vanhoonacker 2011). The member states can create a light structure that receives national information and comes on top of the national expert bureaucracies, or they can completely replace national expert bureaucracies. The demand for expert bureaucracies is likely to vary across policy areas. Scholars have noted that the informational complexity is particularly high in the areas of environment, agriculture, finance, and foreign and defense policy (Moravcsik 1998; Pollack 2003; Epstein and O'Halloran 1999). In addition, foreign and security policy often requires, as has already been noted above, rapid response and therefore efficient informational input. When an EU military intervention needs to be planned, relying solely on information and expertise from the member states might not be the most efficient approach.

The basic unit of analysis so far has been the individual agreement between the member states. Yet agreements are not made in isolation. They fit in with previous and parallel agreements leading to *coordination costs*. Consistency between agreements is generally seen as a condition for optimal payoffs. If an actor takes contradictory action, it signals confusion at the very least. There are various ways in which individual agreements fit into a broader structure. Agreements can be (in)consistent across time, policy areas, and polities. While complete consistency can hardly be fully realized due to bounded rationality, actors have an incentive to avoid excessive inconsistencies. This creates a demand for coordination mechanisms. Coordination over time relates to the continuity of international organizations. In particular, if intergovernmental negotiations between the member states are *ad hoc*, decentralized, and/or led by a rotating chairmanship, there is a strong demand for continuity between these negotiations and the different chairmanships. The functional solution is to establish a standing secretariat that can brief the member states on the decisions they have taken in the past ("institutional memory") and the likely consequences of their actions, as well as international treaty obligations (Lowenfeld 1994; Sandford 1996; Bauer 2006).

Horizontal coordination between different policy areas and vertical coordination between different polities and levels poses similar challenges. Domestic policies and external relations, for example, are increasingly intertwined (e.g. Rosenau 1997; Stetter 2004; Eriksson and Rhinard 2009). Member states themselves can address these challenges through establishing inter-ministerial coordination meetings in the capitals or within the national permanent representations. Coordination within the member states is, however, typically not sufficient. In the EU, for example, many actions are carried out on the EU level by the EU bureaucracies, which may need to coordinate amongst themselves (this also makes coordination an *ex post* transaction cost). It thus makes sense for reasons of efficiency to delegate the task of horizontal and/or vertical coordination to specific bodies or institutions. Those actors that occupy pivotal positions in policy-making are in a particularly good position to lower the coordination costs. These are typically international bureaucracies and chairmanships, but also the permanent representations, which play a role due to their gatekeeping position.

To conclude on the *ex ante* transaction costs of cooperation, the member states face several negotiation, information, and coordination costs when concluding agreements. The delegation of functions is one method that can potentially reduce these costs. It makes the process of cooperation more efficient. Chairmanships, secretariats, and expert bureaucracies are particularly in demand. They are functional solutions to these *ex ante* transaction costs. It is important to note that there are often alternative functional solutions and that various actors can jointly lower the transaction costs. On the other hand, it must be noted that one agent can also serve several functions. Such a combination can yield both positive and negative payoffs. It may be efficient, for example, to get an expert bureaucracy involved in agenda management due to its superior information and expertise. Information and agenda-setting functions, on the other hand, often go badly together with neutral brokerage. By putting content proposals forward, agents almost automatically lose their impartiality. Because there are different solutions to reduce transaction costs and because different agents can provide efficiency, delegation is likely to be debated among the member states.

Ex ante transaction costs are clearly present in the area of foreign and security policy in the EU. Due to the demand of rapid nature of decision-making, negotiation costs can constitute a real obstacle for the successful formulation of foreign policy. It has also been noted that this area of policy requires substantial informational input. When planning a CSDP operation, there is a demand for a strong information-gathering and analysis capability. The planning process, which accumulates into to an agreement between the member states on the Operations Plan (OPLAN), requires the presence of technical expertise. There is thus likely debate between the member states on how to address the information costs of cooperation. Lastly, foreign and security policy are full of coordination challenges. Because this policy is directed towards third actors, continuity over time is of pivotal importance. Security policy furthermore often overlaps with other internal and external policies, such as development, but also migration and fisheries. This involves coordination costs.

Ex post transaction costs

Once an agreement has been concluded, member states face a number of *ex post* transaction costs. An agreement, after all, does not in itself guarantee proper implementation or domestic compliance. Agreements may also be incomplete, which in turn could lead to disagreement on the details. With all such uncertainty, there is thus a demand for member states to credibly commit themselves to the agreement and convince the other parties that they will fully implement the agreement. They can do so by various means and to various degrees. The delegation of monitoring and enforcement tasks to a third party or even the full delegation of implementation tasks themselves constitutes a solution to this credible commitment problem. In addition to the credibility of implementation, implementation may also be costly in itself. Member states might thus be tempted to achieve economies of scale by delegating the implementation functions to the EU bureaucracies. This may make national services redundant, leading to efficiency. Finally, EU bureaucracies may be more effective than the member states when implementing agreements.

The risk of *non-compliance* – that other member states inadequately (or fail to) implement agreements – is among the most important transaction costs of cooperation. For individual member states non-compliance often pays offs.[2] As the member states typically anticipate non-compliance, they will demand credible commitments from the other member states. They may also want to bind future governments to avoid non-compliance over time. There is general agreement in the literature that supranational agents play a vital role in providing member states with credible commitments (Keohane 1984; Moravcsik 1998; Pollack 2003; Tallberg 2002b; Hawkins et al. 2006; Franchino 2007; Milner and Moravcsik 2009). They can independently monitor whether the member states are keeping their promises. By providing transparency, they can contribute to an atmosphere of trust. Commitments become more credible when the member states also delegate enforcement powers to their supranational agents. Courts, for instance, can issue verdicts on instances of non-compliance. In extreme cases, member states can decide to delegate full implementation to a supranational "trustee," which can operate relatively autonomously from the member states (Majone 2001).

Incomplete contracting is another *ex post* transaction cost. Since complex agreements are almost by definition incomplete, some details are likely to be filled in at a later time (Williamson 1985). This leads to two problems: differences in the interpretation of agreements and the need for secondary agreements. Both have distributive effects in terms of payoffs. Interpretation is likely to be a zero-sum game, in which one member state wins and another member state loses. Secondary agreements are more complicated. Unlike primary agreements, to which member states sign up voluntarily, they do not necessarily yield positive payoffs for all the member states. In the primary agreements, member states typically reach compromise proposals (e.g. on the freedom of movement of goods *and* on labor protection). This overall compromise is beneficial for all member states. When the member states start negotiating detailed secondary agreements on, for example, the freedom of movement of goods, some member states are likely to oppose such legislation. If they are capable of obstructing secondary agreements, the whole package may fall apart.

Many of the functionalist solutions for non-compliance also apply to incomplete contracting. The basic function of courts is, after all, to interpret agreements. The solution to the problem of obstruction of secondary agreements is to structure future negotiations on the details between the member states by pooling or delegating sovereignty. This raises the "cost of nondecision or noncompliance" (Moravcsik 1998: 73). The introduction of majority voting (pooling sovereignty) is one functional solution. It allows member states to outvote some of the outliers. Providing a third party with initiation or implementation powers is another case in point. It needs to be said though that member states can also ignore the problem of incomplete contracting. Particularly when the subject is too sensitive and they do not want to be bound by various rules, they can take future scenarios at face value. There are thus again degrees to which the member states can commit themselves and this is part of the negotiations as well.

While credibility is thus a major reason for delegation, the member states may also want to decrease the *implementation costs* (Majone 2001). Domestic implementation, of course, has several advantages, not least in terms of sovereignty (see also below). However, if all member states have to carry out similar tasks, the centralization of executive functions may be more efficient. In particular, when issues are technically complex, relatively non-divisive (Epstein and O'Halloran 1999; Franchino 2000a), and the principals do not have the time nor the ability to take action themselves (Hix 2005), delegation to supranational actors is likely (Majone 1996; Franchino 2007). This reason for delegation fits in with the legislative–bureaucratic literature in domestic politics (Kiewiet and McCubbins 1991; Epstein and O'Halloran 1999). In the context of the EU, scholars focus on the rule-making by the Commission in relationship with the "comitology" machinery and the numerous agencies (e.g. Pollack 1997, 2003; Franchino 2000a, b, c, 2007; Brandsma 2010; Keleman 2002; Groenleer 2009). Efficient implementation is particularly in demand in areas where rapid decision-making is important.

In relation to the demand for efficient daily executive management, there is a need for collective external representation. When the (restricted group of) member states agree on a policy, they will have to communicate their policy outcomes to third parties. This is most obvious in multilateral/bilateral negotiations with other states or international organizations. The delegation of authority to a chairmanship or a supranational agent, acting on a mandate from the member states, constitutes an often-used functional solution to this representation problem (Tallberg 2006). Such an EU agent can more effectively communicate the agreed policies through means of "one voice." On a more strategic level, having one joint representative can also provide a shield function for the member states (cf. Fiorina 1977). By letting an EU representative criticize China's human rights record, individual member states do not have to jeopardize their trade interests.

As with *ex ante* transaction costs, there are various *ex post* costs, which may be reasons for delegation. Credible commitments are among the most important reasons why the member states create strong supranational agents. The delegation of monitoring and enforcement competences is a functional solution for the credible commitment problem. EU bureaucracies can autonomously verify whether the member states are indeed living up to their agreements. Such transparency will lead to an atmosphere of greater trust. There is, however, another rationale for delegation in terms of *ex post* transaction costs. EU bureaucracies can make the implementation process more efficient due to their expertise and specialization (Hawkins et al. 2006). In particular, in policy areas where rapid implementation is a requirement, supranational implementation is beneficial. The EU bureaucracies are, in this respect, more effective. They can do the job better than the domestic administrations. The same holds true when it comes to external representation. EU bureaucracies can provide added value in this respect as well.

Some of these *ex post* transaction costs are also important in the area of foreign and security policy. Collective external representation seems a prerequisite for the EU in order to have a foreign policy in the first place. In the CSDP, the effectiveness of implementation stands out. If soldiers are put in harm's way, command and control must be functional and free from political interference. The "unity of command" is particularly important when it comes to multinational deployments. On the other hand, there seems less reason to provide EU bureaucracies with monitoring and enforcement functions in the area of foreign and security policy (cf. Wagner 2003). Foreign affairs is not subject to extensive legislation or regulatory policy. Ensuring the domestic compliance of member states through lengthy court procedures also seems problematic in foreign and security policy. Finally, as this policy area is about coordination rather than collaboration, it is questionable to what extent the member states will sign up to agreements that they disagree with in the first place. In other words, while there is a clear demand for effective implementation, these is less reason to delegate for the purpose of credible commitments.

Why not delegate: sovereignty costs

In the earliest publications on delegation in international organizations, it was already pointed out that delegation decisions are based on cost–benefit calculations by the member states. As shown above, the benefits of delegation have been well covered in the academic literature. International relations scholars have, in particular, relied heavily on insights from economics. They have, on the other hand, been much less interested in the costs of delegation (with the notable exception of Bradley and Kelley 2008; Hathway 2008).[3] One of the consequences is a bias in case selection with an emphasis on instances where delegation took place rather than a focus on non-delegation. A related effect is the prominence of international economic organizations in the study of international delegation and the absence of security organizations. It is therefore essential to take the costs of sovereignty seriously as a counterweight to the benefits of delegation.

The starting point is to define sovereignty costs. David Epstein and Sharyn O'Halloran measure sovereignty costs "as the distance between the policy that a country would implement if it were not a member of the international organization and the policy that it enacts once it has joined" (2008: 82). Sovereignty costs, in this respect, equal "agency costs" from the economic literature to indicate that the autonomy of the member states to make decisions and take actions is reduced (see also Hathway 2008).[4] The label of "sovereignty" seems to better reflect the language of international relations and the symbolism and uncertainty related to the sovereignty of states than the "agency" of firms in the market economy. Sovereignty costs are most relevant in international organizations involving delegation. They are high "when international arrangements impinge on the relations between a state and its citizens or territory" (Abbott and Snidal 2000: 437) and low if agreements only put limits on the behavior of states in specific circumstances.

Sovereignty costs are intimately related to the process of delegation. As the second part of this chapter will show, the outsourcing of functions and the empowerment of EU bureaucracies will almost automatically give EU officials opportunities to exert a certain amount of influence over the member states. This is, of course, not such an issue as long as the benefits of delegation outweigh the costs. The member states may take anticipated sovereignty costs for granted and they may put in place appropriate control mechanisms to limit influence. The trouble starts when the influence of the EU officials becomes "excessive." Excessive influence is defined, in this book, as the costs of delegation being larger than the benefits for at least one of the member states.[5] In other words, if the member states would have anticipated excessive influence, they would not have delegated tasks in the first place. Principal–agent theory predicts that in such cases, member states may want to take some functions back and will be more reluctant to delegate in future rounds (see also above).

Conceptualizing delegation as a *trade-off between the anticipated efficiency gains and the anticipated sovereignty costs* implies that member states will delegate fewer tasks than would be functionally optimal. Delegation thus has sub-optimal outcomes.[6] First, despite all the possible efficiency gains and functional arguments in the world, states may simply reject delegation when they feel that the sovereignty costs are too high. They may also choose a less efficient functional solution or an underperforming agent over which they can keep control. Second, if the member states anticipate that sanctioning or re-contracting will be difficult given their own divisiveness, they may also decide against delegation (e.g. Stone 2009; Miller 2005; Nielson and Tierney 2003). Finally, as repeatedly noted above, if there exists uncertainty about the consequences of delegation, risk-averse member states are likely to prefer to keep things in-house or delegate step-by-step. In any event, sovereignty costs will result in less delegation than what could have been expected in a fully rational world where agents do exactly what they are told. While efficiency may thus be the rationale, the outcomes do not have to be optimal to support this explanation of delegation.

What is important when it comes to delegation and the role of sovereignty costs is that there are often alternative functional solutions to both *ex ante* and *ex post* transaction costs. In addition to the "in-house" or "outsource" dichotomy, member states typically have to determine the degree of delegation. The jurisprudence of international courts can be either binding or non-binding (e.g. Abbott et al. 2000). International agents can monitor agreements between states or they may also have enforcement powers (ibid.). When it comes to agenda-setting competences, member states can delegate the exclusive right of initiative to an agent or merely the shared right (Pollack 2003). Expert bureaucracies, as noted above, can be relatively light structures that coordinate information analysis or they can completely replace national bureaucracies (Abbott and Snidal 1998). As regards most transaction costs, the degree of delegation is thus a matter of debate. Efficiency alone thus cannot explain why the member states choose one functional solution over another.

There is not, however, choice only in functional solutions. There is also choice in alternative agents. A typical example is whether to go for a permanent, rotating, or elected chairmanship of the member states committees (although rotating becomes less interesting if the membership increases). In the EU, agent selection is very important. Clearly not all tasks go to the European Commission. Fabio Franchino (2007) distinguishes between supranational and domestic agents. Deirdre Curtin (2009) provides an overview of the fragmented executive realm of European integration. Nadia Klein (2010) even argues that member states purposefully employ a "divide and rule" strategy between EU bureaucracies. More generally, agent selection is often seen as a control mechanism to avoid drifting agents. The idea is that principals select agents whose preferences are the closest to their own or which can most easily be controlled (Hawkins et al. 2006). This applies to appointment procedures for leadership positions, but also holds relevance for the choice of EU agents as a whole. Efficiency alone can again not explain the choice between alternative agents.

Sovereignty costs are thus a critical part of international delegation. This is particularly true in foreign and security policy, where "self-help" is an important consideration (Waltz 1979). States, it has been repeated argued, will thus try to avoid being bound by international treaties and delegation. In addition, states will be reluctant to cede control to international organizations when sending their troops in harm's way. This makes sovereignty costs very important in the CSDP. In addition, one can argue that it is more difficult to anticipate or measure sovereignty costs in security affairs than in economic issues, because there are no countable units. Relative rather than absolute gains (Grieco 1988) furthermore typically play a more important role in the area of security, and relative gains are yet again more difficult to calculate. Finally, Charles Lipson (1984) has argued in his seminal article that there is a difference between payoffs in economic and security games. These are all reasons why uncertainty about sovereignty costs is likely to be high in the CSDP and why the member states are thus reluctant to delegate.

Bureaucratic agency in the European Union

Following the delegation of functions, it is worthwhile to study the consequences of delegation, one of which is the empowerment of EU bureaucracies. This book thus asks under which conditions do EU officials exert influence in the area of security and defense? To provide a theoretical answer, this section proposes four steps. First, it discusses the possible preferences of EU officials and the goal conflicts with the member states. Second, it studies the resources of EU officials. Third, it goes into detail about the control mechanisms that the member states have at their disposal. Finally, this chapter provides an overview of the opportunities for agency within the various phases of the policy process. Only in case of conflicting preferences, superior resources, insufficient control mechanisms, and opportunities in the policy process can EU official exert influence. These are therefore the four conditions from a theoretical perspective.

Agent preferences

Studying the influence of EU officials is interesting only if there is actually a goal conflict with the preferences of the member states. When principals and agents want exactly the same, there cannot be influence for the agents. After all, influence is for EU officials to get the member states to do something that they would *not* otherwise do (Dahl 1957; see introduction). In the principal–agent literature, goal conflicts are typically assumed (Waterman and Meier 1998). For example, Roderick Kiewiet and Mathew McCubbins (1991: 5) confidently state that "there is almost always some conflict between the interests of those who delegate authority (principals) and the agents to whom they delegate it." It seems nonetheless a good idea to identify what the EU officials exactly want. This also helps us to understand issues of contention and why agents pursue particular strategies throughout the policy process.

Ever since the budget-maximizing model, as proposed by William Niskanen (1968), there has been a debate in academia on the preferences of public bureaucracies. In the EU, the emphasis has been on competence-maximizing (Majone 1996; Pollack 1997). Mark Pollack (2003) notes, for example, that this assumption is not only central in the theory of rational choice institutionalism, but is also part of neofunctionalism and intergovernmentalism. Competence-maximizing results from bureaucratic politics or self-selection and socialization of personnel (e.g. Peters 1992; Pollack 2003). It comes in two subsequent steps. EU officials will firstly advocate increased competences for the

EU level ("more Europe," e.g. Ross 1995). Yet as mentioned above, it is also important how increased competences at the EU level are divided amongst the EU bureaucracies and other actors. EU officials in the different bureaucracies are thus expected to promote the expansion of their own organizations.

Beyond competence-maximizing, EU officials can also have an interest in policy-seeking (cf. Strøm 1990; Müller and Strøm 1999). Simon Hix (1998), in particular, has made a strong case for studying the left–right cleavage in the EU. Policy-seeking interests, however, often overlap with competence-maximizing, which makes them difficult to distinguish. There are clear examples in the European Commission. Thomas Christiansen (1997: 78), for instance, notes that "inter-departmental conflict is usually related to the conflict between sectoral interests that the respective [Directorates-General] are seen to represent." Thus, Directorate-General for Agriculture and Rural Development (DG AGRI) is generally seen as pro-agriculture, Directorate-General for Health and Consumers (DG SANCO) as pro-consumer affairs, and Directorate-General for Development and Cooperation (DG DEVCO) as pro-development. That having been said, competence-maximizing and policy-seeking are not always complementary. If Directorate-General for Enlargement (DG ELARG) promotes a pro-enlargement policy, it will inevitably lose its *raison d'être* as more countries join the EU.

When it comes to balancing competence-maximizing and policy-seeking interests, the specific functions of the EU bureaucracies are relevant. In particular, expert bureaucracies, which have a role in the formulation and implementation of policy, are likely to have substantive interests. In the process of formulating proposals and in implementing agreements, they make a number of intentional substantive choices. They have to defend these choices before the member states. Agents that play a role in lowering negotiation and coordination costs are less likely to be interested in substance. As a senior official, dealing solely with administrative support and brokerage, once put it: "I don't mind whether [the member states] decide to paint the room black or white, as long as the decision is taken in the correct way" (quoted in Schout and Vanhoonacker 2006: 1054). While staying neutral might not have been his/her default value, it is clear that he/she attaches much less importance to the substantive preferences than to competence-maximizing. Having an impartial reputation is an important prerequisite for honest brokers (see also above).

In the area of foreign and security policy, both competence-maximizing and policy-seeking preferences are relevant. For CSDP officials, it is important to launch missions, as without those they lose their purpose. This creates, needless to say, a goal conflict between the principal and the agent. The member states, acting collectively as one principal under consensus decision-making, may be much more reluctant to launch operations. They will, after all, have to deliver the troops and the finances. In other instances, EU officials may try to block national pet projects by the member states, if they are afraid that such operations are not feasible. The example of the UN is illustrative in that its officials have tried to resist using UN peacekeepers to solve all the world's problems. While conflicts may not be as strong in the EU context, CSDP officials likely have their own ideas and preferences on how to carry out particular operations. They are being kept responsible by the member states, for better or for worse. Their preferences undoubtedly differ from those of the member states.

In addition to preferences for increased competences, budgets, and personnel, EU officials in the area of foreign and security policy also inevitably engage in bureaucratic politics with the other EU bureaucracies. Within the CSDP, there is likely a competition for resources as well as attention between civilian and military crisis management. CSDP as a policy has to compete with other facets of EU external relations, such as foreign and development policy. Budgets can only be spent once and overlapping competences lead to conflict. EU foreign policy as a whole is in competition with other aspects of European integration, such as the financial crisis. In other words, resources and attention for EU affairs are limited and CSDP officials will thus take part in bureaucratic politics. This will, in turn, lead not only to goal conflicts between the different EU bureaucracies, but also to goal conflicts with the member states. Many of the member states have their own interests and will take sides in this EU level competition.

Bureaucratic resources

It has been argued above that delegation in foreign and security policy is likely to be the result of efficiency considerations. Credible commitments, which play such a dominant role in the internal market and regulatory policies, are not of pivotal importance. This implies that member states are unlikely to delegate many formal competences to the EU bureaucracies in the CSDP (Wagner 2003; Majone 2001; Tallberg 2002a). Agents guaranteeing commitments of member states have to stand above the principals and thus require formal autonomy. When agents facilitate the process in order to achieve efficiency gains, formal competences are less important. Member states are consequently unlikely to delegate to the EU bureaucracies formal powers in foreign policy. Influence thus has to come from other bureaucratic resources. Particularly relevant, in this respect, are the "institutional memory" of EU bureaucracies, their continuity, their position in the policy-making web, process expertise, relevant networks, content expertise, and strategic use of time. While these resources may not be available to all EU bureaucracies, it is argued below that in the area of foreign and security policy, EU officials are likely to have an advantage over the member states.

Institutional memory directly results from the centralization of the administrative functions of an international organization. This includes keeping the records, minutes, and archives. The EU officials are not the only ones with archives, but there are several reasons why their memory is superior. First, it is their task. They generally have to write the minutes, which often go for approval to the member states, so it is important that they make sure that the record accurately reflects the deliberations. Second, there is continuity. EU officials typically stay for a long time in one bureaucracy carrying out similar functions. Third, because of the functions that EU officials carry out (e.g. minute-taking), they occupy a key position in the policy-making web. This gives them a better view of unfolding events than the national diplomats, who may only be involved at the margins. Fourth, since EU officials hold superior process expertise (see also below), they generally have a better understanding of what precisely is going on. EU officials are thus expected to have a surplus in terms of institutional memory. It gives them authority on past decisions and knowledge about the historical preferences of all actors.

The *continuity* of agents has further advantages. The literature on relations between politics and administration has long recognized that civil servants typically outlast their politicians. Time is thus to their advantage and EU officials can simply wait until a "window of opportunity" presents itself (Kingdon 1984). Resilience and longevity are indeed two of the main characteristics of a policy entrepreneur. EU officials hold clear advantages in terms of continuity. Again, this was often a rationale for delegation in itself. It relates not only to the rotating diplomats, but to other actors as well, such as the chairmanships of committees. Due to their continuity, EU officials can outlast actors with conflicting preferences. Put the other way around, if EU officials wait long enough they are likely to encounter actors sympathetic to their ideas. National governments, for example, can change as a result of elections. This may affect their foreign policy preferences. In other words, actors are likely to change and continuity pays off.

EU officials typically hold a *pivotal position in the policy-making web*. Depending on their specific functions, this can yield valuable bureaucratic resources. First, it gives them a clear overview of the state of the negotiations (Beach 2005). Since timing is so crucial, this is a valuable asset. Clearly they do not have a monopoly on this information. Other actors closely involved in the negotiations may have such information as well. Some negotiations also go bilaterally via the national capitals to keep EU officials out of the loop. That having been said, EU officials have better information on the state of the art than most of the member states. Second, if EU officials perform brokerage functions, this typically involves becoming party to privileged information (Tallberg 2006). The idea of having an honest broker is to create an opportunity to signal the bottom lines, for the purpose of creating compromise proposals, without necessarily formal commitment. Information on bottom lines may not necessarily be exclusive, as other actors might perform the brokerage functions as well, but it is again likely to result in asymmetries with most of the other players involved.

As a result of their institutional memory, continuity and position in the policy-making web, EU officials often accumulate considerable *process and negotiation expertise* (e.g. Wall and Lynn 1993; Beach 2005; Tallberg 2006). This can help them to point member states at how to make best use of the rules of the game. There is a wide variety of examples of how ignorance over rules has weakened member states' negotiation positions. Margaret Thatcher, for example, found out at the Milan European Council in 1985, whilst being outvoted, that it only took a simple majority vote to convene an Intergovernmental Conference. Process expertise thus puts EU officials in a position of authority (as guardian of the orthodoxy). This is an extremely useful source of information during any negotiation. Derek Beach (2004, 2005) has, for example, shown that the member states do not have the expertise to draft complicated Treaties. They need support or even have to delegate this task. EU officials are happy to make their process expertise available.

Another resource concerns the *networks* of EU officials (Haas 1992; Peterson 1995; Rhodes, Bache and George 1996). What is very important, in this respect, is that many senior officials in the EU bureaucracies have previously held high-level positions in national administrations and other international organizations. This is not only limited to the bureaucratic level, but indeed includes many former politicians as well. Each international organization has such elites and the EU is not an exception. They generally have good networks that often go a long way back and that they can put to good use. The main advantage for a number of EU officials is that they can use these networks to go beyond formal national gatekeepers and veto players, such as the diplomats in the permanent representations. If the national ambassador is not receptive to their concerns, they can contact senior officials in the national ministries directly.

Whereas all these resources may help EU officials in exerting influence, the most important resource is probably *content expertise*. As it is so important, it requires more extensive explanation. When states formulate policy they typically ask expert EU officials to present them with a number of alternatives and anticipated payoffs. The provision of options is a two-step process. EU officials first have to gather relevant data before data can be processed with the use of bureaucratic content expertise. In both steps, EU officials can enjoy informational asymmetries over the member states. They may possess better data if member states do not invest as many resources in information-gathering. They may also have superior content expertise to analyze the data.

Gathering information is a costly process. This may be a reason to outsource these tasks to EU bureaucracies. In the CSDP, for example, member states have delegated the initial fact-finding mission to the CMPD. Consequently, the member states are no longer collecting the data themselves. If they want to check the accuracy of the gathered data, they will need to establish "shadow" expert bureaucracies that perform several of the same information-gathering tasks (Lake and McCubbins 2006). Yet these involve the same costs that were the reason to delegate in the first place. This is the familiar trade-off between the need for policy expertise and the desire for political control (e.g. Bawn 1995). In the absence of parallel information-gathering channels in the national capitals, EU officials thus likely hold information surpluses.

Gathering information is one thing, processing it quite another. EU officials can benefit, in this respect, from their content expertise (Wall and Lynn 1993; Beach 2005; Tallberg 2006). In everyday politics, EU officials are dealing with the diplomats of the permanent representations. These diplomats have to rely on their instructions and informal contacts with the capital for their content expertise. In a boundedly rational world, this flow of information is likely to be sub-optimal (Kassim et al. 2001). Diane Panke (2010), for example, notes that quality instructions result from good cooperation between national ministries and the permanent representations, autonomous lead-ministries, and inter-ministerial conflict resolution mechanisms. If the member states are not able to provide their diplomats with quality instructions, under time pressure, EU officials benefit. Various policies are furthermore

EU-specific in terms of content. This means that the member states do not really have the content expertise in-house (EU trade policy being a case in point). There is thus likely a variation in issues where the EU is pursuing policies similar to those on the national level and those where EU decisions and actions are unique.

EU officials thus typically have superior resources when formulating an agreement. Informational asymmetries and content expertise, however, continue to play a role during implementation. When implementation has been delegated, EU officials are likely to have superior information to the national diplomats, who have to rely on the self-reporting of the agent. Informational surpluses are relevant, but so is the accumulation of content expertise. Dealing on a day-to-day basis with the implementation of tasks leads to specialization on the side of the agents (Hawkins et al. 2006). Their content expertise thus increases compared to the expertise of the principals. These resources are important for the formulation and implementation of policy.

Finally, it is necessary to acknowledge that while EU officials may not have better cognitive skills than national diplomats, *time pressure* can be in their favor. In crisis situations, the member states may not have the time to evaluate policy options proposed by EU officials objectively. This also relates to a previous point. When the instructions arrive late, "it is difficult to shape negotiation outcomes" (Panke 2010: 770). Time pressures negatively correlate with the information-processing capabilities of the member states. Apart from the need for quick decisions under pressure, EU officials can also intentionally play for time. They can relatively easily delay the release of draft documents before important meetings. This increases the pressure on the national diplomats.

To conclude on resources, it has been demonstrated that there are various resources, where EU officials may hold an advantage over the member states in the CSDP. These resources include institutional memory, continuity, their pivotal position in the policy-making web, process expertise, relevant networks, content expertise, and time. What is important, though, is that not all these resources may be at work at the same time. They can differ across issues, time and agents. They also depend on the control mechanisms, which will be discussed below. That said, it is likely that EU officials have some advantages over the member states in the CSDP and that they will use these advantages to exert agency.

Control mechanisms

The delegation of functions to the EU bureaucracies thus leads to a whole range of resources for the agent. This inevitably allows for influence. Delegation cannot be enjoyed without certain agency losses. As David Lake and Matthew McCubbins (2006: 343) succinctly stated "no pain, no gain." This does not, however, mean that agency is always excessive. Principal–agent literature expects indeed that the member states might tolerate some influence for the purpose of efficiency. Several control mechanisms are, however, put in place to limit agency. These can be aimed at restricting the resource asymmetry of the agent *ex ante* or *ex post* and allow for sanctioning. If principals detect excessive influence, the literature predicts a recalculation. With multiple principals, sanctioning may be difficult, as noted above, due to preference heterogeneity. Control mechanisms furthermore *always* involve costs. They lower efficiency and they put extra requirements on principals and agents (Miller 2005). They are therefore part of the cost–benefit analyses of the principals.

The ultimate control mechanism is *re-contracting*. As delegation is a process with feedback loops, member states can take back responsibilities. As Mark Pollack (2003: 391) writes the EU bureaucracies "are causally important actors in the processes of European integration, but they are actors in an intergovernmental play written, and periodically rewritten, by the EU's member governments." None of the EU bureaucracies gets to vote over its own budget, personnel policies, or competences. The ultimate power of re-contracting also works preventively in that EU officials will be cautious to exert excessive influence. Related to re-contracting are institutional checks and balances during day-to-day policy-making. In the CSDP, for example, ultimate decision-making power – to send troops or not – rests with the member states. More generally, the division of labor in policy-making between different agents is a way of limiting excessive influence (Klein 2010). Finally, through using detailed administrative instructions, the member states can put limits on the agents' room to maneuver (Hawkins et al. 2006; Bradley and Kelley 2008).

Another way of controlling agents is to *limit their resources*. Principals can do this in absolute terms. While agents notoriously try to influence budget and personnel decisions (Niskanen 1968), the empirical record shows that states have successfully kept international organizations small (Stone 2009). They are not ever-expanding in terms of budget and staff. It is not, however, just about staff numbers, but also about staff quality. Some international organizations can select their staff members autonomously; others cannot. Salaries are an important control mechanism here as well. From UN desk officers to the judges on the World Trade Organization (WTO) appellate body, low salaries have affected the quality of officials (Myint-U and Scott 2007; Elsig and Pollack 2013). In addition, seconded national officials are an often-used mechanism of control. While they may not act as Trojan horses (e.g. Trondal 2006, 2007, 2008), they undermine the institutional memory, continuity, and expertise of the EU bureaucracies. In the CSDP, seconded experts are omnipresent.

Principals can also undermine agent resources in relative terms by putting in place oversight mechanisms, which limit the asymmetry between the EU officials and their own information and expertise. This involves creating (or keeping in place) parallel information-gathering channels that decrease the dependence on EU officials. In the CSDP, gathering of intelligence is an example. Few member states send troops abroad based on third-party intelligence alone. Moreover, principals can establish their own expert bureaucracies to rely to a lesser extent on the assessments and self-reporting of the agents. The member states are unlikely to replicate everything, as this undermines the rationale for delegation (Lake and McCubbins 2006), but it is to be expected that the member states retain some content expertise to monitor whether the agent is properly fulfilling its job. An analogy can be made with accountancy, where accountants typically do not go through all the invoices, but rather check standard operation procedures and rules (e.g. assets equal liabilities). While such an approach may not be foolproof, it is less costly for the principals than complete monitoring. If agents carry out standard operations, they are easier for member states to control.

Agent screening and selection is another control mechanism. Principals select agents, whose preferences are the closest to their own or which can most easily be controlled. This mainly applies to the appointment of senior personnel, such as Secretary-Generals, Commissioners, or international judges (Kahler 2001; Hawkins et al. 2006; Elsig and Pollack 2013). A problem with this *ex ante* control mechanism is that it may be difficult to read the agent's true preferences in advance, as the agent has incentives to misrepresent its preferences. The functional solution is to appoint senior personnel only for a limited period of time. For them to seek reappointment requires them to take into account the anticipated reactions of the principals. The sanction of not being reappointed is in itself a control mechanism that limits excessive influence by the agent. Agent selection is therefore not only important during the delegation phase, but it plays in day-to-day politics as well.

To conclude, member states have a range of control mechanisms to limit excessive influence by EU officials. They can re-contract, restrict the bureaucratic resources of the agent (including through the means of oversight), and they can select agents. All these measures, however, come at a cost for the member states. They limit the efficiency gains by making the agent less efficient. In addition, member states and EU officials have to invest in control mechanisms through their time and effort. The establishment of control mechanisms in the CSDP is thus expected to be part of the decision on delegation weighing costs and benefits.

Opportunities for agency

EU officials are likely to possess bureaucratic resources. Control mechanisms do not fully compensate in this regard. This leads to opportunities for exerting agency (Thatcher and Stone Sweet 2002). It is thus important to identify these opportunities. For EU officials, there are a number of opportunities to exert influence in the CSDP during the various phases of the policy process. In the agenda-setting phase, they can use their networks and key position in the policy-making web to get their issues high on the EU agenda. During the decision-making phase, they can use their information surpluses and their expertise to affect the construction of policy alternatives. When it comes to implementation, information asymmetries and opportunities for "hidden action" allow for influence. As the dynamics of the various phases of the policy process differ, they will be discussed in turn.

The process of *agenda-setting* essentially relates to the ability of EU officials to get certain issues high on the agenda and to keep them there (e.g. Princen 2007; Tallberg 2003). This has not so much to do with having bright ideas or smart insights. John Kingdon (1984: 71) has noted that "ideas can come from anywhere." Agenda-setting is really about why some issues and not others make it high on the agenda. It is essentially about political competition to determine the agenda. Agenda-setting is, in this respect, not only about formal powers, but indeed also about informal agenda dynamics (Pollack 2003). Guy Peters (2001) has argued that in the case of the EU there are many points of agenda access, because the actors will almost always be able to find a formal power-holder sympathetic to their concerns. CSDP officials can rather easily grab attention by issuing, for example, a statement or publishing a policy paper.

In terms of actual agenda-setting, there are several opportunities for EU officials due to their continuity, key position in the policy-making web, and expertise. Sebastiaan Princen and Mark Rhinard (2006) argue that there is a political and an administrative route to agenda-setting. The political route includes top-down pressure as a result of salient events, while the administrative route is bottom-up with the incremental formulation of proposals and the gradual building of momentum.

They present these as ideal types and argue that a combination may be relevant. What seems indeed powerful is the ability of actors to alternate between these political and administrative venues (Baumgartner and Jones 1991). CSDP officials are well placed in this respect. They are at the heart of the policy-making process and they play an important role in vertical as well as horizontal coordination (Mérand et al. 2010, 2011). Moreover, they are active at both the political and administrative levels where they can push forward their issues. When they get stuck at one level, they can move to the other one and *vice versa*. Most member states do not have the ability to change venues by strategically issuing political statements and at the same time putting forward policy papers in committees. Finally, the timing of agenda-setting is absolutely vital (Kingdon 1984). EU officials have some resources in this respect, as mentioned above. They also have the continuity to test the different venues (Baumgartner and Jones 1991).

During the *decision-making* phase, there are two ways by which EU officials can exert political influence. They can use the negotiations' dynamics to further their interests and they can use their content expertise. The former relates to the ability of EU officials to play a useful role in the negotiations between the member states. It has been established above that there is generally a need for brokerage and that EU officials are well placed to perform it. When carrying out brokerage functions, compromise proposals are important. Given that the broker generally has a good insight into the negotiations, it has the opportunity to craft compromise proposals within the "zone of agreement," but with a bias towards its own preferences (Beach 2005; Tallberg 2006). Even if EU officials do not act as the formal honest broker, they have their ways of providing input. They are often involved in informal negotiations between the honest broker and the key member states, as they hold such important position in the policy-making web. Whether their advice is accepted depends on reputation, which is a built-in control mechanism.

While negotiation dynamics are one possible way for EU officials to exert influence, the opportunities to use private information and expertise may be more significant. It is about their "ability to manipulate either the construction of policy alternatives or information about the consequences of different alternatives" (Bendor, Taylor and Van Gaalen 1985: 1042; Dahl [1963] 2003). Two issues are important. First, EU officials can possess exclusive "hidden information" (cf. Arrow 1985) resulting from their contacts with third parties or autonomous information-gathering. Hidden information is, of course, very valuable when trying to manipulate alternatives or payoffs. Such exclusive information is, however, likely to be limited, as the member states will try to prevent institutional designs that favor the accumulation of exclusive information. Second, the member states may not have the ability to assess all information coming from EU officials, because their information-processing skills are limited (Simon 1987). They may suffer from time pressures and information overload. While the member states thus possess the information they need, they may not be able to process it accurately.

The dynamics of *policy implementation* differ from agenda-setting and decision-making. During the implementation of the decisions made by the member states, EU officials can act on their own preferences rather than "strictly and faithfully [following] the preferences of the member states that created and empowered them" (Pollack 2003: 38). Their ability for "hidden action" is very important (Arrow 1985). This concept implies that "the agent's action is not directly observable by the principal" (ibid.: 37), but that it does partially affect the member states' payoffs.[7] Hidden action thus automatically results in influence for the EU officials. For example, if member states cannot completely observe what a commander is doing during a military operation on the other side of the globe, this gives the commander opportunities to pursue private interests. Influence is, however, restricted by the control mechanisms listed above. These limit the opportunities for hidden action and thus negatively correlate with the influence of the agents.

3
Institutional Development in EU Security and Defense

The previous chapter discussed delegation in the CSDP from a theoretical perspective. It argued that member states are likely to balance the efficiency gains from delegation with sovereignty costs. Given the uncertainty in the process of delegation and the problems of sanctioning resulting from multiple principals, member states may delegate fewer functions than is functionally optimal. The chapter also argued that delegation is not a one-off affair, but that it takes place during subsequent delegation rounds. Member states can use the feedback from previous rounds when making their decisions. With regard to the CSDP, the chapter identified several specific functional demands for delegation. These include the negotiation, information, and coordination costs involved in the planning of operations as well as implementation costs relating to command and control and collective external representation. Credible commitments, which are central in much of European integration, play a less important role. Finally, the chapter pointed at the importance of agent selection in light of anticipated goals conflicts.

Such theoretical argument can only be sustained through sufficient empirical evidence. This chapter therefore analyzes the motivations of the member states during their delegation decisions in the area of the CSDP. The research strategy is to historically trace their reasons during important instances of delegation and non-delegation. The study of cases of non-delegation is interesting, as these highlight instances where sovereignty costs trumped efficiency gains. In tracing the rationale for delegation, this chapter makes use of a range of sources. These include official documents, negotiating positions of the member states and the EU bureaucracies, and formal reports. These "hard" sources are complemented by secondary academic literature and the accounts of officials who have been closely involved in the process. Finally, a number of academic interviews have been conducted to get a better insight into several recent instances of delegation. The combination of sources, of course, makes the findings more robust.[1]

The first section of this chapter analyzes how EU cooperation in the field of foreign policy was originally established (1970–1999). This is important, as the foreign policy structures eventually became the basis for the CSDP bureaucracies. This section emphasizes non-delegation, sovereignty costs, and agent selection. The second section is on the Treaty of Amsterdam of 1999, which led to substantial delegation to the Council Secretariat, making it the EU foreign policy base. The chapter then deals with delegation in the CSDP (1999–2009). The demand for planning and mission conduct capabilities resulted in a rapid institutionalization. This section pays special attention to the different delegation processes in military and civilian crisis management. The lack of a military headquarters and the understaffing of civilian structures are highlighted. The chapter concludes with the Treaty of Lisbon of 2009, which is the most recent step in terms of delegation. The CSDP services of the Council Secretariat were transferred to the EEAS in an attempt to create more consistency in EU foreign policy.

Establishing foreign policy cooperation

EU foreign policy – of which the CSDP is part – was established through several reports (1970–1981) outside the Treaties of the European Communities. They reflected the sovereignty concerns of the member states, which wanted to keep foreign policy cooperation as low-key as possible. Only with the SEA (1987) foreign policy was given a treaty basis. It was still kept legally separate from the other policies of EU integration. This dichotomy of foreign policy and economic issues was further institutionalized in the Treaty of Maastricht (1993). EU foreign policy became its famous second pillar. This section of the chapter traces the limited delegation in foreign policy. It shows that the member states preferred to keep functions in-house by delegating them to the six-monthly rotating Presidency.

The Luxembourg Report of 1970 established EPC. It was a lowest common denominator affair. Previous attempts at foreign policy cooperation had notoriously failed in the context of the Defence Community (1952) and the Fouchet Plans (1959–1962). EPC envisaged only a process of information exchange and a "harmonization of views, concertation of attitudes and joint action when it appears feasible and desirable" (Article II(I)(b)). It was kept separate from the rest of

European integration and was not given a Treaty basis. It was "provided with a bare minimum of institutional support" (Smith 2004: 71). EPC would have consultations at the level of ministers, political directors (in the Political Committee), and diplomats. They would meet in the country of the rotating Presidency. The Presidency became responsible for agenda and procedural management as well as administrative support (Article 8(2)).

The explicit choice of the Presidency and the absence of a permanent secretariat needs to be highlighted. It is an instance of sovereignty costs and agent selection. The reason why the member states did not create a secretariat can be traced to the Fouchet Plans, which ultimately failed, amongst others, due to disagreement on the location of the secretariat. France feared that a Brussels secretariat would create close ties with the other EU bureaucracies. This would lead to an erosion of sovereignty. It therefore proposed a secretariat in Paris. This flew in the face of The Netherlands and Belgium, which feared that such a (French-dominated) secretariat would actually compete with the EU bureaucracies (Nuttall 1992). Individual principals thus anticipated goal conflicts with the agent depending on its location. As the location had been such a sticking point in the Fouchet Plans, the negotiators of the Luxembourg Report avoided the issue altogether. They delegated functions to the Presidency instead.

EPC was revised for the first time in the Copenhagen Report (1973). This report filled in the details of decision-making rules based on experience. The functions of the Presidency were further defined, the role of embassies in third countries was discussed, and an information exchange system (*Correspondance européenne*, COREU) was established. Since a secretariat was still a non-starter, the member states continued to delegate the functions among themselves. They, for example, noted that "experience has ... shown that the Presidency's task presents a particularly heavy administrative burden" (ibid.: Article 8) and decided to allow for administrative burden-sharing between the member states. The costs of cooperation were thus clearly recognized, but creating a secretariat was a bridge too far. The trade-off between efficiency gains and sovereignty costs was almost explicit in the Copenhagen Report.

The end of *détente* gave EPC renewed momentum, as a result of the Soviet invasion of Afghanistan in late December 1979. With the outgoing and incoming Presidencies on holiday, the EPC machinery stopped functioning. Further incompetence by the incoming Italian Presidency meant that the member states were only able to adopt a declaration on January 15, 1980 – three weeks after the event. This provided a feedback loop in terms of delegation. The UK's Foreign Minister called the situation over Afghanistan "frankly ... a bit of a mess" (Hill 1982: 50). He suggested a procedure for convening meetings on short notice and the need for some sort of secretariat "if [the member states] were to coordinate their response to crisis situations in the most efficient way."[2] He thus advocated delegation out of a need for continuity and efficiency.

In reaction to the problems over Afghanistan, the member states adopted the London Report in 1981. It was aimed to improve the efficiency of decision-making. Because a secretariat still ran into French sovereignty concerns (Hill 1982), the member states focused again on strengthening the Presidency (Smith 2004). They established the "Troika secretariat." It consisted of two diplomats from the preceding and succeeding presidencies. They were seconded to the capital of the Presidency-in-office to provide assistance. This would improve continuity between the Presidencies and alleviate the Presidency of the administrative burden without having to create a permanent secretariat. Importantly, the report also stipulated that the Commission was now "fully associated" with EPC. In practice, this meant access to the meetings and information. The involvement of the Commission was useful in terms of coordination and information exchange when foreign policy dossiers touched upon economic issues.

The Single European Act

After the creation of EPC, the ambition in the 1980s was to give it a treaty basis. Integrationist member states – such as Germany, Italy, and the Benelux countries – thought that by bringing EPC and the European Communities together, they would strengthen the role of the EU Commission, Parliament and Court of Justice in foreign policy. This was in line with their preference for "more" Europe. The debate started with the draft European Act, which Germany and Italy presented to the London European Council in 1981. This draft act included a single institutional framework, but it kept the separation in decision-making rules between EPC and the Communities. It also suggested a secretariat to assist the European Council and the ministerial Councils (Article 2(4)(7)). Other member states – notably France and the UK – were not impressed.

Discussions on the draft act led to the non-binding *Solemn Declaration on the European Union* (1983, CVCE). While this declaration was not very relevant, its contents are of interest for the argument of this book. Article 2(2)(3), for example, stated that "to promote the objective of a Europe speaking with a single voice ... the Member States will make a constant effort to increase the *effectiveness* of Political Cooperation and will seek, in particular, to *facilitate* the decision-making process, in order to reach common positions more *rapidly*" (emphasis added). The member states were thus still concerned with lowering transaction costs. The status of EPC was also discussed in the European Parliament, where Altiero Spinelli presented a *draft Treaty Establishing the European Union* (1984, CVCE). The member states were, however, not willing to work on that basis. These attempts at giving EPC a treaty base thus ultimately failed. Yet they signaled increased ambition and eventually served as a springboard for the French President François Mitterrand in the SEA (Nuttall 1992).

Yet before going to the SEA, it is necessary to look at the development of the informal role of the Commission. Its full association with EPC in the London Report marked the conclusion of the endless debates on whether it should be invited at all. From the early 1980s, it started to make use of its resources to yield influence in EPC. Economic sanctions stand out. During the 1970s, the member states had major difficulties agreeing on sanctions. They thus resorted to *Community* sanctions under Article 113 (207 Treaty on the Functioning of the European Union, TFEU). This gave them more flexibility, but it put the Commission in the driving seat. As a result, the Commission was instrumental in negotiating import restrictions against the Soviet Union, South Africa, and Iraq, and over the Falkland conflict. The linkages between EPC and Communities' matters thus gave the Commission a role in foreign policy (Bonvicini 1988).

Following a speech by Mitterrand to the European Parliament on May 23 and the European Council of June 25–26, 1984, the member states appointed the *Ad hoc* Committee on Institutional Affairs "to make suggestions for the improvement of the operation of European cooperation" (Conclusions, CVCE). Its report was modest in its foreign policy ambitions. It stressed the need for continuity and cohesiveness and suggested a permanent political cooperation secretariat using "the back-up facilities of the Council" (Dooge Report 1985, CVCE). There was little development, in this regard, from earlier proposals – also underlined by the 23 reservations made by members of the Committee, including the chairman himself.

Before the member states could comment at the Milan European Council in June 1985, they were faced with two new proposals. The UK tabled a *draft agreement on Political Cooperation*, trumped by the Franco-German *draft Treaty on European Union*.[3] The former was a treaty in all but the name. It constituted a clever reorganization of the existing rules and practices. In terms of delegation, it stated that "the Presidency shall be assisted by a small secretariat ... [which shall] advise the Presidency as necessary on the conduct of Political Co-operation" (quoted in Nuttall 1992: 246). The latter was based on the British proposal. Apart from the rhetorical language and the legal status of the document, there was only one significant difference: the appointment of a high-level Secretary General in charge of "running the general secretariat" (Article 10(2)).

With two competing proposals, it is hardly surprising that the member states did not reach a breakthrough. The Presidency had, however, made it its objective to launch an Intergovernmental Conference. A simple majority vote (under Article 236 Treaty establishing the European Community, TEC) – sidelining Denmark, Greece, and the UK – was its means. The Conference was tasked to present "a treaty on a common foreign and security policy on the basis of" both drafts.[4] It soon became clear that the British "codification" approach was the best way forward (Nuttall 1992). The Commission subsequently issued a draft Treaty in September 1985, which brought the Communities and EPC together in one legal document yet with different "titles." This idea formed the basis of the French draft act of 19 November. This proposal, which formally separated the Communities and EPC, was accepted: the *Single* European Act.

With the SEA, the member states finally created a secretariat in Brussels. It did not have a permanent staff: six diplomats were seconded from the capitals. Nor did it have its own budget. Offices were provided by the Council Secretariat of the Communities, but were separated via a combination lock on the door. The space was symbolically paid for by the Presidency. These constituted *ex ante* control mechanisms to avoid excessive sovereignty loss. The functions of the EPC Secretariat were limited as well. It was given the task to "assist the Presidency in preparing and implementing the activities of [EPC] and in administrative matters" (Article 10(g)). It did not have a mandate of its own. When looking back at the discussions about the secretariat, it is remarkable that it took the member states 17 years before they sent six seconded national officials to Brussels. They were reluctant to delegate functions in foreign policy, despite recognizing that the absence of a secretariat was sub-optimal.

Following the SEA, the Commission also started to play a bigger role. After the fall of the Berlin Wall in 1989, the Commission became a key actor in the discussions over German reunification. Commission President Jacques Delors was among the first to recognize that reunification had become inevitable. He therefore supported the German Chancellor Helmut Kohl, despite resistance of the other member states (Nuttall 1992). The Commission also took the lead in making Eastern Germany compatible with the European regulations (interview with

Commission official). In addition, the Commission became the coordinator of international aid for Central and Eastern Europe. The US, in particular, insisted that the Commission should be delegated this task (after some lobbying of Commission President Jacques Delors). The Commission thus played an extraordinary role in external relations, despite its limited mandate.

The Treaty of Maastricht

The fall of the Berlin Wall created new momentum for treaty change. This would eventually lead to the Maastricht summit in December 1991. The integrationist member states were optimistic that the changing international environment would result in a significant strengthening of EPC. For them the end result was a disappointment. The Treaty of Maastricht made very clear that the role of the EU institutions was secondary to those of the member states. The debate started with a letter from Kohl and Mitterrand on April 28, 1990 (in Laursen and Vanhoonacker 1992). They suggested to "strengthen the democratic legitimation of the union, render its institutions more efficient, ensure unity and coherence ... and implement a common foreign and security policy." Not all member states were convinced. The British Prime Minister Margaret Thatcher responded by presenting a lengthy list of what EPC not should be (Thatcher 1993; Wall 2008). The European Council of June 25–26, 1990 thus launched the Intergovernmental Conference without an agenda.

The Commission was the first to present a formal proposal (October 21, CVCE). It was unsurprisingly on the integrationist side of the spectrum, yet it contained some nuance. Rather than laying "claim to a monopoly of the right of initiative," which it possessed in the Communities, the Commission felt that the "very specific nature of foreign and security policy implies that the right of initiative must be shared" with the member states. Creatively, it suggested creating an expert bureaucracy to prepare foreign policy decisions consisting of the EPC Secretariat and Commission representatives. Decision-making by the member states would take place through a restricted form of augmented qualified majority voting. The Commission would have a key role in implementation.

Several member states also circulated drafts. The Italian Presidency responded by putting forward a compromise proposal on November 16 (Nuttall 2000). Before the member states had the opportunity to discuss this draft at the Rome European Council of December 14–15, they received a second letter from Kohl and Mitterrand (December 6, in Laursen and Vanhoonacker 1992). It was more detailed than the first letter. As a result, it inevitably displayed the compromises both countries had to make among themselves. The contents of the letter were the basis of the Rome Conclusions, which stated, amongst other things, that the institutional framework would be based on (a) a unified Secretariat, (b) the non-exclusive right of initiative for the Commission, (c) adequate procedures for consulting and informing the European Parliament, (d) the possibility of constructive abstention, and (e) the possibility of qualified majority voting for the implementation of agreed policies. This was very close to the final compromise one year later.

While the member states thus agreed on substance, they disagreed about the form. Some had been unhappy with the strict separation of EPC and the Communities in the SEA. They argued that the EU should instead resemble a "unified tree with different branches." Others championed a "Greek temple with separate pillars" in line with the *status quo* (ibid.). This debate came to a head when the Commission tabled the *Development of a Common External Policy* (March 7, 1991, in ibid.). This document brought all external policies together under one title, introduced augmented qualified majority voting for the implementation of dossiers cleared by the European Council, emphasized the role of the Commission, and replaced the Political Committee by COREPER. Most member states felt that this went too far (Nuttall 2000). The Luxembourg Presidency therefore went back to the agreements of the Rome European Council in its "non-paper" (April 12). It introduced the three pillars.

As a result of the break out of the war in Yugoslavia, the member states could not agree on the draft treaty during the European Council of June 28–29. It was now up to the Dutch Presidency to bring the negotiations to a conclusion. Encouraged by the Commission (Nuttall 2000; Van den Bos 2008), it tabled a completely revised draft treaty containing a unified tree structure. It was not so much the content of this draft, but the process that upset the other member states. The Dutch Presidency was given the explicit instruction to work on the basis of the Luxembourg draft. This gave the draft "a legitimacy it had not earned at the Luxembourg European Council" (Nuttall 2000: 170). The Presidency had furthermore lost much of its credibility. The remaining outstanding issues were agreed upon after negotiations on the basis of a final Franco-German initiative (October 11, in Laursen and Vanhoonacker 1992). Despite the modest changes, EPC was renamed. It became the Common Foreign and Security Policy (CFSP).

When looking at the negotiations, one can argue that they primarily dealt with the role of the Commission in the EU foreign policy. On one side of the spectrum was the *status quo* and on the other the

Commission's own proposals of October 21, 1990. The latter included a role for the Commission in the formulation and implementation of foreign policy. However, the member states ultimately decided that the Commission would remain a secondary player in foreign policy (interviews national and Commission officials). Some member states had seen the activism of the Commission following the fall of the Berlin Wall. This made them wary of a further erosion of sovereignty. While re-contracting did not formally take place, one senior Commission interviewee did experience it as such: "the big member states thought that a correction was necessary. The Commission had too much influence. They wanted to limit this. It resulted in the pillar structure." Sovereignty costs thus led to this major instance of non-delegation.

While the Commission generally resented the new arrangements, its leadership decided that its objective should nonetheless be to become an equal player in EU foreign policy on a par with large member states (interview Commission official). The Commission reckoned that since the formal arrangements did not give it such status, it had to employ other means. This included providing the member states with quality information and promoting the cross-pillar synergies between foreign, trade, and development policy (ibid.). Delors thus decided to create the position of Commissioner for External Political Relations and a new Directorate-General (DG). However, for various reasons, these "new arrangements caused more problems than they brought benefits" (Nuttall 1997: 317; Nuttall 2000; Duke 2006; Cameron 2007). The Commission furthermore tried not to confront the member states, given its lack of authority and expertise in foreign policy (interview Commission and national officials). The initiative remained with the Presidency, which increasingly looked at the Council Secretariat for support.

The merger between the EPC and Council Secretariat led to the creation of a CFSP unit. It was based in the Council Secretariat. With around 26 administrators, the CFSP unit was significantly larger than its predecessor. The tradition of seconded national officials was continued, with all member states sending a civil servant to Brussels. The remainder of the unit was made up of permanent staff from the Council Secretariat and from the Commission. The merger of both Secretariats was by no means easy (Nuttall 2000; Dinan 1999). The CFSP unit nonetheless became a useful assistant to the Presidency. While it engaged in conceptual work, its small size meant that it was not a real threat to the Commission bureaucracy. As an official put it, "out of an inborn distaste for too much bureaucracy, we did not consider the idea that there might be a second executive" (interview Commission official).

During the first period of foreign policy cooperation (1970–1999), the member states created a platform for consultation, for which they required little institutional support. There were some modest transaction costs: negotiation, coordination, and representation costs. These were addressed through several delegation rounds. Most important during this period, however, were the anticipated sovereignty costs and the process of agent selection. When delegation took place, it was not to a secretariat, which was the functionally optimal scenario. Instead the member states kept functions "in-house" by delegating them amongst themselves, particularly to the Presidency. During the 1980s, the member states gave foreign policy a treaty basis. In this process, the specific requirements of foreign policy were, time and again, stressed. Foreign policy cooperation was put in a separate legal title and later in the second pillar of the Treaty of Maastricht. The Commission was not given the central role in policy-making, which it enjoyed in the Communities. If the member states delegated functions, it was to the small-scale Secretariat, over which they could keep control. Non-delegation was the major story, despite the acknowledged costs.

The Treaty of Amsterdam

The Treaty of Amsterdam (1999) constituted a major instance of delegation in foreign policy. The failure of the EU to handle the war in former Yugoslavia (1992–1995) led to a demand for a stronger foreign policy machinery. The member states established the Policy Unit to provide them with information analysis and they created the post of the High Representative for the CFSP to make foreign policy more visible, coherent, and effective. Discussions in the treaty negotiations focused on where to locate the Policy Unit and the High Representative. These resources were eventually delegated to the Council Secretariat rather than the Commission in line with sovereignty concerns. The member states nonetheless realized that this was sub-optimal, as they foresaw inter-institutional conflict between both bureaucracies. During the implementation of the treaty, the member states delegated further functions to the Council Secretariat.

The Amsterdam Treaty had already been scheduled at the time of the Maastricht summit. It was to "examine those provisions of [the Maastricht] Treaty for which revision is provided" (Article N). Yet between the Maastricht and Amsterdam Treaties the conflict in Yugoslavia went from bad to worse. Humiliatingly for the member states, in particular, it was the US that brought the war to an end. This may not have been utterly surprising, but it was the opportunity that the US created for the member states ("we do not have a dog in this fight" – US Secretary of State James Baker), the subsequent initiative of the member states ("the hour of Europe has dawned" – Luxembourg Foreign Minister Jacques Poos), and the eventual failure that was shocking.

The process started in June 1994 with the creation of a Reflection Group. While its report is considered as modest (Edwards and Pijpers 1997; Dinan 2004), the provisions on EU foreign policy are very interesting. They were strikingly rationalist and comprehensive. Because the members of the Group did not fully agree, the report gives a good overview of the main debates at the time. It is therefore worthwhile studying the report in depth. For the preparatory phase of foreign policy, the majority of the Group thought "that an analysis, forecasting, early warning system and planning unit should be set up" (paragraph 153). Such a unit could ensure from the outset "the necessary follow-up to crisis situations" and could prepare "possible response and decision options." The unit "could, moreover, encourage a common vision and greater cooperation among the Member States. The latter and the Commission should in the unit share the information they possess so that correct analyses of the situations may be done" (ibid.). There was thus a very clear informational rationale behind the creation of this unit.

With regard to composition and location of the unit, the report weighed functional needs with sovereignty concerns:

> Most representatives advocate locating it in the [Council Secretariat, because of] the merit of abiding by the present institutional framework by not creating any new bodies, and [most representatives] highlight the advantage of situating the unit at the Council on account of the central role played by the States within the CFSP ... A broad majority of members point at the same time to the need to involve the Commission in forecasting and analysis ... in order to avoid inconsistency between the political dimension and the external economic dimension of the Union. For a large majority, it is understood that the unit should include Commission staff as well as staff from the national foreign ministries. (ibid.)

The report also stated that "it is widely considered that ... the analysis and forecasting unit ought to be a preparatory body and therefore have no formal right of initiative, which could be a source of conflict or confusion of powers between Member States, the Council and the Commission" (ibid.). The Group thus identified a need for information, which could be supplied by establishing an expert bureaucracy. This bureaucracy would not have formal powers, because it was to encourage greater cooperation among the member states, leading to joint gains. Moreover, the member states made an explicit choice in agent selection (Council Secretariat over Commission), they anticipated potential inefficiency resulting from the inter-institutional conflict and tried to mitigate these by including Commission staff, and they implicitly noted continuing sovereignty concerns.

The discussions over decision-making were mainly about the question of introducing some sort of majority voting. The report was, however, again very specific with regard to implementation (paragraphs 156–161). It primarily focused on the "Personification of CFSP" in order for the Union "to implement its external actions with a higher profile" (preamble). While some members of the group favored a "Mr or Ms CFSP" to be located in the Commission, "for the majority, this would be someone in the Council." The report went on to discuss several functional alternatives. It concluded that "there is no consensus on the personification of CFSP," but that inter-institutional conflicts were to be avoided. Thus yet again the member states anticipated that there might be consequences as a result of agent selection. Finally, the report stated that "the central role of the Presidency must be maintained in the external representation and implementation of CFSP."

Little progress was made in the negotiations following the publication of the report (e.g. Moravcsik and Nicolaides 1999; Devuyst 1998). For the UK in particular there was little on the agenda that seemed palatable. Moreover, for Prime Minister John Major any advance in political integration was electorally potentially toxic (George 1997). Only in December 1996 did the process start moving again after pressure from the Irish Presidency and a joint letter by Kohl and the French President Chirac. The elections in the UK were, however, close at hand, and it was clear that European partners had to wait (Wall 2008). After the landslide victory of the Labour Party on May 1, 1997 and the appointment of Tony Blair as the British Prime Minister, the negotiations were resumed.

The renewed momentum came, however, very late. There were only six weeks to the summit in Amsterdam on 16–17 June. It meant that the agenda was overcrowded. This led to a lack of clarity, leftovers, and post-Intergovernmental Conference meetings. The *cohabitation* of the French delegation also made matters worse. In the area of foreign policy, however, the planning unit as suggested by the Reflection Group proved uncontroversial (Duke 2002a). The personification of CFSP, on the other hand, became a night-long affair. The exact standing of "Mr CFSP" was particularly an issue. Eventually the member states agreed to combine the position of Secretary-General of the Council with the functions of High Representative for the CFSP. In a complicated deal, the treaty also created the post of a deputy Secretary-General in order to increase the foreign policy profile of the "Mr CFSP." The question left open was whether the High Representative should work on the political or bureaucratic level (Regelsberger 2011; Dijkstra 2011).

According to the Treaty of Amsterdam, the High Representative would "assist" the rotating Presidency in external representation functions (Article 18(3) TEU_{Nice}). He/she would also "assist" the member states in the "formulation, preparation and implementation of policy decisions" (Article 26 TEU_{Nice}). This was in line with the EPC and Council Secretariat assisting the Presidency under the SEA and Maastricht Treaty. The Amsterdam Treaty furthermore codified the position of the European Union Special Representatives (EUSRs), who would represent the EU abroad (Article J(8)(5)). The Policy Unit was established in a separate declaration attached to the Amsterdam Treaty. It was to be an expert bureaucracy, which would provide foreign policy assessments and "argued policy option papers" during the decision-making process. It consisted of civil servants from the member states, the Council Secretariat, the Commission, and the Western European Union (WEU), and it was located in the Council Secretariat.[5] The provisions of the Treaty of Amsterdam were thus about functionality.

At least as important as the provisions in the Treaty was its implementation. Following the ratification of the Treaty, the member states delegated additional tasks and resources to the Council Secretariat. First, they appoint Javier Solana as the High Representative. Solana was a high-level politician and the NATO Secretary-General at the time. His appointment must be seen in the context of the Kosovo crisis (1998–1999). For the second time in less than a decade, the EU was incapable of bringing a conflict on its continent to a close. When the Heads of State and Government met to appoint the High Representative at the Cologne European Council in June 1999, American aircraft were bombing targets as part of the NATO air campaign. Given this international context, the earlier ideological discussion on whether to have a politician or a bureaucrat for the job seemed suddenly a non-issue. Member states had been impressed by how Solana had kept the North Atlantic Alliance together. This intentional choice to have a high-level politician proved at least as important as the decision to have the position of a High Representative in the first place.

Second, the EU experienced a proliferation of EUSRs. Previously, there had been two *ad hoc* envoys. The codification eventually led to there being 11 when the Lisbon Treaty entered into force in 2009. While the EUSRs are appointed by the member states, they report to the High Representative and support his/her work (Adebahr 2011). Each EUSR furthermore has a couple of staff members paid for by the member states. As a result, the establishment of the EUSRs has created substantial (indirect) bureaucratic support for the High Representative. Third, the Policy Unit, which contained one seconded national official per member states increased with the subsequent enlargement rounds. Because this caused bureaucratic rivalry with the Council Secretariat's Directorate-General External Relations (DG E), parts of the Policy Unit were merged with the regional units of this DG (2004 onwards) (Duke and Vanhoonacker 2006). This has led in turn to economies of scale. These bureaucratic reorganizations have made the Council Secretariat stronger.

The post of High Representative, however, did not only involve the Council Secretariat. It indirectly also had an impact on the Commission. Despite the general fear that it would lead to inter-institutional tensions, such conflicts have been surprisingly limited (Crowe 2003; Patten 2005; interviews Commission and Council Secretariat officials). Solana was mainly busy with establishing his position *vis-à-vis* the Presidency, while Patten reorganized the Commission's aid budgets, external delegations (Spence 2006a, b) and at the same time gave some room to the new chief in town (Patten 2005). While the relation between Solana and Commissioner Benita Ferrero-Waldner was not as good (Bengtsson and Allen 2011), the consultative practices at the bureaucratic level continued.

To conclude, the member states delegated new functions in the context of the Amsterdam Treaty following the wars in former Yugoslavia. They created the post of High Representative and the Policy Unit for the purpose of external representation and information analysis. They decided to delegate these resources to the Council Secretariat rather than the Commission. This case of agent selection was the result of sovereignty concerns, despite the fact that the member states anticipated that it might lead to inter-institutional conflict. They thus explicitly chose a sub-optimal scenario. Delegation in the treaty was, however, only one step. Instances of delegation also took place when implementing the treaty. For example, the member states appointed a political high-level High Representative, installed a range of Special Representatives, and reorganized the Council Secretariat. The delegation of foreign policy functions in the Treaty of Amsterdam created the basis for the establishment of a security and defense machinery.

EU security and defense policy

The Kosovo crisis not only played a role in the appointment of Solana. It also created momentum for the CSDP.[6] At the bilateral St Malo Summit on December 4, 1998, France and the UK decided that the EU should have "the capacity for autonomous action" in order to become a more prominent actor. This idea was endorsed by the other member states at the Cologne European Council in June 1999. The EU launched its first police and military missions four years later. The desire to deploy civilian and military operations immediately triggered a range of new functional demands, which subsequently led to delegation to the EU bureaucracies. Delegation was, however, not automatic. Anticipated sovereignty concerns continued to be important. The absence of a standing military headquarters is a case in point. Civilian crisis management remained under-institutionalized as well, due to uncertainty about where this policy would lead. Efficiency gains were weighed against sovereignty loss.

The St Malo Declaration was rather short on the institutional structure of the CSDP. Yet interestingly, it already stated that "the Union must be given appropriate structures and a capacity for analysis of situations, sources of intelligence and a capability for relevant strategic planning, without unnecessary duplication, taking account of the existing assets of the WEU" (paragraph 3). From the outset, France and the UK thus anticipated specific functional needs. They also recognized that those needs were costly and that they had to be met efficiently. The Vienna European Council on December 11–12, 1998, welcomed the Franco-British declaration and invited the incoming German Presidency to "further this debate" (Article 78). This accidental timing thus gave Germany the chance to put its mark on the CSDP after having been initially ignored by France and the UK.

Despite an already challenging agenda, Germany made full use of this opportunity. It proved instrumental in bridging the divide between France and the UK on the actual content of this new policy (e.g. Howorth 2000). On February 24, 1999, it issued a discussion paper titled *Informal Reflection at WEU on Europe's Security and Defence* (in Rutten 2001) discussing several options for the member states to engage in crisis management missions. Defense commitments, the paper stated, were "not the first priority." This was the task of NATO. The options for European states to launch crisis management operations included (a) NATO operational scenarios, (b) the possibility of European-led operations using NATO assets, and (c) autonomous European-led operations without NATO assets. The paper went on to discuss a whole range of implications for the last two options. It also posed questions in terms of the new functional demands – such as "what are the *minimum* requirements for an *effective* decision making capability in the field of defence and security ... what institutional arrangements would be *required* ... what should be the organisational link with NATO ... do we need regular meetings of the General Affairs Council together with Defence Ministers ... *do we need* a EU military Committee" (emphasis added)?

Three weeks later, the German Presidency tabled a new paper during an informal meeting of foreign ministers in Reinhartshausen (March 13–14 in Rutten 2001). It no longer asked questions, but made a number of points. These points formed the basis for the conclusions of the Cologne European Council (see below). As for institutional support in the field of security and defense, the paper effectively stated that three types of bodies are required: (a) political decision-making organs, (b) intelligence, situation analysis, and strategic planning units, and (c) an operational headquarters. The paper thus suggested that the EU requires "regular meetings of the General Affairs Council, including Defence Ministers; a permanent body consisting of representatives with pol/mil expertise; an EU Military Committee consisting of Military Representatives; a Military Staff including the Situation Centre." With regard to the headquarters, the member states "could use either European capabilities pre-identified within NATO ... or national European means outside the NATO framework." This would avoid "any unnecessary duplication with regard to existing capabilities within NATO."

After the US gave its blessing during a summit of the North Atlantic Council on April 24, 1999, the member states finalized the CSDP during the European Council in Cologne (June 3–4). The Presidency Report, which was attached to the Conclusions, reiterated the institutional structures of the Reinhartshausen paper. While the Report was comprehensive on institutions, the all-important discussion of capabilities was rather short. It was therefore not surprising that the UK and Italy, shortly after the Cologne European Council, issued a joint declaration on capabilities (19–20 July, in Rutten 2001). Capabilities are beyond the scope of this book, but it needs to be said that the incoming Finnish Presidency took the lead in developing benchmarks. It led (via an Anglo-French summit, November 25, in ibid.) to the famous Helsinki Headline Goals formulated during the European Council on December 10–11.

In the summer, Chirac sent to his colleagues an *Action plan of European Defence* (July 22, in ibid.). It went beyond the Cologne Report by proposing a stronger EU machinery. Chirac suggested the creation of an operational headquarters, an autonomous chain of command and autonomous intelligence sources. He also noted implicitly that the High Representative should play a role in the CSDP (Howorth 2000). The Action Plan also elaborated on the new institutional bodies that were mentioned in the German Presidency Report. For example, it stated that the Political and Security Committee (PSC) was to be a high-level body with its own ambassadors (not shared with NATO through "double-hatting"). The EUMC, on the other hand, could consist of the same military representatives as NATO's Military Committee for countries, which were also members of NATO. While few of the innovations of this action plan were accepted, it did point at several contentious issues that would remain on the agenda for the future.

The European Council in December 1999 finalized the decision-making procedure of the CSDP. It established a PSC, which would deal with the CSDP matters, an EUMC, and an EUMS. Since it was at the time not yet clear whether the CSDP would require a treaty change, the European Council decided to set up interim bodies. The interim PSC was to work under the guidance of the Political Committee and the Military Staff would consist of military experts from the member states seconded to the Council Secretariat. This choice of agent selection was pretty obvious, as it had become clear that the Council Secretariat was the main institution in EU foreign policy. The extensive use of seconded national experts constituted an important control mechanism. The creation of the Military Staff meant in practice that the resources of the WEU Military Staff were transferred to the EU. Compared to previous documents, the European Council was innovative in one other aspect. It discussed – after an intense Swedish lobby (Björkdahl 2008) – the possibility of having a parallel track in the CSDP with a "non-military crisis management capability." This became civilian crisis management.

Delegation in military crisis management

Following the decisions of the European Council, the Council (of Ministers) created the interim bodies and seconded the military experts to the Council Secretariat through Council Decisions (February 14, 2000). In a subsequent Council Decision (2000/178/CFSP), it laid down the provisions for the secondment. Apart from trivial issues such as insurance and hours of work, these also included the task description of the seconded national officials. This was short but comprehensive. The military experts seconded to the Council Secretariat were to "provide *military expertise* to the interim [Military Committee] and to the ... High Representative" (Article 4, emphasis added). They were not meant to carry out operational functions during the implementation of military operations. They were rather appointed as interim experts to help the member states develop the CSDP.

On the same day that the provisions for secondment were adopted, the defense ministers discussed the "arrangements and procedures" for the permanent bodies under the Portuguese Presidency (February 28, in Rutten 2001). They stressed that the Military Staff will *not* act as an OHQ, but would provide military expertise. During "peace time," it would perform early warning and monitor potential crises as to enable the EU to react quickly. In crisis management situations, the Military Staff would request and handle intelligence, provide situation assessment to the member states, provide them with military strategic options, and coordinate with national planning staffs that might participate in EU-led operations. These are typical expert bureaucracy functions. During implementation, the Military Staff would assist the member states and particularly the Operations Commander in the OHQ. The defense ministers thus delegated particular supportive functions to the Military Staff in all the phases of the policy process. Command and control functions were not delegated to the Council Secretariat.

Apart from these discussions on the Military Staff and allowing the High Representative to establish a small Joint Situation Centre (SITCEN) for intelligence analysis, the Presidency did little in military crisis management. The European Council Conclusions of 19–20 June, 2000, refer only to the establishment of the three new bodies. For the incoming French Presidency, the institutional structures of the military track of the CSDP were again on top of the agenda. In Annexes III–V of the Presidency Report attached to the Nice Presidency Conclusions (7–9 December, in ibid.), the details for the establishment of the three permanent CSDP bodies are worked out. The Military Staff is to perform "early warning, situation assessment and strategic planning" and amongst its extensive list of "roles," "tasks" and "functions," features prominently that "it is the source of the EU's military expertise." These annexes were turned by the foreign ministers into a Council Decision establishing the Military Staff as a permanent department in the Council Secretariat (2001/80/CFSP) under the guidance of the EUMC and the High Representative.

In addition to the establishment of the PSC, the Military Committee and the Military Staff, the member states also created a Directorate for Defence Issues (DG E VIII) in the DG E of the Council Secretariat in 2001. This small Directorate would support the intergovernmental decision-making bodies dealing with the military operations (i.e. the Military Committee and the working groups). This was in line with the regular tasks of DG E. DG E VIII contained permanent staff and seconded national officials. The permanent staff was recruited from the WEU Secretariat, NATO's International Staff and the member states via an open competition (*concours*). This caused some frictions within the WEU Secretariat, whose staff members were under the impression that they would automatically be transferred (since they knew their languages and had security clearance and experience with crisis management). Only three officials passed the competition eventually. NATO gratefully employed the remainder of the WEU Secretariat (interview with WEU official).

Although the CSDP led to substantial institutional development in a short period of time, it is important to emphasize that the member states did not delegate to the Council Secretariat and its Military Staff any autonomy or authority to implement joint actions or decisions. They kept the decision-making power in-house. The intergovernmental bodies – PSC, Military Committee, Council, etc. – call the shots. The Military Staff provides only military input into the deliberations. When a situation emerges, the ambassadors can convene on an emergency basis and coordinate a reaction. At the operational and tactical end, it is the Operations Commander in the OHQ (at NATO or in one of the member states) and the Force Commander on the ground who have some discretion. By deciding not to delegate these functions, through for example a standing military headquarters, the member states kept a close rein on the implementation of the CSDP in order to keep sovereignty loss as limited as possible.

While France and other Europeanist member states were happy to sign up for these arrangements at the European Council in Nice (December 2000), their ambitions went further. After the establishment of the Military Staff and the mentioned decision-making bodies, the debate therefore shifted – in the context of military crisis management – to developing an EU OHQ which would have some executive discretion (under the guidance of the PSC). This would clearly be a more efficient scenario, which would decrease the dependence on NATO and on the availability of national facilities (see also below). Yet the idea of an EU OHQ ran counter to the argument of US Secretary of State Madeline Albright to avoid the duplication of scarce military resources (December 7, 1998). The issue of the OHQ therefore put the Europeanist member states on collision course with the Atlanticists (UK, Portugal, Spain, Denmark, The Netherlands) in the EU, many of which were reluctant to give up sovereignty in this area.

This second round of institutional questions and delegation in the military field started with a letter from the Belgian Prime Minister Guy

Verhofstadt to his British and French counterparts, carbon copied to the complete European Council (July 18, 2002, in Haine 2003). He felt that after the events of September 11, 2001 – and despite the Laeken Declaration (December 15, 2001) – the CSDP was losing its momentum. He even felt "the risk of renationalisation." He therefore posed the question to Blair and Chirac "why not [to] consider the establishment of a European Headquarter [sic] ... and why not [to] put all the multinational forces ... under this integrated command?" While this letter was ill-received at first by almost all member states, the European split over the American invasion in Iraq (fall 2002–spring 2003) provided it with new support. The Franco-German proposal to the European Convention on November 21, 2002 (in Haine 2003, own translation), for example, talked about the need for a "harmonization of military planning, the pooling of capabilities and resources and a division of labour."

Yet only with the prospect of the Iraq war approaching did the risk that NATO facilities would not be available for Europeanist pet projects (such as peacekeeping missions in Africa) become more pertinent. It also turned out that using NATO assets made the coordination between the EU military operations and its other instruments, such as assistance policies, much more difficult. In the case of national headquarters, much time had to be spent on making the headquarters truly European. During the much televised Franco-German summit of January 22, 2003, on the occasion of the 40 years anniversary of the Elysée Treaty, the possible transformation of the CSDP into a European Security and Defence Union was suggested. This entailed little more than the proposals for the Convention, but these statements were misinterpreted by an over-enthusiastic Verhofstadt. He invited all his counterparts to discuss the possibility of a European Headquarters during a meeting in Tervuren on April 29 (in Missiroli 2003). Only France, Germany and Luxembourg showed up, and they did not in fact share the Belgian enthusiasm.

The significantly watered down declaration called for all kinds of things, but one line stood out: "the creation of a nucleus collective capability for planning and conducting operations for the European Union." While this was unacceptable to most other member states, the UK did feel the need for reconciliation after the split over Iraq. It agreed to set up a small planning cell in the Military Staff for missions with a specific civil–military character (Howorth 2007). For military operations, it was argued, there were the NATO and national headquarters, and the civilian missions were supported by some *ad hoc* structures in the Council Secretariat (see below), but for civil–military operations – supposedly the EU's key selling point – there was no planning cell.[7] In the words of the UK, the cell would be "a key tool in improving ESDP's *efficiency* and developing *expertise* in civil/military crisis management ... the cell [would] strengthen the EU's strategic planning for joint military and civilian missions, thus enabling more *coherent and effective* action" (UK Presidency Priorities, 2005, emphasis added). The civil–military cell became operational in 2005.

While this civil–military cell has met political resistance from several member states, it has also become the basis for the small-scale EU Operations Centre, which was finally established in January 2007. After the member states had great difficulty in finding an OHQ for their CSDP operations in Congo (2006), they decided to create this third operational scenario (in addition to the possibility of using NATO and national headquarters). This Operations Centre would also address some of the inefficiencies related to using NATO and national assets. Yet it remains a long way from a standing military headquarters, which many observers deem necessary. The UK and several other member states went to great lengths to ensure that the small Operations Centre would not grow into something bigger. It can be activated on an *ad hoc* basis using personnel from the Military Staff and from the member states.

Establishing a military headquarters has come back time and again to the EU agenda. The most recent attempt was made by France, Germany, and Poland. Following their "Weimar Letter" of December 6, 2010, on July 11, 2011, Lady Ashton published her report on the CSDP. Among a number of measures to make the CSDP more effective, she suggested a permanent civil–military OHQ with approximately 250 officers. This suggestion was immediately vetoed by the UK on the basis of the "no duplication of scarce resources" argument (EUObserver 2011a). As a result, no conclusions were reached on the CSDP at the Council meeting of July 18. Shortly after the summer, the three member states took yet another initiative – this time together with Italy and Spain – to establish an OHQ (September 2) (EUObserver 2011b). The compromise was to activate the Operations Centre for the first time in 2012 to facilitate the coordination between the various operations in the Horn of Africa. The Operations Centre, however, did not get a formal command role, remained an *ad hoc* structure and was given only two dozen officers for this facilitation role.

Delegation in military crisis management thus took place during two subsequent delegation rounds. Shortly after the member states had expressed their wish to engage in military operations, the rotating Presidencies quickly identified the new functional demands and suggested institutional solutions. This led to the delegation of resources to the EU bureaucracies (Military Staff and the DG E VIII). Importantly, however, the member states decided not to delegate implementation functions out of sovereignty concerns. There thus remained clear institutional checks on the EU bureaucracies. Using mostly seconded national officers also put limits on agency. During the second delegation round, a number of member states tried again to establish a standing OHQ. In functional terms, it would clearly be a more efficient scenario than using NATO and national assets. Several member states blocked such delegation, however, out of sovereignty concerns. In the end, and after much debate, they went along with a small Operations Centre. This is an instance of the member states' excessively limited delegation.

Delegation in civilian crisis management

Delegation in military crisis management has been more extensive than in civil crisis management. While military bureaucracies were furthermore quickly established, delegation in civilian crisis management took a different pace. The civilian aspects of the CSDP were for a long time regarded as a by-product of military crisis management. Some member states accordingly refused to invest in expensive civilian structures. Moreover, the member states were very wary of delegation in civilian crisis management, as it was an innovative policy area that lacked operational doctrine and standard operating procedures to keep the agents in line. It turned out, however, that the EU civilian crisis management instruments were in much demand. The civilian missions soon outnumbered military operations. When various ambitious civilian missions furthermore appeared on the horizon – most prominently EULEX Kosovo (see Chapter 8) – the member states decided to strengthen the civilian CSDP bodies in a second delegation round.

The European Council of December 1999 suggested the creation of a parallel track in CSDP for civilian crisis management. It tasked the incoming Portuguese Presidency to carry the work in civilian crisis management forward, despite little genuine Portuguese interest (Björkdahl 2008). During the European Council on March 23–24, 2000, the member states established the Committee for Civilian Aspects of Crisis Management (better known by its acronym CIVCOM) as a working party under the guidance of Committee of Permanent Representatives (COREPER), albeit with links to the PSC. While the member states established CIVCOM via a Council Decision, which was not strictly necessary, it did not have the standing of the Military Committee, which can be regarded as its military equivalent (see Cross 2010; Chapter 4). The European Council on June 19–20 subsequently identified four priority areas (police, rule of law, civil administration, and civil protection) for civilian crisis management. This was somewhat surprising, as the Commission was already carrying out many of these activities, leading to possible duplication.

As the incoming French Presidency was busy with the Nice Intergovernmental Conference and paid much attention to military crisis management, civilian crisis management was brought forward by CIVCOM (Duke 2002b). The Nice European Council Presidency Conclusions summed up their major conclusions, stating on delegation: "the Union's policing activities should be integrated, as from the planning stage, into a coherent overall crisis management operation. This requirement means that the [Council Secretariat] should be provided with a permanent policy expertise as soon as possible." The incoming Presidency and the High Representative were charged with specifying "requirements for planning and conduct of European policing operations." This effectively meant that the bureaucratic services were to be developed in the Council Secretariat rather than in the Commission, despite the fact that the Commission had previous expertise. Agent selection is thus again of importance in this instance of delegation. While the Commission could probably have played a useful role, the member states wanted to keep it out of the CSDP.

A Police Unit was established in the Council Secretariat as part of the new Directorate for Civilian Crisis Management (DG E IX). This Directorate consisted of a mix of seconded national experts and permanent staff members (cf. DG E VIII). Its main tasks consisted of "integrated planning and co-ordination, situation assessment, preparation of exercises, and preparation of legal frameworks and rules" (Göteborg European Council, in Rutten 2002). DG E VIII could, however, rely on the Military Staff and an OHQ for the conduct of military operations. DG E IX did not have such civilian equivalents. As one observer (interview Council Secretariat official) put it, "DG E IX [was] at once the DG E VIII, the EUMS and the OHQ of civilian crisis management." It had to do everything, from creating standard operating procedures and protocols to logistics, procurement, and third country contacts during the actual civilian CSDP missions. No wonder that it borrowed heavily from their military counterparts and that it used the military's in-house expertise. The creation of DG E IX was in fact a major instance of non-delegation. The member states did not know what to do with civilian CSDP. Under such uncertainty, they preferred to keep the functions in-house.

The Swedish Presidency also convened a conference for National Police Commissioners in Brussels on May 10, 2001. This meant the involvement of the national ministries of interior in the CSDP. These had so far only played a very small role in foreign policy. The Swedish Presidency then drafted a Police Action Plan. This document emphasized the institutional needs for police missions in the CSDP. These included "arrangements for planning and conduct of police operations at political-strategic level" – such as "the development of a capability for generic, contingency and operational planning for police operations, the integration of police expertise and input into EU structures for early warning and timely assessment (including EU fact-finding missions), [and] the development of an ability to rapidly set up operational headquarters" – as well as "concepts and systems for command and control of police operations." The Göteborg European Council fell short of creating new institutions in what was yet again a case of non-delegation.

As civilian crisis management was institution-poor compared to military crisis management, it is no surprise that the Joint Action establishing the first European Union Police Mission in Bosnia-Herzegovina (EUPM) (March 11, 2002, 2002/210/CFSP) was very detailed on the institutional division of tasks. For example, it established an *ad hoc* Planning Team "to deal with functions ensuing from the needs of the mission." The services in the Council Secretariat were tasked with drawing up the Concept of Operations (CONOPS). The Planning Team would subsequently draw up the OPLAN and "develop all technical instruments necessary to execute the [Police Mission]." The Council would approve the CONOPS and the OPLAN. The Joint Action determined the location of the Headquarters and Monitoring Units on the ground as well as the appointment procedures. The formal link between the Police Mission on the one hand, and the member states and the Council Secretariat on the other went through the EUSR on the ground. The unusual detailed character of the planning process and division of labor in the Joint Action is evidence of the fact that there were no generic concepts for civilian crisis management. In this Joint Action, the member states wanted to keep incomplete contracting, and thus uncertainty, to a minimum.

Other civilian missions quickly followed and discussions over the institutional structures continued. The CSDP Police Mission in Macedonia, for example, worked in parallel with police training by the Commission. Interestingly the seniority of the Commission officials was much higher than those of the CSDP mission, although the latter had more visibility. This inevitably led to some personal tensions (interview Commission official). The division of labor between both missions was unclear also (Ioannides 2006). The negotiations over the mission in Georgia were of a more complex nature. The Commission simply stated that Georgia was not in a state of crisis and that as a result a CSDP mission (rather than using development instruments) was not justified (Kurowska 2008). The Commission and the member states clashed again over the AMM (see Chapter 6). The result was that the member states excluded the Commission from their negotiations and dealt with the Council Secretariat instead.

The European Council met at Hampton Court on October 27, 2005. On its agenda was the strengthening of civilian crisis management, with a view to more challenging future missions in Kosovo and Afghanistan. The member states asked the High Representative to submit proposals for crisis management structures that could meet the new demands and the CFSP budget. One day before the European Council on December 15–16, Solana sent the paper *Follow-up to Hampton Court: CFSP and ESDP* to the Presidency. It stated that after 12 civilian missions "we are currently close to the limits of our capacity" (Article 12). Therefore he argued that "arrangements for management and control of these missions need to be strengthened [and] steps should be taken to clarify the chains of command and responsibility and to ensure access to the planned operational facilities, so that we can deal with such situations twenty-four hours a day/seven days a week" (Article 16). He suggested to "put in place more robust arrangements for the management and control of missions and operations, involving clearer chains of command and responsibility and ensuring access to planned operational facilities" (Article 19).

These requirements eventually led to the creation of the CPCC (operational since August 2007). This body can be seen as the civilian equivalent of the Military Staff and the OHQ. Following the establishment of the CPCC, civilian missions have a unified chain of command. The Civilian Operations Commander has the highest authority. Like the Military Staff, the CPCC supports the decision-making process and the implementation of the actual missions (see also next chapter). The creation of this new civilian body was therefore the result of the new functional demands, posed by challenging future missions in Kosovo and Afghanistan, for professional civilian crisis management. To run those challenging missions more efficiently, civilian crisis management required supportive bodies in Brussels. This second delegation round in civilian crisis management was an intentional decision by the member states weighing efficiency with delegation loss. Despite the significance of the CPCC, it needs to be said that this body currently employs some 70 civil servants. This remains minimal compared to the 200 in the Military

Staff and the 150 in an OHQ, particularly taking into account the high number of civilian missions.

The Treaty of Lisbon

The Treaty of Lisbon of 2009 is the most recent step in the institutionalization of EU foreign policy and the CSDP. It brought about three major changes. First, on the political level, it merged the position of the High Representative with that of the Commissioner for External Relations. Second, on the bureaucratic level, it has merged the external relations services of the European Commission with those of the Council Secretariat into the EEAS. The EEAS also consists of a number of seconded national diplomats. Third, the Lisbon Treaty has transformed the existing Commission delegations in third countries into EU delegations, which have a stronger political and diplomatic function. In the area of the CSDP most changes have been cosmetic. While all the CSDP bureaucracies have formally moved from the Council Secretariat to the EEAS, they still are housed in the same building. It is nonetheless important to discuss the reasons behind the reorganizations of the Treaty of Lisbon. This section highlights the coordination costs between the EU bureaucracies, policies, and representation, and stresses agent selection and re-contracting.

The reforms of the Lisbon Treaty have some history. As discussed above, the member states decided in the Amsterdam Treaty to strengthen the Council Secretariat rather than the Commission. They were conscious at the time that this might bring inter-institutional tensions. When the treaty was negotiated during the mid-1990s, however, it was unclear that the foreign policy bureaucracies in the Council Secretariat would grow as dramatically as they did in the period 1999–2002 (the various reasons have been mentioned above). This made the inter-institutional tensions and the coordination costs worse than anticipated. It created a feedback loop for the European Convention when it met in the early 2000s. The objectives became to merge the relevant services of the Council Secretariat and the Commission. The merger of the High Representative and the Commissioner would result in the Union Minister for Foreign Affairs and Security Policy. The bureaucratic merger would lead to the EEAS and the Union delegations.

The European Convention was launched with the Laeken Declaration (2001). It the area of foreign policy it asked three modest functional questions: "How should the coherence of European foreign policy be enhanced? How is synergy between the High Representative and the competent Commissioner to be reinforced? Should the external representation of the Union in international fora be extended further?" During the Convention, these questions were discussed in the context of the "External Action" working group. When reading their final report, it is clear that most energy went to debating the synergy between the High Representative and the Commissioner. For future relations, the Convention made four suggestions: closer cooperation, integration of the High Representative into the Commission, a truly double-hatted position, and a higher level double-hatted position with a bias towards the member states (CONV 459/02).

The discussion within the Convention was thus not unlike the earlier discussion under the Treaty of Amsterdam in the Reflection Report. There were again functional debates. For example, the Convention report noted about the first option that "a considerable number of members felt that closer cooperation, while maintaining the two distinct functions of HR and Relex Commissioner, would not be sufficient to ensure coherence ... they considered that more bold institutional changes were needed" (ibid.: paragraph 30). There was thus an efficiency rationale. Sovereignty costs, however, stayed important as well. "For a considerable number of members [option 2] would represent the most effective solution to overcome the challenge of coherence and consistency in external action. At the same time they noted that it might not be attainable at this stage, as there was no consensus among Member States to turn foreign policy into an exclusive/shared competence" (ibid.: paragraph 32). The third option was therefore "presented as a compromise solution" (ibid.: paragraph 33). It was a trade-off between sovereignty and efficiency and at the same time an instance of agent selection.

The Convention working group debated the bureaucratic services much less extensively. Duplication and inefficiencies had to be avoided. Services therefore had to be merged. The delegations of the EU in third countries furthermore had to be upgraded to achieve a higher presence. In addition to the working group "External Action," there was also a working group "Defence," which made several general recommendations, few of which concerned the institutional setup. Both reports were used for the drafting of the Constitutional Treaty, in which the name of the High Representative was talked up from "European External Representative" to "Union Minister for Foreign Affairs," which in terms of terminology was close to option 4. In addition, all the relevant external relations services of the Commission and Council Secretariat would be merged into the EEAS. The Treaty, as is well known, failed ratification in 2005. The resulting Lisbon Treaty toned down the rhetoric by turning the "Minister" again into a "High Representative." It is fair to say that few people could predict, at the time, the exact effects of the one line in the Constitutional and Lisbon Treaty on the EEAS. From the very beginning it was clear that the EEAS would require further contracting through Council Decisions. In such delegation decisions all member states would have a veto. Everyone involved, from the member states to the EU institutions, knew that negotiating the EEAS would be a tremendous task. Simon Duke (2003: 19), for example, noted that the negotiations over the EEAS "have the potential to reopen traditional intergovernmental and *communautaire* tensions and, at a human level, to introduce a good deal of uncertainty and anxiety." That intensive political negotiations thus materialized on the EEAS in 2005, in 2007–2008 and in 2009–2010 was not a surprise.[8] Those who did not expect "guerrilla warfare over the tiniest details" (Howorth 2010b: 2) are well-advised to read about the history of EU foreign policy. With the EEAS, the member states were rearranging their foreign policy machinery and this involved a lot of power politics.

When looking specifically at the outcome of the negotiations and the institutional design of the EEAS, the rational institutionalist model provides us with several insights. The first relates to agent selection. The member states explicitly decided not to make the EEAS part of the European Commission or the Council Secretariat, but to make it a *sui generis* third institution. It has been noted above that the member states, time and again, did not equip the Commission with foreign policy functions due to its diverging preferences and significant bureaucratic resources. Instead they chose this role for the Council Secretariat. While foreign policy never fitted comfortably within the Council Secretariat (Dijkstra 2010a; Christiansen 2002), the member states chose the Council Secretariat because of "the merit of ... not creating any new bodies" (Reflection Group, Article 153). With the foreign policy services in the Council Secretariat becoming significantly larger than anticipated, the relative costs of creating a third body decreased compared with the costs of keeping them in the Council Secretariat. Agent selection thus continues to be important.

It is also interesting to take a look at the Commission. As the dust of the negotiations begins to settle, it becomes clear that the Commission has lost much of its resources to the EEAS. The Commission had to give up its external relations expertise Directorate-General External Relation (DG RELEX) and its desks from DG Development.[9] It has lost its strategic control over the sizable development budget and it has had to hand over most of the important Head of Delegation positions to national diplomats. The record is thus pretty sobering. In fact, the creation of the EEAS can be seen as a major attempt by the member states to re-contract. The member states were arguably never entirely pleased with the Commission carrying out external relations tasks under the first pillar. With the increase in the number of delegations during the 1990s, the Commission touched upon national sensitivities. The EEAS presented member states with an opportunity to take some of these resources back in the name of consistency.

The Lisbon Treaty and the EEAS are an important step in the institutional development of EU foreign policy. They bring together the foreign policy services of the Council Secretariat, the Commission and the member states. While certainly not everything is rational or intentional about the EEAS, some of the defining characteristics of this delegation decision fit well with the principal–agent model. Agent selection was one of the main points of the EEAS. By creating a *sui generis* institution, the member states continued to keep the Commission at arm's length. They made the Council Secretariat once again a traditional body for the Council. In this major restructuring of the foreign policy machinery, the member states have used the opportunity to re-contract some resources of the Commission in the field of external relations: its expertise, management of funds, and delegations. On the CSDP machinery, the Lisbon Treaty has had little effect.

Conclusion

This chapter has analyzed many historical instances of delegation and non-delegation in the context of EU foreign and security policy. It has shown that member states constantly balanced between the functional need to delegate and their sovereignty costs. As a result, they generally delegated fewer functions than was optimal. What is somewhat surprising – yet completely in line with the argument of this book – is how explicit the deliberations of the member states have been in terms of the efficiency/sovereignty balance. Equally surprising is the continuous importance of agent selection: first the explicit choice of the member states to keep tasks in-house through the Presidency; later the choice for the Council Secretariat over the Commission; currently the choice of making the EEAS a *sui generis* institution. Finally, there has been a strong link between the desire of member states to engage in certain foreign policy activities (exchange of information, diplomatic initiatives, CSDP operations), the related transaction costs (negotiation, coordination, information, and implementation costs) and the delegation of functions. These empirical observations provide powerful evidence for the overall argument.

The first period under analysis concerned the creation of foreign policy cooperation. In terms of delegation, the member states recognized the need for administrative support. Yet given the history of the Fouchet Plans, they decided intentionally to do without a secretariat. Instead, they delegated tasks to the Presidency, while realizing that this was a sub-optimal scenario. Inefficiencies were acknowledged, but this did not lead to delegation in the Copenhagen and London Reports. In the SEA and the Maastricht Treaty, efficiency and sovereignty continued to play an important role. EPC and the Communities were kept separate, despite increasing overlap and the need for coordination. When the EPC Secretariat was finally established, it was a small affair with seconded national officials. The member states furthermore explicitly decided not to make the European Commission a crucial actor in EU foreign policy as part of the Maastricht Treaty. They preferred to rely on their Council Secretariat, over which they had more control.

The second section of the chapter has studied the Amsterdam Treaty and its implementation. The desire of the member states to upgrade foreign policy cooperation, following the failures in the Western Balkans, led to the creation of the Policy Unit and the position of High Representative. Both addressed transaction costs related to efficiency (information and representation). What was important about the Amsterdam Treaty, however, was that the member states made the choice to delegate these resources to the Council Secretariat rather than to the Commission. This was a clear case of agent selection. The member states anticipated that they would be able to exert more control over the Council Secretariat. That their choice would lead to potential inconsistency and possibly to inter-institutional tensions, they appreciated. They nonetheless preferred the sub-optimal functional option out of sovereignty concerns.

The delegation decisions in the CSDP closely resemble those in foreign policy. From the very start it was clear to the member states that a new institutional structure was necessary if they wanted to send civilian and military operations abroad. The most prominent transaction costs were already mentioned in the St Malo Declaration and the early German Presidency documents. The EU would need the capacity for information analysis in the planning phase and would need to have a structure for implementation. While the member states quickly addressed these demands through the delegation of functions, they did not deal with all the costs of cooperation. Sovereignty costs were yet again important. The member states have to date rejected equipping EU bureaucracies with a standing military headquarters. They have also kept the supporting bureaucracies for civilian CSDP small, despite the fact that there are strong functional needs resulting from ambitious operations in Kosovo, Afghanistan, and Georgia. Moreover, the CSDP bureaucracies were packed with seconded national officials, which is an important control mechanism that limits expertise and continuity.

Finally, this chapter has looked at the recent changes of the Treaty of Lisbon. While many of the innovations are often overstated, particularly in the CSDP, rationalist theories continue to have relevant explanatory value. The rationale for the Lisbon reforms was very much one of coordination and external representation. The member states wanted to further limit bureaucratic politics between the Commission and the Council Secretariat. They also want to create synergies between the various EU external relations policies. The institutional design of the EEAS is also particularly striking. The member states made the explicit choice to create a third institution and to keep strict control over its mandate, budget, and structure.

The evidence thus provides support for the theoretical argument, which was outlined in the previous chapter. That said, there are always a number of anomalies that rationalist theories have difficulty explaining. In the context of the Maastricht Treaty, there were repeated references to getting the European Parliament involved. Reducing transaction costs cannot be an explanation. In addition, the appointment of Solana must be seen in the context of the ongoing Kosovo war. Finally, the EU relied to a certain extent on NATO concepts in the development of the CSDP. This may be to some extent evidence for constructivism. These individual anomalies do not, however, convincingly challenge the argument that in the majority of instances the member states carefully weighed efficiency gains with sovereignty costs. Neither do they challenge the claim that the member states made intentional decisions on institutional design in terms of the formal autonomy of agents and agent selection, as well as control mechanism.

In addition to directly competing alternative explanations, it is also worthwhile to point out the limits of delegation theory as empirically analyzed in this chapter. The principal–agent model is a middle-range theory that helps us to better understand relations between the member states and the EU bureaucracies. It does not explain the whole world.

The relations between principals and agents are, of course, conditioned by structural developments in the international system as well as third actors. Indeed, this chapter has regularly indicated the importance of major world events and the US in understanding the development of EU foreign policy cooperation as a whole. Without reference to such events and third actors, one cannot explain the empowerment of the EU bureaucracies in security policy. They affect the preferences of member states and thereby indirectly the institutional development of the EU.

4
Policy-Making in EU Security and Defense

The previous chapter traced the delegation of functions to the EU bureaucracies in the CSDP. This chapter comprehensively describes their role in the CSDP policy process. It provides the basis for the case study analyses in the remaining chapters, which focus on the military operation Althea in Bosnia, the monitoring mission in Aceh (Indonesia), the military operation in Chad and the Central African Republic, and the rule of law mission in Kosovo. While this chapter reflects the state of the art in terms of the CSDP policy process, it will make mention of previous structures as well to provide sufficient background information. After all, the planning of the military operation Althea, for example, started almost a decade ago and the EU bureaucracies looked a bit different then. The starting point is the agenda-setting phase of civilian and military missions. The chapter then moves on to the planning phase. It concludes with the implementation. The chapter uses practical examples from the four case studies to illustrate the process.

Agenda-setting

Agenda-setting is best seen as a process during which different actors try to put and keep their issues high on the agenda (e.g. Princen 2007; Tallberg 2003). It is the first step of the policy process. Without agenda-setting, it is not possible to take decisions or actions. The starting point for analysis is the formal agenda-setting powers of the EU bureaucracies. In the CSDP and in foreign policy, the right of initiative is shared by the member states and the High Representative (Article 30 TEU). These actors "may refer any question relating to the common foreign and security policy to the Council and may submit to it ... initiatives or proposals" (ibid.). This provision of the Treaty of Lisbon marks a change from previous treaties, in which the right of initiative was shared between the member states and the European Commission. While the Commission thus no longer holds the shared right of initiative, it needs to be noted that the High Representative is also the Vice-President of the Commission. As such he/she can also take initiatives "with the Commission's support" (ibid.).

The right of initiative, as defined in the Lisbon Treaty, is a reflection of the previous practice of agenda-setting in the CFSP/CSDP. Under the Treaty of Amsterdam, the High Representative and the Council Secretariat did not enjoy formal agenda-setting power. After all, they formally only assisted the Presidency and the member states in the conduct of foreign policy. Yet in practice it was not difficult for Javier Solana and his civil servants to put issues on the EU agenda. Many of the formal CSDP planning documents came from them. Moreover, they had agenda access via the Presidency or like-minded member states. Finally, Solana could simply raise the attention of the member states by traveling to trouble spots or by giving a statement to the press. Officials in the Council Secretariat could put forward policy and options papers or they could make comments in the relevant foreign policy working groups. The lack of formal agenda access was in practice not a problem for Solana and the Council Secretariat.

The Commission, on the contrary, had had the power of initiative since the Maastricht Treaty, but it did not made much use of it. Following the Maastricht Treaty, there were reorganizations in the bureaucratic structure of the Commission. These severely undermined its capacity to be a foreign policy player (Nuttall 2000). Some observers have also argued that the Commission simply did not have the content expertise in the field of foreign policy to come up with good initiatives. This was particularly the case in the area of military CSDP, where the Commission did not have in-house expertise. It made it impossible for the Commission to draft planning documents (interview Commission official). Other observers noted that following the defeat of the Commission's ambitious proposals in Maastricht, it has focused on other areas. The fact that initiatives in the area of CFSP/CSDP did not come from the Commission, despite its formal powers, is now reflected in the Treaty of Lisbon, which has delegated the right of initiative to other actors.

Access to the agenda is, however, only one part of the story. The point is how to get issues *high* on the agenda. In the case of the CSDP, this is only partially a matter of the big member states pursuing their interests openly as they have done in Chad and Afghanistan (with mixed results). It is more likely to be a delicate process, which requires the use of diplomatic skill and networks. A number of operations, for example, resulted from requests by the UN.[1] Many operations in the Western Balkans were "logically" taken over from NATO and the UN. The CSDP operations in Aceh and Rafah were the result of intense entrepreneurship by Solana himself. The monitoring mission in Georgia was a response to an emerging crisis (though promoted by France), while the Security Sector Reform mission in Guinea-Bissau came on the agenda as a result of the Portuguese Presidency. In other words, to get a mission on the agenda, actors need to have access to the center of CSDP policy-making. The High Representative and the CSDP officials in the EEAS are very well-placed in this respect (Mérand et al. 2010, 2011).

In the EEAS, there are several actors involved in the agenda-setting phase of the CSDP. At the highest level, there is, of course, the High Representative, the cabinet and the "corporate board," consisting of the Secretary-General and Deputies-Secretary-General. In addition, desk officers from the Regional Departments are typically involved to provide country and region-specific expertise. The lead in CSDP is, however, with the CMPD. This Directorate is a merger of the two Crisis Management Directorates (DG E VIII for Defence Issues and DG E IX for Civilian Crisis Management) of the Council Secretariat and includes some former officers of the Military Staff. While the CMPD is an integral part of the EEAS, it reports directly to the High Representative. In case of an emerging crisis, officials of the CMPD often write an options paper. This is still part of what is called "advance planning" (Simon and Mattelaer 2011). When the member states want to take the work forward, the options paper may become the basis for formal Crisis Response Planning.

While the CMPD of the EEAS is thus in the lead during agenda-setting, some of the Directorates-General of the European Commission can play a supportive role. Before the AMM was launched, for example, the Commission funded the mediation activities of the former Finnish President Martti Ahtisaari between the Aceh rebels and Indonesian government through its Rapid Reaction Mechanism. During the agenda-setting process of the military operation in Chad, the CMPD and Commission officials wrote a joint options paper. In the case of EULEX Kosovo, Commissioner Olli Rehn co-authored several reports with the then High Representative Solana on the future EU presence. By being closely involved, the Commission can lend weight to certain topics. This is important for some member states. The Commission plays a role through its desk officers in the various Directorates-General (DEVCO, Humanitarian Aid and Civil Protection (ECHO), ELARG).

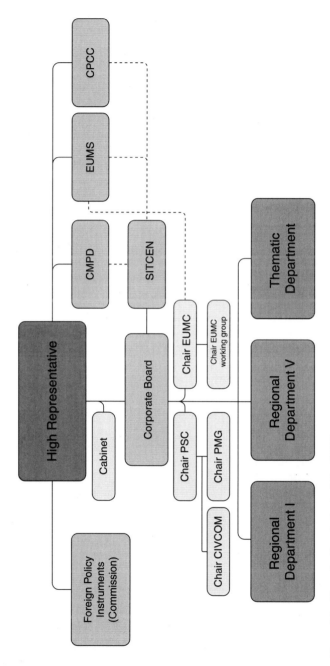

Figure 4.1 Organizational chart of the EEAS

After a possible options paper by the EEAS – in some cases there is no time or need for an options paper – the member states discuss whether "action is appropriate." The most relevant body is, in this respect, the PSC, consisting of national ambassadors. While the PSC was previously chaired by the rotating Presidency, since the Treaty of Lisbon, it has been chaired by a representative of the High Representative, who is formally part of the EEAS. In other words, the PSC currently has a permanent chairmanship. Once the member states have agreed that action is appropriate, the EU moves to Crisis Response Planning. The next step is generally to send a team of CSDP experts on a fact-finding mission to the operations theater. This is the beginning of the formal decision-making process.

Decision-making

Fact-finding mission and Crisis Management Concept

The decision that EU action is appropriate is already an important decision in itself, as it creates external expectations. Sending out a fact-finding mission, in particular, is a strong diplomatic signal (interview national official; Council 2001). This creates a Catch-22, as member states are reluctant to sign up for civilian and military missions if they do not have sufficient information. Yet they can only get such information by sending out a fact-finding mission. The involvement of CSDP officials and the contacts with third parties often leads to a *fait accompli* for the member states. The presence of EU officials during the Aceh negotiations raised expectations, while the fact-finding mission to Chad in August 2007 created momentum. This problem, where the member states have a lack of information and face uncertainty and subsequent contracting, seems difficult to resolve.

The fact-finding mission generally takes one week. It consists of a handful of EU officials, but its composition is flexible. A policy officer, planner, logistical officer, and intelligence officer are part of the core team. These are all EEAS officials. They come from the Regional Departments, the Planning Directorate (CMPD), the EUMS or the CPCC, and the Intelligence Centre (INTCEN; previously Joint Situation Centre, SITCEN) for intelligence. The missions also include senior staff from the EEAS or the member states, who will play a leading role in the future mission. Moreover, Commission officials have recently been added to most of the fact-finding missions. Finally, officials from other international organizations may join as well. In the case of Aceh, for example, officials from Association of Southeast Asian Nations (ASEAN) states joined, since they would contribute monitors to the operation. For the Chad fact-finding mission, the UN sent a team of officials, as it would deploy a parallel police training mission. Fact-finding missions thus fit purpose, but the EEAS makes up the core of the team. A report on the fact-finding mission is sent to the member states.

Shortly after an international crisis starts, the Crisis Platform within the EEAS is activated.[2] The purpose of this platform is to bring together all the actors involved in the planning of an operation, including Commission officials, to ensure coherence. It has no formal planning authority, which remains with its constituent actors. The meetings take place throughout the whole planning process. The platform includes senior officials, which implies, in practice, directors from the EEAS and desk officers from the Commission. Needless to say, the role of the Crisis Platform and its predecessor structures has changed over time. Obstructive behavior by the Commission during the planning of the military operation in Bosnia (see Chapter 5) meant that it quickly found itself excluded from these meetings (interview EU official). During the military operation in Chad, on the other hand, the Commission played a constructive role and its desk officers thought that it was very helpful venues to raise their concerns (interviews Commission officials).

The first topic for discussion is the *Crisis Management Concept*. This is the first planning document (see Table 4.1). The concept is based on information resulting from the fact-finding mission. It is formally drafted by the CMPD. The concept benefits from the input of the other actors in the Crisis Platform and moves up the EEAS hierarchy. It is then sent to the member states in the Political and Security Committee. Before the national ambassadors take a look at it, they ask their working groups for advice. The EUMC, its working group and the Political-Military Group (PMG) deal with military concepts.[3] The CIVCOM is in charge of the civilian ones. In some cases, the EUMC also comments on

Table 4.1 Overview of the planning documents

Military operations	Civilian operations
Crisis Management Concept	Crisis Management Concept
Military Strategic Options	Civilian/Police Strategic Options
Council Decision (pre-Lisbon: Joint Action)	Concept of Operations
Concept of Operations	Council Decision (pre-Lisbon: Joint Action)
Operation Plan	Operation Plan

civilian concepts. The civilian monitoring mission in Aceh, for example, included a disarmament capability, which consisted of military officers (in civilian clothes). It was therefore necessary that the Military Committee also presented its views.

It is important to elaborate a bit on the composition of the EUMC and CIVCOM. These are the main intergovernmental control bodies of the member states. Mai'a Cross (2010) shows, however, that they are quite different. The Military Committee consists of the Military Representatives, who are two- and three-star generals in the Permanent Representations. Many of these generals are also the Military Representative in NATO. Considering the importance of NATO to almost all defense ministries, they are at the top of the national military hierarchy. On average, they have 35 years of experience and about half of them have received mid-career training in the US. As a result of their shared military background, Cross (2010) notes, they generally do not have major problems finding agreements on military issues. They know how to apply military doctrine. As they have such senior positions in their national defense ministry, they encounter few problems in getting quality expertise and instructions from the national capitals. As noted, they are also supported by a working group. Finally, the Military Committee has a permanent chairperson in the form of a four- or five-star general, who is supported by a small permanent office.

CIVCOM is, in comparison, a much more junior body. It consists of early to mid-career diplomats. Importantly, Cross (ibid.: 25) states, "most CIVCOM delegates do not come to Brussels with experience in either civilian crisis management or EU affairs." Their lack of technical expertise is explicitly acknowledged (ibid.). It is also important that these diplomats cannot rely on a working group, nor necessarily on their national capitals. There is a serious absence of civilian doctrine with clear standard operating procedures (Benner and Bossong 2010). Moreover, the expertise in the national capitals is limited and it is available in ministries (i.e. interior and justice) other than the foreign ministry, where most CIVCOM delegates come from. Given coordination problems at the national level, this limits the possibilities for CIVCOM to get quality instructions in a short amount of time (e.g. Vanhoonacker and Jacobs 2010). The difference between the Military Committee and CIVCOM is partially overcome by the ambassadors in the PSC, who have the final say over the Crisis Management Concept and the other planning documents. The PSC is, however, a very senior body. It therefore does not have time to deal with details that should be addressed at the level of CIVCOM.

On the basis of the CIVCOM/EUMC advice, the PSC can amend and/or adopt the Crisis Management Concept. The concept is then forwarded to the Council for formal adoption. It is adopted by the foreign ministers meeting in the Foreign Affairs Council. If necessary, the Crisis Management Concept can be adopted via silence procedure.[4] In case of a military mission, the adoption is the moment to identify the future OHQ. The EU can, in this respect, rely on the NATO command and control structures. It can use national assets of the member states. It can also decide to activate its Operations Centre within the EEAS. In practice, the choice of the OHQ is generally straightforward. The NATO assets were used in the follow-on operations in the Western Balkans. The French headquarters was the obvious choice during Operation Artemis in Congo (2003) and in Chad. In EUFOR Congo (2006) and Operation Atalanta (2008–date), there were serious negotiations, but the informal choice was made early (Grevi, Helly and Keohane 2009). For civilian operations, the EEAS performs mission support functions in-house through the CPCC.

Strategic Options

Following the adoption of the Crisis Management Concept, the EEAS drafts the *Strategic Options* (the second planning document). In the case of a military operation, these are the Military Strategic Options; for civilian missions, these are the Civilian or Police Strategic Options. The Military Strategic Options are written by the officials of the EUMS, which is a hierarchical international military bureaucracy that reports directly to the High Representative and the Military Committee. As such, the Military Staff is an integral part of the EEAS. It is led by a three-star general, who also holds the rank of Director-General in the EEAS. It employs around 200 military officers and some civilian personnel. The EUMS consists of five main directorates: concepts and capabilities, intelligence, operations, logistics, and communication and information systems. The Military Strategic Options are drafted by the EUMS' Operations Directorate in cooperation with the staff of the CMPD, which previously had the lead on the Crisis Management Concept.

The Civilian and Police Strategic Options were initially drafted by the predecessor of the CMPD (DG E IX of the Council Secretariat). This difference with the military planning process resulted from the fact that there was no civilian equivalent of the EUMS until 2007 (see Chapter 3). With the creation of the CPCC, however, the asymmetry was rectified. The body has become responsible for the drafting of Civilian and Police Strategic Options. It is located in the EEAS and employs around 70 civil servants, many of whom are seconded. While the CPCC is in various ways the equivalent of the Military Staff, it is important to note that it is *also* in charge of mission support as well as operational command and control. In a way, it is the Civilian OHQ. Tellingly, the CPCC is led by the permanent Civilian Operations Commander. As noted above, the Military Staff does not perform such functions. During military operations, the EU uses a separate OHQ.

The Strategic Options themselves are directly based on the Crisis Management Concept. They give very general possibilities for engagement. In the case of the military operation in Chad, for example, four strategic options were proposed (from training the local army to deploying up to four battalions). The military has to consider all options, but by also including the ones that are not politically feasible, the EEAS can focus attention squarely on one or two options. Military Strategic Options are accompanied by a reference amount for the common costs of the operation. These common costs are to be shared by all the member states proportional to their gross national income. The common costs include costs related to the headquarters as well as infrastructure costs. The bulk of the costs – such as salaries/transport – are borne, however, by the troop-contributing countries themselves. Since the financing of the civilian missions is differently organized, a reference amount cannot be given at this stage. After the Strategic Options have been written, they go to the member states in CIVCOM, the Military Committee, the PSC, and finally the Council, which chooses the preferred option.

Civilian and military planning to this point are very similar. Following the formal adoption of the Strategic Options, however, they go different ways. In essence, military planning moves away from Brussels to operational planning within the designated OHQ, while civilian planning remains with the CPCC. This difference also explains the different order of the planning documents (see Table 4.1 above). The Council Decision is the next step in military planning. The emphasis in civilian planning is, on the contrary, on the CONOPS. Because planning differs, military and civilian planning will be described separately below.

Once the Military Strategic Options have been agreed, the military planning process moves from strategic to operational planning. However, before this step can be made, the EU has to adopt a Council Decision (previously Joint Action), which is the formal legal basis of the operation. The Council Decision formally designates the OHQ, appoints the Operations and Force Commanders, and makes funding available for the common costs. In practice, the Council Decision is not a military planning document, but rather a codification of the Military Strategic Options and the Crisis Management Concept. Earlier in the process, the OHQ and both Commanders have been identified. The Council Decision is drafted by legal experts. It is then discussed by the RELEX Counselors, who are the legal and financial experts in the permanent representations. The Council Decision subsequently goes up to the Council, but is also discussed in COREPER, because of the institutional and financial aspects. The member states generally quarrel over money.

In civilian crisis management, Strategic Options do not lead directly to a Council Decision. This is mainly for financial reasons. As mentioned, the financial aspects of military operations are rather straightforward. The common costs are covered by all member states, whereas member states individually pay for their contributions.[5] In civilian crisis management, it is more complicated. Apart from the nationally borne salaries of seconded mission staff, most of the costs are covered by the CFSP budget. This is administered by the Commission's Service for Foreign Policy Instruments (which falls under the High Representative/Vice-President; see Figure 4.1). Because mission staff are recruited within civilian missions on an individual basis (rather than as a contingent in the case of military missions), it is not yet clear at the stage of the Strategic Options what the exact costs will be. If the ratio between seconded and non-seconded staff, for example, changes, it has budgetary consequences. Much more detailed plans thus have to be made before the budget can be established in the Council Decision. Moreover, at this stage, there is also no need to designate an OHQ, as civilian missions use EEAS facilities. In other words, more in-depth planning can take place first within the EEAS.

After the adoption of the Civilian and Police Strategic Options, the CPCC thus drafts the *CONOPS*. This is a much more detailed plan of the mission. The CONOPS is sent for approval to the member states. At the same time, the Commission, in consultation with the EEAS, prepares the budget for the operation. The ceiling of the CFSP budget has been set in advance as part of the overall EU budget and cannot, in practice, be amended. The Commission is not going back to the European Parliament to ask for more money (interview Commission official). Needless to say, this is the world upside-down, because crisis situations are difficult to plan in advance. The budget then has to go to the member states, which discuss it in the Group of External Relations Counselors (RELEX group). Ultimately it becomes part of the Council Decision, which has to be adopted by the member states. The Council Decision appoints the Head of Mission, who becomes personally (!) financially responsible for the whole mission to the Commission through signing a contract. This is the last step in the decision-making phase of civilian CSDP missions.

Implementation

The adoption of the Joint Action by the member states as the formal legal basis concludes the decision-making phase. It simultaneously starts the operational planning of civilian and military missions, which in turn leads to launching operations on the ground. The civilian and military operations again differ during this phase. In military operations, the operational planning takes place in the OHQ.[6] In civilian missions, the emphasis is already on establishing the operation on the ground. The launch of the civilian and military operations will thus be discussed separately.

Military planning and launching of the operation

Once the Council Decision is adopted, the OHQ can finally be activated. The EU has three scenarios: (1) it can make use of the NATO OHQ (Supreme Headquarters Allied Powers Europe, SHAPE); (2) it can use the OHQ of the member states (France, Germany, Greece, Italy, UK); or (3) it can decide to activate the Operations Centre in the Military Staff. These three options all have their advantages and drawbacks. The EU can use SHAPE under the Berlin Plus agreement. It means that the EU seconds a dozen of military officers – the EU Staff Group – to SHAPE. These officers support the EU Operations Commander, who also happens to be NATO's Deputy Supreme Allied Commander Europe (DSACEUR). The EU furthermore relies on NATO assets, such as the communication and information systems. While NATO provides a powerful machinery, there are three problems. First, EU–NATO relations are complicated as a result of asymmetrical membership (the Cyprus–Turkey problem). Everyday work is undermined as a result of all kinds of rules (e.g. military officers from neutral EU countries have restricted access). Second, because SHAPE is a powerful machine, some of the member states feel that they cannot exert adequate political control over the military missions. Third, cooperation between SHAPE and EU actors is difficult. The Berlin Plus scenario has therefore only been used in follow-on operations when the EU took over from NATO.

The second operational scenario is the use of member states' assets. The idea is that one of the member states makes its headquarters available. This OHQ is then "Europeanized" by the other member states sending some 150 military officers ("augmentees") within weeks.[7] The process is managed by the Military Staff, which sends liaison officers. In reality, this operational scenario has been problematic. By making the headquarters available, a member state accepts a leadership role during the operation. Most member states are reluctant to do so, not least as a result of costs and commitments elsewhere. The Europeanization of the headquarters is also a tiresome affair. In the case of the Chad operation, it took nearly three months before the headquarters was fully up to speed (interview Council Secretariat official). This was somewhat mitigated given that France had already unilaterally activated the headquarters six weeks in advance. Having the headquarters in a national capital also creates unwanted national political influence. Since this scenario is sub-optimal, various member states have advanced a standing European OHQ (see Chapter 3). As a compromise, an Operations Centre was created in 2007, which can be activated on an *ad hoc* basis. This happened for the first time in 2012 to facility coordination between the EU's operations in the Horn of Africa.

The first task of an OHQ is to draft a *CONOPS*. The Military Strategic Options and the Joint Action are a starting point. Because the headquarters has not been involved in the previous discussions, the Military Staff drafts an Initiating Military Directive (IMD), which translates the earlier documents into military guidance. This directive is formally issued to the Operations Commander by the EUMC. In practice, the IMD itself is not enough. As mentioned above, liaison officers are sent to the OHQ as well. In addition, the Operations Commander generally has the support of a number of Political Advisors (POLADs), at least one of whom has been intensively involved in the negotiations about the previous planning documents. The CONOPS itself is much more detailed than the Strategic Options (up to a hundred pages). This is also the first time that the Operations Commander can provide his/her input. Given that he/she will have to take operational command and thus final responsibility, several adjustments can still be made. The CONOPS, after consultation with the relevant bodies in the EEAS, is sent to Brussels and is adopted by the member states committees and the Council.

The CONOPS includes a Provisional Statement of Requirements (PSOR) that lists in detail the number of required troops and the enabling capabilities (e.g. medical, transport, logistics, communication). This document is the starting point for the force generation process. In practice, however, (several) informal force generation conferences will already have taken place to have an idea about the possibilities. The OHQ and/or the Commanders also come from lead nations, which thus have to be identified before the Council Decision. On the basis of the Statement of Requirements, the Operations Commander organizes various rounds of formal force generation conferences. During these conferences, the member states pledge troops and capabilities. At the end of each round the shortfalls are identified, and these form the basis for the next round. In the case of EUFOR Chad, it took five formal force generation conferences over several months. This was an extreme case, yet overall force generation is difficult. What is also important is the variation between the member states in their ability to quickly pledge commitments. Some member states need parliamentary approval.

When shortfalls remain after several rounds of force generation conferences, the Operations Commander faces a difficult choice. He/she can organize another conference, with the risk that the member states are not forthcoming, or he/she can decide to launch the operation with the pledged forces, while taking full responsibility for the results. If the Operations Commander decides to launch the operation, the OHQ forwards a draft *OPLAN* and the Rules of Engagement to Brussels for the approval of the member states. The OPLAN is a completely worked out version of the CONOPS (now several hundreds of pages). It is based on the actual pledged troops and enabling capabilities, whereas the CONOPS was still based on the Statement of Requirements. Before the OPLAN is sent to the member states, the Military Staff is consulted to give some final input. The moment that the member states adopt the OPLAN, the military mission is launched.

So far the policy process has primarily been discussed with reference to the situation in Brussels and the OHQ. It is now time to turn to the situation on the ground. It needs to be said, in this respect, that there is an important difference between military follow-on operations where the EU takes over and completely new operations.[8] In the former case, while there may be some issues related to the follow-on agreements, the infrastructure is already in place. In the latter, it is not and this requires several preparations. Before the troops can actually arrive, various visits are made by officials from the EEAS, the OHQ, and the member states. One of the most important is the fact-finding mission in preparation of the Crisis Management Concept. The fact-finding mission is, however, by no means the only visit to the ground. The Operations Commander is likely to go on reconnaissance missions. Most, if not all, of the contributing member states make their own security assessments. Some may send their military intelligence officers, others may collect information by going to some of the important member states and/or international organizations. In addition, member states may have a bilateral presence on the ground, such as an embassy, that can make preparations for the arrival of troops.

Before the formal launch of the operation, the Force Commander will fly in with a small team of officers to start making preparation for the establishment of the Force Headquarters on the ground.[9] A number of

POLADs support the Force Commander in this respect as well. At the launch of the operation, the member states send many more officers to the Force Headquarters. At full capacity, the Force Headquarters can be even bigger than the OHQ.[10] The number of staff in both headquarters depends, needless to say, on the military operation. Apart from the headquarters, the EU still has to sign a Status of Forces Agreement (SOFA) with the host state to arrange the details of the stay and the diplomatic immunities of personnel. The member states send their own contingents and sort their logistics out themselves. Once the mission has established itself, it declares Initial Operational Capability (IOC). When the mission is ready to fully carry out all tasks listed in the OPLAN, it finally declares Full Operational Capability (FOC). There can be a number of months between the adoption of the OPLAN and the declaration of IOC. There can also be several months between IOC and FOC.

Civilian planning and launching of the operation

After the adoption of the CONOPS and the Council Decision, the CPCC continues to work towards the *OPLAN*, which needs the approval of the member states. The Civilian Operations Commander in the CPCC works, in this respect, closely together with the designated Head of Mission on the ground.[11] Because the CPCC is relatively small, it often makes use of the expertise of the EUMS. This gives it extra weight *vis-à-vis* the member states. During the final phase of operational planning, however, the most important task is for the Head of Mission to recruit his/her staff members. They are all recruited on an individual basis.[12] Vacancies for individual posts are circulated to the member states, which can put forward their candidates on a seconded basis. If vacancies remain unfilled they are published for open competition. This huge task cannot be highlighted enough. It concerns not only the selection of senior officials in the mission, but indeed all staff members and also local staff. In addition, new rounds of recruitment are necessary if mission staff leave when contracts end. Recruitment is done by the CPCC and the civilian mission on the ground.

The next challenge is to establish the mission on the ground. This requires a lot of procurement procedures. For all buildings, cars, computers, and other materials, mission staff and the officials in the CPCC have to go to the Commission and ask for money in the context of the previously agreed budget. Some improvements have been made in recent years, but these procedures have often been experienced by staff members as traumatic. In particular, it has proven difficult to make use of resources before the formal adoption of the Council Decision. In instances of rapid response – such as the monitoring missions in Aceh and Georgia – it was necessary to establish a presence before the ministers had the chance to formally agree. As a result of these problems, preparatory measures have been introduced which allow for the pre-financing of missions. This has already been used in the case of Kosovo (see Chapter 8) and the monitoring mission in Georgia (Grevi, Helly and Keohane 2009). Overall, financing remains a problem. In many operations theaters, it is difficult to acquire resources following Western procurement standards. The police mission in Afghanistan is a case in point.

Since the CPCC and the Head of Mission play a bigger role in the implementation with regard to staff recruitment and procurement than their military equivalents, it has been important to send advance parties as soon as possible. In the case of the rule of law mission in Kosovo, a Planning Team was on the ground for more than two years before the formal launch of the mission. This is an exception. Yet also for the purpose of the AMM, staff were sent immediately to the ground to start preparing for the mission – e.g. find an appropriate location for the headquarters and field offices, start the local procurement procedures, etc. Two weeks after the core staff arrived in Aceh, the first monitors flew in to create an initial monitoring presence. Four weeks later, the mission reached full capacity.

The conduct of the operation

Once the operation is established on the ground, the implementation phase can start. With regard to the substance of implementation, there is tremendous variation across the operations (Merlingen and Ostrauskaitė 2008; Grevi, Helly and Keohane 2009). Several military missions have the mandate to contribute to a "safe and secure environment" through merely being present and having a deterrent function. Some police and rule of law missions focus on pro-active training of local officers and officials through "monitoring, mentoring and advising." Other civilian missions perform executive tasks and include riot control capabilities, such as integrated police units. As a result of these differences, it is difficult to describe implementation in any general terms. A small-scale advisory Security Sector Reform operation in Africa quite naturally does not have the same type of command and control structure as the executive rule of law mission EULEX Kosovo. This section therefore makes some general remarks on institutional structures during the implementation phase of CSDP operations.

The key actor on the ground is the Force Commander in military operations and the Head of Mission in civilian missions. He/she is in charge of the (Force) Headquarters and has the main responsibility for the day-to-day running of the operation. This includes commanding authority over a number of tactical decisions, such as authorizing covert action against war criminals in Bosnia, deploying the integrated police units for riot control in Kosovo, or increasing the number of patrols in areas with high levels of reported human rights violations in Chad. Such decisions either cannot wait for the OHQ or the political actors in Brussels, or they play at such a tactical level that there is no need to get the headquarters and Brussels involved. Force Commanders and Heads of Mission normally get considerable autonomy from the OHQ. Brussels and the headquarters do not want to "micro-manage" the Force Commander or the Head of Mission on the ground.

It is difficult to generalize from the four case studies of this book, because personalities matter tremendously in the relations between the Force Commander and Head of Mission on the ground and the Operations Commander in the headquarters. Yet the Operations Commander of the military operation in Chad, Lt. General Pat Nash, provided his French Force Commander, B. General Jean-Philippe Ganascia, with a lot of autonomy (interview EUFOR official). One of the Force Commanders in Operation Althea in Bosnia, M. General David Leakey, had even more autonomy to implement the operation on the ground (see Chapter 5). The Bosnia operation was not such a priority for SHAPE and the DSACEUR that they did not feel the need to get actively involved in the running of the mission. The Head of the AMM, Pieter Feith, practically ran the operation from the ground with little between him and the PSC in Brussels.[13] The Heads of Mission of EULEX Kosovo, Generals (r) Yves de Kermabon and Xavier Bout de Marnhac have also substantial independence, despite the creation of the position of the Civilian Operations Commander in Brussels.

The Head of Mission of civilian missions, in this respect, seems to have more autonomy than the Force Commander of military operations. In military operations, it furthermore depends whether the EU makes use of NATO assets or of a national OHQ. In the latter case, the whole OHQ is dedicated to one particular mission, while SHAPE and the DSACEUR have other business to do. What also plays an important role is the functional need for extensive communication between the Operations and Force Headquarters. Interesting, in this respect, is that Force Commander Leakey in Bosnia reportedly tried to talk via telephone directly to DSACEUR only once per week, but that they sometimes did not talk for a whole month (interview Althea official). The number of contacts between generals Ganascia and Nash was higher.

It ranged from several times per day to at least a number of times per week (interview EUFOR official). In addition, Lt. General Nash visited Chad some 10 times within the course of only a year-long military operation. Their contacts were thus much more intense, mainly because the military operation in Chad was more challenging.

It is not only the chain of command between the Force and Operations Commander that is interesting. There is an important link as well between the Operations Commander and the PSC, which has political control and provides strategic direction. As civilian and military operations require certain discretion to carry out their functions, the member states in the PSC do not provide the Operations Commander with detailed tactical instructions. Rather, the Operations Commander informs Brussels at regular intervals about the implementation of the mission. This takes a number of forms. First, the operation sends regular reports. Depending on the mission, these can be daily, weekly, monthly, and six-monthly reports. It is quite a formal exercise and most operations have their own reporting units for this purpose. On the basis of these reports, the member states can ask questions to the EEAS, which acts as a liaison. Second, the Operations Commanders come to the PSC, CIVCOM, and the Military Committee for an exchange of views. This generally happens on the occasion of the six-monthly report, which is the main opportunity for the Operations Commander to make his/her views known regarding the overall course of the mission.

In addition to these formal reporting requirements, there are a lot of intensive relations between the OHQ and the EEAS. Moreover, member states have, of course, direct contacts with the EEAS and the OHQ. The unity of command and the hierarchies need to be respected, but contacts are rather extensive. The POLADs of the Operations and Force Commanders play an important role in this perspective. They maintain contacts with the outside world and provide clarification. With regard to reporting, it is important to realize that the ambassadors and diplomats in Brussels do not merely wait passively for information to come to them: they go on field trips to the operations to see the implementation for themselves. The member states have their own reporting channels as well via bilateral embassies and their national contingents. The latter is stronger in military missions, where contingents remain national, than in civilian operations, where staff are recruited on an individual basis. Mission staff in civilian operations are nonetheless repeatedly contacted by their national embassies, although this practice varies across the member states (interview EULEX official).

One important institutional aspect is the coordination with EU and international actors. The civilian and military operations are generally only one foreign policy instrument of the EU. There may be other operations, the presence of a EUSR, and generally there is a Union Delegation. Particularly in the Western Balkans and the Democratic Republic of Congo, there are often several CSDP operations taking place at the same time. Military operations can be implemented in parallel with civilian missions or multiple civilian missions may take place in one country. If there is functional overlap between missions, coordination is of utmost importance. In Bosnia, for example, both the EUPM and Operation Althea had the fight against organized crime in their mandates (see Chapter 5; Juncos 2007; Merlingen 2009). The Special Representative or the Union Delegation can, in this respect, act as an important coordination agent. It is problematic, however, that the unity of command in civilian and military operations does not allow for the Special Representative and the Delegation to play a formal role. Operations have their own chain of command and they cannot be told what to do.

Coordination also needs to be ensured between the CSDP missions and the activities of the Commission on the ground. There is the risk of conflicting interests. CSDP missions are inherently short-term, focusing on crisis management. They often take ownership away from local institutions. (Development) instruments of the Commission, on the other hand, focus on the medium to long term. They are about capacity building and have a strong notion of local ownership. Interests are thus often conflicting. The emphasis is therefore on coordination between the CSDP missions and activities of the Commission "without prejudice" to individual competences. With the member states, coordination takes place through regular Heads of Mission meetings on the ground. These include the ambassadors of all the locally represented member states plus the delegation and mission staff.

Coordination with EU actors is one issue; that with other international actors quite another. There are two issues at stake. First, there has to be coordination with other international actors involved in crisis management. In Kosovo, for example, the EULEX mission works closely together with NATO's military operation in terms of riot control. In the case of Chad, the military mission was part of an international multi-dimensional presence, in which the UN was training local police in a parallel effort to provide a safe and secure environment. At the tactical, operational and sometimes even strategic level, these international organizations will make (formal) arrangements and coordinate their actions. EULEX riot police, for example, need communication channels with NATO if local riots turn into larger civil unrest and paramilitary violence. Second, as with the donor coordination in most developing countries, there is generally a coordination mechanism for all international actors involved on the ground. In Bosnia, for example, there is a Board of Principals meeting, consisting of major international agents, such as the World Bank, International Monetary Fund, European Commission, Organization for Security and Cooperation in Europe (OSCE), NATO, EU missions, etc. Political actors, such as the member states and third states, are not involved. This Board of Principals meeting is chaired by the High Representative of the international community.

Coordination on the ground is thus a major affair. While there is a lot of inefficiency, duplication, and competing mandates between the actors, the general impression is that international officials want to make the best of it and make things happen. Institutional problems are often bigger at headquarters than on the ground. Practical solutions are frequently found. Informal contacts are also important, as the international community on the ground tends to be rather small.

Prolongation and termination

Most CSDP missions are so-called end-date rather than end-state missions, which means that they are deployed for a limited time and that withdrawal is not subject to achieving the objectives (Mattelaer 2010). In the military operations in sub-Saharan Africa, in particular, the member states know precisely when the troops will come home. Even if a final date for withdrawal is not explicitly set from the outset, mandates need to be formally prolonged through Council Decisions. EULEX Kosovo, for example, was authorized a budget for "a period of 16 months starting from the approval of the OPLAN" (2008/124/CFSP: Article 16(1)). The commitment of the member states to end-dates makes political sense, as they fear becoming indefinitely involved in expensive operations or "mission creep." It clearly makes much less sense from an operational point of view, and it might not necessarily raise the right expectations with third parties. Given the use of end-dates, there is always a moment during implementation that prolongation or termination has to be discussed. In addition to the limits to the duration of operations, the six-monthly report is the occasion to discuss the future of the operation.

Since the Council Decision and formal planning documents have to be amended, the process of prolongation follows the decision-making phase, as discussed above. The Operations Commander and the relevant bodies of the EEAS draft the necessary documents, which are discussed by the member states in Brussels. Interestingly, the preferences of the member states and the EEAS are not fixed in this respect. During the military operation in Chad, all actors pushed for the termination to be ready on the scheduled date. With regard to the termination of Operation Althea in Bosnia, the Operations Commander has repeatedly made clear that the military job has been done and that he would like to conclude the mission. The member states, on the other hand, have been hesitant, pointing at potential instability in Bosnia in the long run. Moreover, while the EU decides on the length of its missions, the international context often plays a role as well regarding prolongation and termination. The AMM was prolonged at various times by several months because it took the government of Indonesia some time to adopt a local election law. The EU was, of course, pushing for this, but it felt that it could not withdraw its troops before local elections were held in the province of Aceh in accordance with the peace agreements.

Decisions on prolongation and termination have proved to be very political or, as mentioned above, conditioned by external factors. As such, the EU agents have difficulty exerting influence. An interesting case, in this respect, was the military mission in the Democratic Republic of Congo (2006). Prolongation was openly discussed. It was, however, unacceptable for Germany. Because the German OHQ was used, this was the end of the discussion. CSDP missions are most easily prolonged in the Western Balkans, where many member states have direct interests in stability. The police and military operations in Bosnia have existed for a long time. When prolongation and termination are on the agenda, it is thus also a key moment to make changes to the direction of the mission. Downsizing is a serious option. In the case of Operation Althea, the total authorized strength went in 2006–2007 from about 7,000 troops to around 2,500.

A recurring theme during the termination of CSDP operations is what to do with local assets. For the purpose of the missions, the EU often invests sums of money in local infrastructure and buildings. Unlike other assets, such as cars and computers, these cannot be shipped back to Brussels or relatively easily be sold. Deals therefore have to be made with the host state in the SOFA or with a possible follow-on mission by other international organizations (e.g. UN). This is inevitably tricky, as the departing force has generally very little leverage when leaving the scene. In the case of Chad, the host country notoriously used the situation for its own benefit (Seibert 2010; Dijkstra 2010b). The final task of bringing the troops and equipment back to Europe is – like the initial deployment – the responsibility of the contributing states. Following the termination of the operation, the Operations Commander still has to send to the member states an account of all expenditures.

Conclusion

This chapter has given an overview of the CSDP policy process. It has taken a practical rather than formal approach and has included many examples of the four case studies, which will be discussed in the subsequent chapters. What needs to be acknowledged is that CSDP has a lot of flexibility when political will is present.[14] This is important in crisis situations. Various formal rules, such as the Crisis Management Procedures (Council 2003), are in place to facilitate member states in the planning of operations. They are not carved in stone. In many missions, member states have deliberately skipped steps in the planning process or have turned the order around. Flexibility is also present in, for example, the composition of fact-finding missions. While their core consists of EEAS officials, they may also include civil servants from the member states or other international organizations, if this is deemed useful. The intensity of contacts between the Commanders depends much on the need in particular operations. Procedures fit the specific needs of the missions, and not the other way around. The conclusions of this chapter may therefore not be applicable to all CSDP operations, as most missions have their own anomalies.

When it comes to the role of the EU bureaucracies in the policy process, their first obvious function is in the *agenda-setting phase*. EU officials are generally involved in CSDP operations from the very beginning. They are at the heart of the policy-making process and can shape the EU agenda to their benefit. Their pivotal position allows them to frame the parameters around which the mission will be established. During the subsequent *decision-making phase*, EU officials again play a leading role. They make up the core of the fact-finding mission, and draft the Crisis Management Concepts, Strategic Operations, and Council Decision. These planning documents have to be approved by the member states, but the initiative is with the officials of the EEAS. This chapter has also noted, in this respect, variation between the control bodies of the member states in civilian and military crisis management. While the Military Committee is very senior and has enough resources, CIVCOM is rather junior and ill-equipped.

During *implementation*, there is a notable difference between civilian and military missions in the launch of the operation. In the military CSDP, the lead is with the OHQ. It writes the CONOPS and the OPLAN and is in charge of Force Generation. The Military Staff supports the headquarters in this respect, and performs an important liaison function, but it is not in the lead. In civilian missions, the CPCC inside the EEAS drafts the final planning documents and carries out, in close cooperation with the Head of Mission, the selection of individual mission staff members. EU officials are also much more closely involved in setting up base on the ground in civilian than in military operations. In civilian missions, officials from the Commission play an administrative role in procurement and other financial tasks. During the conduct of the mission, the lead is with the Force Commander and Operations Commander and with the Head of Mission and the Civilian Operations Commander within the EEAS. For the prolongation and termination phase similar dynamics are at work as for the decision-making phase. While EU officials make assessments, prolongation and termination are eventually political decisions taken by the member states.

5
Military Operation in Bosnia

On December 2, 2004, the EU launched the military operation Althea in Bosnia-Herzegovina. Althea is still ongoing and remains the largest CSDP mission ever deployed. It was not a completely new mission. In fact, the EU took over a well-functioning operation from NATO after the North Atlantic Alliance had ensured a "safe and secure environment" following the Dayton agreement of 1995. Through its Implementation and Stabilization Force (IFOR; SFOR), NATO had contributed to security in Bosnia. NATO handing over command to the EU fitted with the strategy to put Bosnia "irreversibly on to the road to statehood and membership of Europe" (Ashdown 2007: 299). An EU-led military operation would serve EU foreign policy better than the continuing NATO presence. After the takeover, NATO remained involved in Bosnia through the Berlin Plus agreement (see Chapter 4) and through its own residual activities. Operation Althea started with the same troop levels as SFOR, but the member states soon reduced their presence from the approximately 7,000 soldiers to 1,300 in 2012.

This chapter traces the influence of the EU officials throughout the CSDP policy process. It first discusses how Althea came on the agenda (December 2002–Spring 2004). Subsequently, it analyzes the decision-making process from the moment that the member states started to consider the takeover until the adoption of the Joint Action on July 12, 2004. The chapter then looks at the period leading up to the handover in December 2004. It analyzes the implementation phase of operation Althea (December 2004–Spring 2006) and discusses the restructuring process (fall 2006–date). In the conclusion, the chapter gives an overview of the influence of the EU officials during the phases of the policy process. These empirical results will provide input for the conclusion of this book, which brings all the case studies together.

Agenda-setting

The preference of the US to withdraw troops from Bosnia was well known. In 2001, the International Crisis Group issued, for instance, a report stating that there was "no early exit." NATO had "to maintain a credible military presence" and "the U.S. and UK [sic], in particular, should not undermine the NATO mission in Bosnia by continuing to make disproportionate cuts in the size or capacity of their forces" (2001: 4). The US had already reduced its average troop level from one-third of the soldiers in IFOR (20,000/60,000) to one-sixth in SFOR (3,300/20,000) (ibid.). SFOR would be further reduced to 7,000 soldiers at the time of the handover in 2004. Only 900–1000 troops were still from the US (International Crisis Group 2004; Bertin 2008).

While the military involvement of the US in Bosnia was thus decreasing, the EU was making an increased effort. For example, it appointed Lord Ashdown as the first EUSR to Bosnia in 2002 – a post he carried out in addition to his work as the High Representative of the International Community.[1] Ashdown therefore had two superiors. He reported to the Steering Board of the Peace Implementation Council, which consists of states representing the international community. As the EUSR, he also had to report directly to Javier Solana and the member states. This was a signal that the EU was increasingly taking the lead. In parallel to his appointment, the EU decided to take over parts of the United Nations Mission in Bosnia-Herzegovina (UNMIBH, 1995–2002), which became the EUPM (2003–date). Finally, the Thessaloniki European Council in June 2003 noted that the Western Balkans had a "European perspective." This meant that they were seen as potential candidates for membership.

While the first CSDP mission (EUPM) was of a civilian character, the rationale had been military. By 2002, all the military structures had been established and there was a desire to deploy operations. The Western Balkans, being the backyard of Europe, was the most likely theater. The EU would be able to take over ongoing NATO operations in Macedonia, Bosnia, and Kosovo, which would require relatively little planning. Under the foreseen Berlin Plus agreement, the OHQ of NATO could be used. Such continuity would increase the chances of success. Taking over a mission from NATO furthermore fitted with the American preferences to withdraw from the Western Balkans *and* the CSDP operating through NATO. Finally, increased ownership over the military missions would give the EU more visibility and more coherence in its foreign policy instruments. It would also send a political signal to the Bosnians about who is in charge.

The idea of the takeover was first suggested in 1996 by Commissioner Hans van den Broek (Reichard 2006). The CSDP, of course, did not exist, but in light of the American presidential election, questions were raised about future commitment of the US. The US stayed, yet the idea remained a topic of debate in academic circles (interview national official). In the context of Operation Althea, one national interviewee "clearly remembers" that the "first clear political signals [to consider the transition from NATO to EU-led military operations in Macedonia and Bosnia] came from Solana himself." Solana had an interest in launching a military operation after he had invested considerable effort in developing the CSDP machinery. "The proof of the pudding is in the eating" (ibid.). Jamie Woodbridge (2002: 3) similarly confirms that a possible takeover was "aggressively pushed by the High Representative."

Solana was clearly not alone in suggesting the handover. He was supported by France and the UK (Pohl 2009). France wanted the military missions to start and the UK was sensitive to the concerns of the US. Moreover, both member states had had negative experiences in Bosnia being large contributors to the United Nations Protection Force (UNPROFOR, 1992–1995). They wanted to set the record straight (Reichard 2006). Following suggestions by Solana and both member states, the European Council of December 2002 "indicated the Union's willingness to lead a military operation in Bosnia" (Presidency Conclusions, paragraphs 28–29).

There were two important prerequisites before the EU could take over the SFOR operation. First, the EU and NATO had to reach agreement on the use of NATO assets for the EU-led operation under the Berlin Plus agreement. Second, these structures had to be tested before the EU could be trusted with the responsibilities. It was therefore decided that a small military operation in Macedonia (Concordia, March–December 2003) would serve as a test-case (interviews national and NATO officials). The negotiations over Berlin Plus, however, proved difficult (e.g. Reichard 2006; Cascone 2008; Howorth 2007), which resulted in severe delays before operation Concordia could be launched in Macedonia (Guardian 2002). Agreement on Berlin Plus was finally reached in December 2002. It was ratified in March 2003. The military operation in Macedonia started the same month (see Mace 2004; Gross 2009b; Howorth 2007).

The conclusion of the Berlin Plus agreement and the launch of Concordia took place at the height of transatlantic tensions over Iraq, but the war seemed initially to have little impact. The CSDP acting through NATO was, after all, in line with American preferences. It increased burden-sharing and lessened the need for autonomous EU military action. The transatlantic tensions themselves, however, created a whole new rationale for autonomous action. What if the NATO assets would *not* be available for EU-led operations? Shortly after the Iraq invasion, Belgium invited Luxembourg, France, and Germany to discuss the possibility of having an autonomous military headquarters in addition to NATO facilities. This "chocolate" summit (April 2003) re-opened the duplication debate. It made the US and the UK hostile towards further CSDP developments. Several months later, the EU launched its first autonomous military operation (Artemis in the DR Congo, June–September 2003). The mission ran almost exclusively on French resources and was viewed with great suspicion in the US (Giegerich et al. 2006).

These developments were reason for the US to block the transition from SFOR to Althea in Bosnia in June 2003 (FT 2003a; European Security Review 2003; Robertson, Papandreou and Solana 2003).[2] To the Europeans, this decision came as a surprise (FT 2003a). While the NATO Secretary-General, Lord Robertson, stated that both NATO and the EU had been too busy to actually plan this mission (Robertson, Papandreou and Solana 2003), the opposite was true. At an earlier bilateral Anglo-French summit in Le Touquet on February 4, 2003, the initial planning for the takeover had already started. Both member states had produced a paper, which was complemented by a paper from Solana. These two papers had been approved by the Council on February 24, 2003. If the US had not blocked the takeover in Madrid, one national interviewee stated, "the whole preparation [for Althea] could have taken place in 2003. Theoretically, the launch of the mission could then have taken place at the end of 2003 or the beginning of 2004." EU officials in the *Financial Times* (2002) confirmed that the handover could have taken place mid-2004.

This deadlock continued for several months. It was overcome when transatlantic relations improved and the ideas about an EU Headquarters was gradually abandoned (Reichard 2006). During a meeting of NATO defense ministers on October 8–9, 2003, the transition from SFOR to Althea was put back on the agenda. Lord Robertson indicated that the EU could take over within 12–18 months (FT 2003c). This time frame was confirmed during December 2003, where the NATO ministers stated that "we will consider how to adjust the [SFOR] operation further, including its possible termination by the end of 2004 and a transition possibly to ... a new EU mission within the framework of the Berlin Plus arrangements" (Final Communiqué). December 2004 thus became the scheduled date for the handover instead of early/mid-2004.

104 Policy-Making in EU Security and Defense

Table 5.1 Chronology of Operation Althea

November 21, 1995	Dayton Peace Agreement
December 20, 1995	Start of NATO-led IFOR
December 20, 1996	Termination of IFOR; Launch of NATO-led SFOR
May 27, 2002	Lord Ashdown as EUSR/High Representative
December 12–13, 2002	European Council indicates "willingness to lead"
December 16, 2002	Berlin Plus agreement between EU and NATO
January 1, 2003	Start of EUPM in Bosnia
March 31, 2003	Start of EU-led Operation Concordia via Berlin Plus
February 4, 2003	Anglo-French Le Touquet Summit
February 23, 2003	Approval of Anglo-French & Solana planning paper
March 20, 2003	Start of US-led Operation Iraqi Freedom
April 29, 2003	Chocolate Summit in Tervuren
June 3–4, 2003	EU-NATO Summit in Madrid
June 12, 2003	Start of autonomous EU-led Operation Artemis
October 8–9, 2003	NATO Defence Ministers in Colorado Springs
December 1–2, 2003	NATO Defence Ministers in Brussels
February 23, 2004	Solana's Report on a Possible EU Deployment
April 26, 2004	Adoption of Crisis Management Concept
June 2004	EU planning team to Bosnia
June 28–29, 2004	NATO Summit in Istanbul
July 9, 2004	Adoption of UN Security Council Resolution (UNSCR) 1551
July 12, 2004	Adoption of Joint Action
July 15, 2004	Joint visit of Solana/de Hoop Scheffer to Bosnia
September 13, 2004	Adoption of CONOPS
October 11, 2004	Adoption of OPLAN
October 2004	Force Commander David Leakey arrives in Bosnia
November 22, 2004	Adoption of UNSCR 1575
November 25, 2004	Council launches Operation Althea
December 2, 2004	Handover NATO; Start of Althea
May 30, 2006	Departure of Lord Ashdown
Summer 2006	Common Operational Guidelines Althea-EUPM
October 17, 2006	Solana–Rehn Report on Reinforced EU Presence
December 12, 2006	Adoption of revised CONOPS
February 27, 2007	Adoption of revised OPLAN
November 8, 2007	Adoption of revised Joint Action
January 25, 2010	Council agrees on non-executive functions
October 10, 2011	Council effectively ends executive role

Decision-making

The decision-making phase of operation Althea started shortly after NATO had given the go-ahead. It lasted until July 12, 2004, when the EU adopted the Joint Action. This was the formal legal basis of the CSDP operation. Given that the EU was taking over the operation from NATO, the negotiations were not especially difficult. That said, the member states found plenty of issues for debate. First, the EU actors discussed the mandate of the operations, including the coordination on the ground. Second, the EU had to negotiate with NATO over the delineation between Althea and NATO's residual activities.

Althea's mandate

NATO had run a very successful operation since the Dayton agreement of 1995. When the possible takeover by the EU was discussed, it had accomplished a "safe and secure environment," which was one of its key military tasks (interview national official). With few potential spoilers on the horizon, it was felt that NATO's passive presence as a deterrent force had been part of its success. A report of the International Crisis Group (2004: 1) states that SFOR "has been widely seen as the strongest guarantor that war will not break out again." NATO had acquired such a strong brand name mainly due to American involvement (despite the fact that the US contingent was only a small part of it). The European troops did not enjoy a similar reputation. In fact, as the same report notes, "the reputations of the main EU powers continue to suffer among Bosnians due to their inglorious performances during the 1992–1995 war, when they provided the commanders and the bulk of the troops for the UN Protection Force" (p. 2).

In addition to the deterrent function, the presence of SFOR was widely seen as support for the political activities of the Office of the High Representative. The High Representative has an executive mandate and possesses the so-called Bonn-powers. These allow him to sack politicians and judges, and to impose legislation within the Dayton framework. Having a military presence strongly increases his authority (interview national official). Then there was the situation in Kosovo, which remained a potential source of instability throughout the Western Balkans (interview national official; International Crisis Group 2004). An independent Kosovo could potentially set a precedent for *Republika Srpska*, which makes up approximately half of the territory of Bosnia. While NATO would continue to keep the peace in Kosovo through its Kosovo Force (KFOR) operation, there was thus also a need for a continuing military presence in Bosnia.

For these reasons, it was widely understood that Althea should in the first place be seen as a *continuation* of SFOR (interviews national officials). The early Anglo-French paper presented to the Council on February 24, 2003 stated, in this respect, that "the EU force should not be weaker than the Nato force it replaces" (quoted in FT 2003b). The accompanying report of the Solana stressed "the need for the future mission to retain a robust mandate" (Council Presidency Conclusions 2003: 9). It goes without saying that the US, which was skeptical of the EU's power projection, had a preference for such a mandate as well. It is thus unsurprising that Althea ended up with the same strong mandate as SFOR ("to take all necessary measures," United Nations Security Council Resolution (UNSCR) 1551) and the same number of troops at the date of the handover.

And yet it was also clear that Althea had to have added value for the activities of the EU as a whole in Bosnia. In other words, Althea had to contribute to the overall objective of helping Bosnia on "the road to Europe" (see above). The joint declaration of France and the UK at Le Touquet on February 4, 2003, in this respect, stated that "we see [the EU's intention to undertake a military operation in Bosnia] as supporting the efforts of Lord Ashdown ... to pursue the EU's agenda in Bosnia-Herzegovina and to complement the EU's efforts to promote the development of that country." The accompanying report of Solana noted "the opportunity that an EU-led operation would offer in terms of an integrated EU approach towards the country (notably with the presence of the EU Police Mission in [Bosnia])" (Presidency Conclusions 2003: 9).

The idea that Althea would be part of a broader EU effort was strongly emphasized in Solana's *Report on a Possible EU Deployment in Bosnia and Herzegovina* presented to the Council on February 23, 2004. This report argued that Althea should be a "new and distinct mission" rather than a simple continuation of SFOR. It noted that Althea would be in a "very different position from that when NATO first deployed in 1995." It therefore proposed "two fundamental objectives." First, the mission would "guarantee the secure environment required for the core objectives in [Office of the High Representative's] Mission Implementation Plan and the Stabilisation and Association Agreement, and should contribute directly to them." Second, it would "have a particular focus on the fight against organised crime." The Council stressed indeed the comprehensive approach, and asked Solana "to ensure expeditious follow-up with a view to the development of a General Concept for early consideration by the PSC" (Presidency Conclusions 2004: 8).

It is necessary to take a critical look at the report. By stressing that the military mission should be "new and distinct" rather than a continuation, it took issue with the existing discourse of the member states. This was partially cosmetic, as the mission would still "be credible and robust" with a UN chapter VII peace-keeping mandate, but nonetheless important in terms of the framing of the operation. Moreover, while the "safe and secure environment" remained a key objective, Althea was explicitly linked with the Office of the High Representative's Mission Implementation Plan and the Stabilisation and Association Agreement. What is more, Althea was tasked to "contribute directly to them." On ensuring coherence between the EU actors in Bosnia, the report stated that:

> [it] can best be achieved by cooperation and leadership on the ground. At the centre of this should be a reinforced co-ordinating role for the EUSR. He needs to be able to function as *primus inter pares* among the heads of the different EU missions in [Bosnia]. In particular the EUSR should ensure complementarity between the implementation of the Dayton/Paris provisions and progress in the Stabilisation and Association Process.

This proposal was, of course, not institution-neutral. As the Special Representatives reported to Solana, it would give the Council Secretariat a stronger role in Bosnia. It was therefore not well received by the Commission, which is in charge of the Stabilisation and Association Process. The main rationale of the Commission's effort is local ownership. Local politicians are given a carrot, if they obey the international rules. Such ownership conflicted with the Bonn powers of the High Representative and an executive military presence. Yet not only was the link between the military operation and the Stabilisation and Association Process a problem for the Commission. The Commission also took issue with the proposed objective of fighting organized crime. As Solana's report rightly stated, "the EU is already involved in these areas through the CARDS programme and EUPM [and the] eventual aim is a [Bosnia] that can tackle organised crime on its own." Thus the possible involvement of soldiers in fighting organized crime would create problems of functional overlap with other EU instruments (interviews Commission and EU officials).

Given its various reservations, the Commission started to speak up in order to defend its own position. It did not have formal decision-making power in the CSDP, but it did get a number of the member states on board. The Crisis Management Concept, which is the first major planning document, is fascinating in this regard. It allegedly mentions some 10–20 times (!) that Althea should carry out its tasks "without prejudice to Community competence" (interview EU official). The Commission insisted until the Council's legal service gave in. These references also come back a number of times in the actual Joint Action – not just to guarantee Community competences, but also to safeguard the formal military chain of command from any unwanted political influence (Article 7(2); Article 10). The Commission thus successfully defended its competences, but it did not improve the coherence of EU instruments within Bosnia. The behavior of the Commission was also the main reason why the CRCT stopped functioning months before the end of the planning phase.

The Commission was, however, not the only actor with concerns. The member states also did not appreciate the "new and distinct" approach. They decided in their Joint Action of July 12, 2004 that the emphasis should remain on the safe and secure environment and the Dayton tasks. Althea's primary objective thus became to "provide deterrence, continued compliance with the responsibility to fulfill the role specified [in the Dayton agreement]" (Article 1(1)). However, as a second key objective, the member states included a reference to the Mission Implementation Plan by stating that Althea will "contribute to a safe and secure environment in [Bosnia], in line with its mandate, required to achieve core tasks in the OHR's Mission Implementation Plan and the SAP" (ibid.). The fight against organized crime was not included as a key objective. It became a key supporting military task instead (Leakey 2006). The coordination role of the Special Representative was restricted as well:

> The Council shall ensure the maximum coherence and effectiveness for the EU effort in [Bosnia]. Without prejudice to Community competence, the EUSR shall promote overall EU political coordination in [Bosnia]. The EUSR shall chair a coordination group composed of all EU actors present in the field, including the EU Force Commander, with a view to coordinating the implementation aspects of the EU's action. (Article 7(1))

Ultimately, Solana was not successful in pursuing his interests with regard to Althea's mandate. The member states took a conservative approach that left little room for entrepreneurship. They fell back on traditional doctrine and standard operating procedures. Coordination on the ground was encouraged by the member states, but the military chain of command and the division of competences between the EU actors on the ground had to be respected.

Delineation of EU and NATO activities

The relationship between EU actors on the ground was thus a topic of debate in the decision-making phase. Another concern was the relations between the EU and NATO. The Berlin Plus agreement had been tested during the Concordia operation in Macedonia, but the relationship between both organizations was wider in scope. From the beginning of the planning process it was clear that NATO would keep a residual presence on the ground in the form of its headquarters in Sarajevo (Bertin 2008). NATO's principal remaining task was non-executive. Under NATO's Partnership for Peace agreement, it would continue to assist the Bosnian government with high-level defense reform. This function was complementary to the EU's responsibility as the stabilization force after the handover from SFOR. However, the US insisted that the NATO headquarters would also continue to carry out some executive tasks. With two friendly military forces in one operational theater, there was a need for coordination and a delineation of mandates.

Within the US, there were clearly doubts about whether the EU could do the job. It therefore insisted on keeping the opportunity to redeploy NATO troops in a worst case scenario. For this purpose, NATO had to retain all its executive prerogatives (interview Althea official). It meant that the NATO headquarters would need to continue to enjoy its United Nations chapter VII mandate and that NATO would need to continue to keep its "silver bullet clauses" of the Dayton agreement. These gave the NATO Commander "the authority, without interference or permission of any Party, to do *all* that the Commander judges necessary and proper" (Annex 1A, Article 6(5), emphasis added). As a cover story to retain these powers, the US argued that the NATO headquarters should continue to play a role in counter-terrorism activities in Bosnia and support the International Criminal Tribunal for former Yugoslavia (ICTY) in The Hague in bringing persons indicted for war crimes (PIFWCs) to justice.

The US presented its conditions as a *fait accompli*. This greatly annoyed the EU member states, which noted that "you can't have two forces in the same country, under two political command and control regimes, with two commanders, and two armed forces under the same mandates" (interview Althea official). Given that the tasks of the NATO headquarters included covert actions, the potential problems were obvious: Althea could unintentionally interfere with the NATO mission and *vice versa*. These institutional difficulties regarding the delineation of mandates proved so controversial that an agreement could not be reached in Brussels. Instead, the military commanders of both organizations on the ground made arrangements among themselves (ibid.; Kupferschmidt 2006). To facilitate coordination, it was decided to co-locate the EU and NATO headquarters in Bosnia rather than to co-locate all the EU actors.

Another issue in the EU–NATO relationship was the availability of "over the horizon forces." This concept had been introduced under SFOR, when NATO started to decrease its troops. With the low number of troops in Bosnia, SFOR would have been unable to stop major deteriorations in the security environment. Instead, it could rely on reserves within the member states and the NATO troops that were part of the KFOR operation in Kosovo (interview NATO official). It was quite quickly agreed that when the EU took over the SFOR operation, it would continue to be able to rely on these NATO reserves. Yet this obviously raised a number of questions. The most difficult issue was through which procedures the EUFOR Commander could request these NATO troops, particularly given that reserves normally have to be used at short notice. It was decided that while the EUFOR Commander was allowed to ask for such reinforcements, the North Atlantic Council had the final say. Given that DSACEUR acted as the EU Operations Commander under Berlin Plus, it was not such a major difficulty in the end.

The final issue in the EU–NATO relationship, which became a topic of debate, was the role of NATO's Allied Forces Southern Europe (AFSOUTH) based in Naples. As the Joint Force Command for NATO's activities in the Mediterranean, it coordinated all operations in the Western Balkans. This made functional sense. The region was one operational theater and many tactical issues could be better dealt with regionally than in SHAPE (interview NATO official). Thus when the EU launched operation Concordia in Macedonia, it was decided to leave this structure intact, albeit with a European Union Command Element (EUCE) in AFSOUTH. One of the lessons learned, however, was that such an extra layer in the chain of command made it more difficult for the PSC to exert control (Mace 2004). There was another implication. AFSOUTH had traditionally been led by an American. When France tried to negotiate its way back into NATO in 1997, it unsuccessfully demanded this position (e.g. Bryant 2000). Thus the fact that an American had an important position during the EU-led Concordia operation was something France had difficulty with.

For Althea, it was decided to take the EUCE element at AFSOUTH out of the formal chain of command. The Force Commander would directly report to the Operations Commander (DSACEUR) in SHAPE. Yet AFSOUTH continued to be in the chain of command of the residual NATO operation. It also owned some of the assets of the Althea operation, such as the headquarters at Camp Butmir (interview NATO official). The member states recognized that AFSOUTH continued to fulfill a useful regional function for the Western Balkans, even after the operations in Macedonia had ended. The EUCE at AFSOUTH therefore became an "enabler" for Althea (interviews Althea and NATO officials). It consists of eight liaison officers (McColl 2009; interview national official). AFSOUTH supplies intelligence and situation assessments.

In all these discussions, EU officials played a facilitating role. Deputy Director-General for External Relations, Pieter Feith, for example, had previously worked for NATO and was involved in the nitty-gritty details of the inter-organizational relationship. Solana himself had, of course, been Secretary-General of NATO, which was useful in terms of contacts. Both men were undoubtedly important in making sure that the agreements finally materialized. In terms of actually shaping the relations between the EU and NATO, their role was smaller. These relations were so politicized that some sort of *status quo* or pragmatic agreement was the only possible outcome. There were no obvious goal conflict, in this respect, between the EU officials and the member states.

Finalizing the joint action

Most institutional questions were addressed during early 2004. Some final outstanding issues were presented to the Council meeting of the Ministers of Foreign Affairs, the Ministers of Defense, the PSC ambassadors and the national Chiefs of Defense (May 17, 2004). With these key actors present, this was the place to finalize matters (interview national official). After agreement on the remaining issues, there were still a number of formalities. First, NATO had to declare that it was concluding its operation, which it did during the Istanbul summit on June 28–29, 2004. Second, the UNSC had to approve Resolution 1551 to give the Althea (and the continuing NATO activities) formal legitimacy under chapter VII. After this hurdle was cleared, the member states adopted the Joint Action on July 12.

When looking at the decision-making procedure, it is clear that the member states did not rush things (interviews national officials; Pohl 2009). The EU (and the US) took at least 18 months to think about the mission between the agenda-setting in December 2002 and the adoption of the Joint Action. This relatively long period had not so much to do with planning issues, as with political and institutional discussions. Apart from the delay caused by the US, the phase itself was also rather lengthy. One national interviewee noted that the military documents (see below) could have been done by April 2004. Yet when it became obvious that December 2004 was the target date of the handover, the process was almost automatically delayed. Another national interviewee notes, in this respect, that "without a sense of urgency nothing happens ... if there is time, it is being used fully for diplomatic and political games. When the decision finally has been taken, the member states ask the general the next day why his forces are not yet deployed."

Implementation

Launching Althea was relatively easy. As it took over from SFOR, the supporting structures and most of the troops were already in place. There were no difficult logistical issues, the force generation process was not challenging, and the planning documents had already been drafted for the NATO operation. It is, in this respect, telling that the future Force Commander, General Leakey, who had been appointed as part of the Joint Action of July 12, 2004, continued his job in the UK before he took up responsibilities. Only in October did he move to Bosnia with a small support staff to set up the Force Headquarters (interview Althea official). On the day of the handover, most of the troops switched their badges and continued the same activities under EU flag. As a national interviewee notes, "I am not sure whether they actually changed phone numbers, as the NATO communication assets were still being used."

The first thing to do, after the decision on the handover had been taken, was to reassure the Bosnian population that nothing would change in the security situation. Solana and NATO Secretary-General Jaap de Hoop Scheffer therefore went on a joint visit. During the press conference, Solana stated (2004b) that "continuity and development are precisely what this change-over is about ... I want to make it very clear that EUFOR will begin its operations with all the material and personnel that it requires – the same troop strength as SFOR. It will have what it needs to do the job." While the overarching message for the population was thus one of continuity, he also noted (yet again) that the EU's "objective is to put [Bosnia] irreversibly on the road towards EU membership – and that involves a broad and profound reform effort, which has only recently got properly underway. [Althea] is the latest element in a comprehensive EU strategy to help [Bosnia]."

At the bureaucratic level, the planning took place in Bosnia and at SHAPE. Already, in June 2004, the member states had sent a planning team to Sarajevo to set up camp inside the local SFOR Headquarters (Bertin 2008). This planning team performed a liaison function and arranged a number of technical details for the arrival of General Leakey. After the approval of the Joint Action, the military planning process could also formally start. An Althea EU Staff Group was formed within SHAPE to support the Operations Commander DSACEUR, consisting initially of nine military officers drawn from the Concordia EU Staff Group (NATO 2008). The Staff Group increased over time to 19 officers (McColl 2009). It was in charge of planning. The CONOPS and OPLAN were largely based on NATO documents (interview national official).

The force generation process took place in parallel with drafting the planning documents. There were still some 900–1000 American troops under SFOR when Althea took over responsibility. They had to be replaced, which required a series of force generation conferences. Overall, this did not present a problem. It was relatively easy (interview national official). Several non-NATO EU member states (Finland, Sweden, and Austria) stepped up their commitments. Finland became framework nation of the Task Force North. All the gaps left by the US were quickly filled. After the force generation, the Security Council adopted on November 22, 2004, Resolution 1575, which formally gave the EU the green light to take over from SFOR. Three days later, the Council set December 2 as the handover date. On the day itself, most of the soldiers of the contributing member states changed their badges. The handover was thus not particularly spectacular.

The conduct of the operation

As noted above, Solana wanted Althea to be a "new and distinct" operation. It would send a signal to the Bosnians about the new EU leadership. Since he only partially achieved this aim during the decision-making phase, he tried again during implementation. Before Force Commander General Leakey left for Bosnia, he was summoned to the office of the High Representative. During this meeting, Solana made three clear points. First, Leakey had to be "his general." This meant reporting to him through the chain of command and not directly to the member states (interview Althea official). Second, the operation had to make a difference. The handover from SFOR to Althea, Solana argued, should lead to new political leverage for the EU in Bosnia (interview national official). Third, Solana told General Leakey that the operation, in this respect, should be "new and distinct" (Leakey 2006: 60). With these instructions General Leakey went to Bosnia in October.

In a reflective article written after his posting (ibid.), General Leakey noted that he initially found these instructions strange and unclear. After all, he had had extensive experience with Bosnia – as the UK's Military Representative during the Dayton peace talks, as commander under IFOR and SFOR, and as Director of Military Operations. He was very well aware of the success of SFOR as a stabilization and deterrent force. "Why change a winning formula" (ibid.: 60)? General Leakey noted that he did not completely understand these instructions until he actually had a look at his official mandate and started to read the Office of the High Representative's Mission Implementation Plan. This plan, as it turned out, gave the Force Commander a lot of leeway and General Leakey interpreted the role of Althea in the widest possible sense. As a result, Althea became quite new and completely distinct from what SFOR had been before.

As stated in the OPLAN, the first two key military tasks were to continue to ensure a safe and secure environment in Bosnia as well as compliance with the Dayton agreement. These had been the objectives of the SFOR's mandate. At the Istanbul Summit in June 2004, however, NATO had already declared "mission accomplished" (Leakey 2006; Bertin 2008). It effectively meant that the military job was done. During Althea, the safe and secure environment was indeed never at risk. The presence of 7,000 troops as a deterrent force, to achieve the key military tasks, was of symbolic importance. Bertin (2008: 67) notes:

> Althea's main function is reassurance, which is at least partly a psychological concept. The international military presence is a key element contributing to a sense of safety among the local population. The citizenry are convinced that renewed inter-ethnic fighting is impossible thanks to the continued presence of an international military force.[3]

As part of this deterrent function, Althea engaged in extensive patrolling. By simply driving around in army vehicles, it showed its presence. In the first months, this gave the EU visibility as well. Althea furthermore continued with the weapons-harvesting operations of SFOR. Soldiers went through the towns and villages and granted people amnesty for handing in their weapons. In addition, soldiers conducted searches for weapons if they had intelligence. Such intelligence often came in through the Liaison and Observation Teams (LOTs). These teams were living in local communities throughout Bosnia (Bertin 2008). Finally, in ensuring compliance with Dayton, Althea helped the Bosnian army to secure and/or destroy weapons and ammunition storage sites. Althea was also in charge of weapon transports. Thus the soldiers made "themselves useful and busy" (interview Althea official).

The key military task to support the High Representative's Mission Implementation Plan was less straightforward. The Plan consisted of four sections: the economy, the rule of law, the police, and defense reform. Yet as Leakey (2006: 61) notes, the military has little to contribute to the economy or the rule of law. The police tasks were done by the EUPM and defense reform was still the prerogative of NATO. This made it difficult for Althea to really contribute something militarily to the Mission Implementation Plan without stepping on someone's toes. Yet without acting actively on this key military task, Althea would not be new and distinct. Leakey went to see the High Representative Ashdown, who made a point about the "obstructionism which was preventing [Bosnia's] progress and process towards membership of the EU" (ibid.: 61) resulting from organized crime intertwined with endemic corruption in Bosnian politics.

Leakey decided to make the fight against organized crime the "centrepiece of his agenda" (Bertin 2008: 68). It seemed to him that corruption, organized crime, fraud, and the black economy were undermining growth and foreign direct investments. This had negative effects on the well-being and the tax take of the government. Both were in the long run potential spoilers and causes of instability. Given that the fight against organized crime was a key supporting military task, Leakey thought it legitimate for Althea to take appropriate action (Leakey 2006). This would indirectly support a second key supporting military task – bringing to justice the remaining persons who were indicted for war crimes by the ICTY (Bertin 2008).

It is important to note that Althea could formally only *support* the fight against organized crime. After all, Althea was not a law enforcement agency. Leakey (ibid.: 63–64) interpreted this support function as follows:

> Soldiers would create the conditions in which the [Bosnia] law enforcement agencies not only "could" but "would have to" do their duty. In other words, [Althea] would help discover a crime or illegality (e.g. fuel smuggling or illegal timber cutting), but would "freeze the scene" and hand it over to the [Bosnian] authorities to deal with the legal and law enforcement technicalities. This avoided [Althea] soldiers being involved in the specialised police work of handling evidence or appearing as witnesses in subsequent legal proceedings.

In the fight against organized crime, Althea had, of course, the integrated police units. As military police, they were well trained for such jobs. Yet there were only 500 of them. Leakey understood that he would also require the remainder of his troops. If he wanted to employ them in a flexible manner, he first had to deal with national territorial caveats. These caveats, which dated from the IFOR period, prevented troops from one member state being used in a sector of another member state. When IFOR was initially deployed with about 60,000 soldiers, these caveats made sense. The operational theater was decentralized to prevent states from operating in each other's space. Yet with only 7,000 troops in Bosnia, it was necessary to have some flexibility in deploying them. While many member states were reluctant to give up the caveats, their Chiefs of Defense were effectively lobbied by the Operations Commander (Leakey 2006).

After the caveats had been lifted, General Leakey started targeting several of the Gross Domestic Product (GDP)-earning industries, most notably the fuel and timber industries. The former was relevant, because Bosnia imported all its fuel and the levies charged at the border were an important source of tax revenue. Based on calculation it was clear that much fuel was imported illegally. In support of the Mission Implementation Plan, the EU soldiers started to stop fuel tankers at the borders. They put surveillance on border crossing points, where tankers could pass illegally, and they checked all the tankers coming over the border legally by photocopying their documents. Furthermore, they dipped the fuel tanks and took samples of the fuel in order to check the quality, because the levies on lower quality fuel were different from those on higher quality fuel. The effect of these measures was that after three months of inspections the tax revenue on fuel imports increased by 12–14%. Moreover, it made various politicians, who were in charge of the government-owned fuel industry, extremely annoyed. It exposed the corruption in the various law enforcement agencies. The problem was, of course, that Althea could not follow up on these issues nor carry out these tasks indefinitely.

One of the reasons why these military activities were not very successful was the lack of EU support. Leakey's activism was met with resistance from various member states, the Police Mission, and parts of the Commission. At least five of the major contributing member states were at the highest levels "very, very unenthusiastic, if not in opposition, to their military being used in this way" (interview Althea official). They thought that these were not military tasks. The departure of Leakey at the end of 2005 was a good moment for the member states to reconsider Althea. First, they appointed General Chiarini, who had a more conservative view on things. Second, the member states reduced Althea by 1,000 soldiers. Given that Althea had a number of other key military tasks, such as the harvesting of weapons and patrolling, this meant that General Chiarini simply had too few troops to carry out extra tasks to support the Mission Implementation Plan. Through these two steps, the member states thus eventually got what they wanted.

The problems between Althea and the EUPM were at least as serious. The officials from the Police Mission pointed out that they were "trying to tell the Bosnians that you don't use the military to sort out the internal political problems in a country" (interview Althea official). The problem, however, was that no one dealt with executive rule of law enforcement. Thus in the end, Althea carried out these tasks because the EUPM did not. Still, in the words of a Commission official, "the feeling on the [EUPM] side was that the military were going in with big heavy boots, but not really achieving anything. In the end, if they stop someone, they never got into a place where they could have real evidence that could be used in court." An Althea interviewee similarly notes, "you can't do the fight against organized crime with military. You need to have police and prosecution involved, because otherwise you lose it."

The relationship between the Police Mission and Althea was also particularly tense because of personalities at the top (interview Commission official; Merlingen 2009). This was partially resolved when the leadership left in December 2005. Leakey's one-year term was over and Commissioner Carty's term was not extended. In addition, Althea, the EUPM and the Special Representative agreed on seven principles for coordination (Juncos 2007), which led to a stronger coordinating role for the latter. On this basis, in 2006 the EU adopted the Common Operational Guidelines between the Police Mission and Althea. These guidelines stress that the ownership is with local law enforcement agencies and that they, with the endorsement of the Police Mission, can ask Althea to support them. The guidelines work well in practice. While the Police Mission has a strong role to play here, it is worth noting that Althea shortly afterwards downscaled. Finally, after the 2007 changes in the formal Joint Action, the Special Representative received an even stronger coordinating mandate and more staff.

Restructuring and termination

During General Leakey's period in Bosnia the member states had already reduced the strength of Althea from approximately 7,000 to 6,000 troops. This left his successor with fewer resources. Thus after a very ambitious first year, Althea scaled down its military activities. Real change to Althea, however, came in 2006, when the UK announced that it would unilaterally withdraw all of its almost 600 troops from Bosnia. The country was overstretched, with ongoing operations in Iraq and the newly launched military operation in South Afghanistan under NATO's International Security Assistance Force (ISAF) (mid-2006). It is also worth noting that with the conclusion of its Presidency (fall 2005), the end of the mandate of Ashdown (May 2006) and with Leakey leaving, there was no real political purpose for the UK to stay involved in Bosnia.

Pohl (2009: 29) describes how this move of the UK was perceived by France and Germany as "'rather brutal' and 'un-British in style.'" Yet the UK was not the only member state with other commitments. Germany was also deeply involved in Afghanistan and Kosovo. When the German government considered taking up the leadership of the EU military operation in Congo (July–November 2006), this led to fierce resistance in the German parliament, partially because of over-involvement (IHT 2006a). When Germany, during the summer of 2006, also agreed to send its navy to the coast of Lebanon as part of an effort to bring stability after the Israeli–Lebanese war, it became clear that things had to change. At the end of October, the German defense minister announced that he would withdraw his troops from Bosnia (IHT 2006b; FT 2006).

The situation was not very different in many of the other major contributing member states. In 2006, France became involved in Congo and Lebanon. Italy even accepted the commanding role of the United Nations Interim Force in Lebanon (UNIFIL) operation in Lebanon. The Netherlands launched an operation in South Afghanistan under ISAF. Only Spain and Turkey and some of the neutral countries had reason to stay in Bosnia. With the risk that other member states would follow the bold move of the UK, the Operations Commander faced the problem of ending up with too few troops. It was thus decided to change the key military tasks with the result that Althea could continue with fewer troops. A new CONOPS was tabled in June 2006, which was accepted in December. The ministers stated that the "security situation in [Bosnia had] evolved enough" (Council Conclusions). The OHQ was tasked to revise the OPLAN so that a transition could take place, which would reduce the force to 2,500. The OPLAN was accepted on February 27, 2007, by the PSC. The force reduction was completed by April.

While the formal mandate was not amended, Althea could only continue as a deterrent force and carry out some of the Dayton tasks. In this respect, it would continue to be able to rely on the "over the horizons forces" of KFOR in Kosovo, which was extensively communicated to the population. As part of the transition, Althea concentrated all the troops around Sarajevo. This meant that it could no longer do extensive patrolling. It kept a number of "liaison and observation team" houses open to continue to gather intelligence from the local population. The reduction in force thus changed the sort of operation that the EU was carrying out. Parallel to these developments, the US withdrew its national contingent from Tuzla. As a result, the NATO headquarters in

Sarajevo no longer has any operational capability at its disposal. While it continues to enjoy its executive powers, NATO is no longer capable of counter-terrorism activity and the hunt for war criminals (interview NATO official).

It was not long after the transition that questions were raised over the complete phasing out of the Althea operation. In the original CONOPS, the end-state of the military operation was defined on the basis of three objectives (interview Althea official):

1. The military and stabilisation tasks [of the Dayton agreement] have been accomplished;
2. Democratically controlled [Bosnian] security capabilities are in place, able to maintain lasting stability;
3. The [Office of the High Representative's Mission Implementation Plan] no longer needs support by military means to back the EU's short and medium term political objectives.

Following continuous assessments of the Operations Commander, the first two objectives have been achieved (interview Althea official). The third objective was foreseen for 2007. Solana and Rehn issued a joint report on a reinforced EU presence in Bosnia after the closure of the Office of the High Representative already on October 17, 2006. It stipulated a stronger mandate for the Special Representative, who would replace the High Representative. Once the international community would accept to close the Office of the High Representative, the third objective of the end-state of Althea would be achieved.

It is quite embarrassing that the international community to this date has not decided to close the Office of the High Representative. More than seven years after the idea was first tabled, the debates are still ongoing in the Steering Board of the Peace Implementation Council. There are two reasons for this stalemate. First, since the secession of Kosovo from Serbia, Russia has been extremely reluctant to give up its veto position, which it enjoys in the Steering Board. Second, the political situation in Bosnia has deteriorated, which makes a number of EU member states and the US wary of giving up the executive powers of the High Representative.

With the closure of the Office of the High Representative under debate, the future of Althea has also been in a limbo. In 2008, for example, France decided to withdraw its remaining troops. A number of the other member states followed France's example, bringing the Althea operation down to fewer than 2,000 soldiers. This (again) led to a situation

120 *Policy-Making in EU Security and Defense*

where the Operations Commander was faced with the risk of not having enough troops. Future options for the operation were therefore discussed. On this point, however, the member states disagreed. Some member states were still afraid of future instability. Other member states argued that the time had come to give full ownership to Bosnia, because otherwise they will never take their own security seriously (ibid.).

This discussion played throughout 2009. Whereas the reduction in 2007 still allowed for future reinforcements, the discussions over withdrawal implied that the EU would give up its UN chapter VII mandate. This meant that it is no longer possible to redeploy peace-keeping troops in the event of future instability. In early 2010, it was decided that Althea would take on a training function in addition to the work of the integrated police units and the LOTs. This would be part of the further downscaling of the operation. In October 2011, the EU finally decided to end the executive military role of Althea after many of the remaining member states also unilaterally withdrew their troops (ISIS Europe 2011). Althea retains its chapter VII mandate and has over the horizon troops that can be deployed in the worst-case scenario. The presence on the ground is, however, very small. Only Austria, Turkey, and Hungary still have a significant number of troops in Bosnia.

Overview of the findings

This chapter has provided an analysis of the policy process of the military operation Althea in Bosnia-Herzegovina. Special emphasis has been paid to the role of Solana and other EU officials. The chapter concludes by assessing their influence. For this purpose, the yardstick presented in the introduction of this book will be used (see Table 1.1). This allows for a comparison between Althea and the other case studies. To briefly repeat the main indicators for influence: EU officials have a high amount of influence when they take the lead (together with one/two member states) during a particular phase of the policy process. For them to have a medium level of influence, they should constitute a necessary condition to explain the outcome during a particular phase of the policy process. In order to have a low amount of influence, they would be required to be actively involved in the deliberations. If they were not involved, they would have no influence.

EU officials played an important role in the *agenda-setting phase* of the Althea mission. Javier Solana was particularly active in promoting the idea that the EU should take over from NATO. This idea had been around before, but he spent political capital to put it high on the agenda. The main reason for Solana to promote Althea was a bureaucratic interest in actually using the CSDP services, which had been established since 1999. The Western Balkans were considered a good testing ground for the CSDP. By taking over an operation from NATO under the Berlin Plus agreement, the EU would not undermine its relations with the US, which had been very skeptical about the CSDP. From an operational perspective, taking over from NATO was also relatively easy given that all the planning documents were ready and the troops already in theater. The risks of having a military operation in the Western Balkans were thus low. This was ideal for the development of the CSDP and clearly in the interest of the Brussels-based Council officials.

Solana was not the only actor pushing for a military operation in Bosnia. The idea was also supported by France and the UK. These three actors worked closely together in getting the European Council in December 2002 to approve the Macedonia and Bosnia takeover from NATO. Afterwards, they wrote the early planning documents together (February 2003). The problem for Solana – and the EU as a whole – was that they did not determine the timing of the handover. At the end of the day, this decision was made in Washington. The transatlantic tensions in the spring of 2003 resulted in severe delay. For at least six month, the US managed to keep the plans for the military operation in Bosnia off the table. EU officials thus played a front-running role by putting earlier ideas on the political agenda. They were, however, not alone within the EU. Moreover, they were not fully capable of autonomously carrying these plans through. Their influence within the EU was therefore medium in the agenda-setting phase.

EU officials played a particularly active role during the *decision-making phase*. Yet activity does not equal influence. From the beginning, Solana and his civil servants recognized that a takeover from SFOR would give the EU an opportunity to improve the coherence between its instruments in Bosnia. A comprehensive approach, in which the military operation complements the other activities of the EU, was strongly emphasized in a report of Solana to the member states (February 24, 2004). Solana advocated a "new and distinct" approach when it came to military deployment. Althea, in his view, would not merely be a continuation of SFOR, but would be used to give the EU political clout in Bosnia. An example of the new and distinct approach was the role of the military operation in the fight against organized crime. In Solana's report, this was even a key military objective.

The member states decided not to go for this new approach. They took a conservative view and in their deliberations stressed continuity.

The key military tasks, which were eventually accepted, followed the objectives of SFOR. The member states did not, however, completely reject Solana's proposal. In the formal Joint Action, they referred to the Mission Implementation Plan and they made the fight against organized crime a key supporting task. Yet the main idea to make Althea new and distinct and to increase the powers of the Special Representative was not accepted. On other topics, such as EU–NATO delineation, the EU officials had little influence. These were typically issues where some of the member states had strong views, which in the end prevailed. The details of EU–NATO delineation were indeed so sensitive that they had to be decided on the ground rather than in Brussels. Thus, despite all activity, the influence of Solana and other EU officials in the decision-making phase was low.

The *implementation phase* of Althea has been rather long (2004–date). It is therefore difficult to make generalized statements on influence. When looking at the various facets of implementation, the contribution of the EU officials has been limited. To start with, consider the launching of the operation. This was rather simple and straightforward. Most of the military planning decisions were taken in SHAPE based on previous SFOR documents. The limited force generation processes, which only required the replacement of the American troops, took place under the leadership of the Operations Commander. Of course, the EUMS was involved, but looking from a counterfactual point of view, it is difficult to see where the EU officials would have made a difference.

Regarding the conduct of the operation, it is difficult to miss Leakey's activism. This was partly the result of the explicit instructions, which he received from Solana. Furthermore, Leakey's good working relationship with Ashdown also facilitated his actions. Through his instructions, Solana tried to pursue his preferences after he had failed during the decision-making phase. It is worth noting, in this respect, that Leakey initially got away with it, despite the opposition of the member states. The costs of removing Leakey during his term would be too high. One should also recognize, however, the limits of Solana's influence. Once Leakey left as Force Commander, the member states appointed a more conservative Italian general and cut the size of the force. These can be seen as *ex post* control mechanisms. Such cases of agent selection and re-contracting are to be expected after the member states detect excessive agency.

The restructuring and termination process of the Althea operation continues to date. Overall, there is only one conclusion. No matter what sorts of reports the EU officials and the Operations Commander

Table 5.2 Influence of EU officials in Operation Althea

Agenda-setting	Medium
Decision-making	Low
Implementation	Low

send to the member states, member states make their own decisions. Both the transition of the operation and the talks on the termination were triggered by unilateral military withdrawals of individual member states. They had to do with concerns exogenous to the EU. For both the UK and France, it was about their national military services being overstretched and about the financial burden of continuing endless military operations. EU officials were involved in the decisions about future options, such as a possible non-executive mission, but they did not call the shots. In conclusion, the overall influence of the EU officials during implementation was therefore low. They clearly tried to pursue their own policy interests, but they failed to take on the member states.

When taking an overall look at operation Althea, one can clearly identify goal conflicts between the EU officials and the member states. Particularly with regard to the mandate of the operation, Solana wanted different things. He failed, however, to completely change the mandate in light of member state opposition. The member states preferred the existing military template, were wary about the uncertainty that changes would inevitably bring, and stuck to their standard operating mechanisms. Their control mechanisms thus functioned as expected. The implementation of operation Althea nonetheless created opportunities for influence. Through the Force Commander, Solana asked for a wide interpretation of the mandate. This did not go undetected, however, and the member states again stepped in by means of replacing the Force Commander. The existing control mechanisms were thus sufficient in this case to avoid too much shirking by EU officials amidst conflicting preferences.

6
Monitoring Mission in Aceh

The AMM was one of the first serious civilian CSDP missions outside Europe. For 15 months (September 2005–December 2006) some 250 monitors from the EU and ASEAN member states oversaw the implementation of a peace agreement between the Government of Indonesia and the Free Aceh Movement (*Gerakan Aceh Merdeka*; GAM), which had been brokered after the tsunami had devastated the province of Aceh in December 2004. It included overseeing several rounds of decommissioning of weapons by the Free Aceh Movement and the subsequent withdrawal of the Indonesian army. The task of these monitors was by no means easy. On the eve of the signing of the peace agreement, the International Crisis Group (2005) issued a report warning that "no one should underestimate the difficulties of bringing an end to a 30-year-old conflict … peace is not a done deal" (see also Aspinall 2005: 1). The EU, however, got the job done and the Head of Mission, Pieter Feith, claimed in retrospect that the AMM was "nothing less than a success" (Feith 2007). The mission wonderfully showed the added value of the EU's civilian crisis management.

As with the previous chapter, this chapter analyzes the influence of EU officials by means of process-tracing following the different stages of the policy process. It starts with how the AMM came onto the EU agenda (January–June 2005). It shows the early involvement of EU officials through their close relations with former Finnish President Martti Ahtisaari, who mediated the peace agreement between the Government of Indonesia and the GAM. It then moves on to internal decision-making (July–August). In this period, EU officials presented member states with a *fait accompli* and it found innovative means of financing to get the endeavor under way. The chapter then focuses on implementation (August 2005–December 2006). The emphasis is on the Interim Monitoring Presence (IMP), pro-active monitoring and the lengthy termination process. The chapter concludes by analyzing the influence of the EU officials in the different phases of the policy process.

Agenda-setting

The AMM was a direct result of the Memorandum of Understanding of August 15, 2005, which the Government of Indonesia had negotiated with the Free Aceh Movement under the facilitation of the Crisis Management Initiative (CMI) of former Finnish President Martti Ahtisaari. Contrary to previous peace initiatives, such as the talks under the guidance of the Geneva-based Henry Dunant Centre (2000–2003), these negotiations were arguably successful due to a changing political environment. First, the GAM had suffered an enormous military defeat following a large-scale Indonesian military campaign (2003–2004). This meant that independence had become an even more distant prospect. Second, in September 2004, the first ever democratic Presidency elections in Indonesia were held. This event went hand-in-hand with processes of democratization and security sector reform. It made Indonesia more accommodating. Finally, the devastating tsunami of December 26, 2004, put the attention of the international community on the Aceh province, where the situation was worst.

The military campaign and martial law, which the Indonesian government introduced shortly after the final breakdown of the previous round of peace talks (Tokyo, May 17–18, 2003), proved decisive. The government deployed 35,000 soldiers to the province of Aceh, who killed and captured within a year a significant proportion of the Acehnese rebels (Huber 2008). Yet the Indonesian government realized that this was not a sustainable solution. It therefore remained open to further peace talks through "back channels." This process was facilitated by the Finnish businessman Juha Christensen, who had connections with the Indonesian leadership and the GAM government-in-exile in Sweden. From mid-2004, when martial law was replaced by a "state of civil emergency," the Indonesian minister Jusuf Kalla became involved in these talks through his personal advisor Farid Husain (Huber 2008). During a trip to Iran in February 2004, with a "slight" unofficial detour to Helsinki, Husain met with Ahtisaari to explore whether the former President would mediate (Merikallio 2008; interview in Accord 2008). The contacts intensified after Kalla was elected Vice-President of Indonesia on September 20, 2004. Just before Christmas, Ahtisaari was told that both sides were willing to negotiate (Ahtisaari 2008; Huber 2008; Helsingin Sanomat 2006; interview in Accord 2008).

Before a meeting could be scheduled between the Government of Indonesia and the GAM, the tsunami of December 26, 2004, hit the coastal states of the Indian Ocean. With over 100,000 casualties in Aceh alone, it became the center of world media attention. Despite difficult access to the hard-hit areas during the first few days, the EU quickly took the lead in terms of humanitarian aid. Commissioner Louis Michel traveled through the most-affected countries. He was later joined by Commission President Barroso during various donor conferences. Given that the Commission is one of the largest humanitarian donors, its role was only natural. In addition to this attention, and with international officials getting access to the province of Aceh (something which had been difficult before), the tsunami led to a temporary halt of hostilities – albeit informal and unilateral, rather than a mutually agreed ceasefire (FT 2004). This sparked some hopes that the tsunami had presented a "window of opportunity" to put the peace talks back on track (ibid.).

The prospect of renewed talks gained more prominence on the international agenda when foreign minister Fischer made German aid conditional upon new peace initiatives (January 5, FT 2005a). This forced the GAM back to the negotiating table and left them with little negotiating leverage. The people of Aceh were most desperately in need of international help. Whereas previously the Indonesian reluctance to allow international mediation and the drive of the rebels to fight for independence had caused a stalemate, the tsunami removed these obstacles. The first round of formal negotiations took place in Helsinki on January 27–29, facilitated by Ahtisaari and his CMI. Apart from some confidence-building conversations, little was actually achieved during this round. The rebels refused to give up their objective of full independence. Ahtisaari nonetheless invited the parties for a second round.

The first round of negotiations was – apart from the negotiating parties and CMI – attended by two officials of the Finnish Ministry of Foreign Affairs, who acted in the capacity of observers. President Ahtisaari introduced them to the parties as the ones "paying for the electricity" (interview with participant in negotiations). Indeed, the Finnish Foreign Ministry was paying for the expenses. What was, however, not told to the parties is that these observers were already reporting to the other member states by means of COREU and during meetings in Helsinki and Brussels. Moreover, President Ahtisaari himself kept the EU informed. Already, at this stage, he envisaged that some kind of governmental monitoring mechanism would be necessary and that the EU's "involvement would be desirable" (quoted in Accord 2008). The EU was probably the only party that could send monitors who would have credibility in the eyes of the GAM and who could be acceptable to the Indonesian government.[1] After the first round, he thus called Javier Solana, whom he personally knew well. Solana told him to "go ahead" (Merikallio 2008: 80), though naturally stating that it would be up to the member states to decide.

In addition to contacting Solana, the CMI contacted the European Commission with a request for funding for its mediation activities. This request was positively received and even politically supported after Commissioner Ferrero-Waldner had discussed Aceh with Indonesian counterparts during a visit to Jakarta (March 9–12, 2005) (interview Commission official). The funding details were worked out between the staff of the CMI and DG RELEX, including during a short trip of CMI staff to Brussels. As one of the staff members from the CMI writes:

> From the beginning of February, CMI was in daily contact with [the desk officer] to seek assistance from the Commission ... the submission of an application was not a "one off" affair. Indeed a number of proposals were submitted, each one reflecting lengthy discussions with [the desk officer] who worked with his hierarchy to find a suitable formula. (Herrberg 2008)

The Commission finally approved the proposal for funding under the Rapid Reaction Mechanism (Commission 2005). Antje Herrberg (2008) suggests that the involvement of the Commission and the endorsement of Solana made them shareholders of the project and created a sense of ownership. This would "pave the way for ... European monitoring of the eventual peace agreement."

The second round of negotiations under the guidance of the CMI (February 21–23) was more successful than the first. The Acehnese negotiators understood that if they continued to pursue independence, the talks would break down (Nur Djuli and Abdul Rahman 2008). Rather than accepting "special autonomy," which the Indonesian government had proposed during earlier negotiations, Ahtisaari suggested instead that they would pursue "self-government" – a synonym "without the same abhorrent connotations" (ibid.). This opened the door for substantive talks. Ahtisaari stated during the concluding press conference that both parties recognized the need for monitors, but that the UN was not an acceptable party. The parties would instead consider monitors of the regional organizations, such as ASEAN and the EU (FT 2005b). For this purpose he had kept Solana informed (IHT 2005).

Table 6.1 Chronology of the AMM

December 4, 1976	Declaration of independence
December 9, 2002	Cessation of Hostilities Agreement by Dunant Centre
May 17–18, 2003	Tokyo negotiations
May 19, 2003	Martial law in Aceh
February 2004	Initial contacts with President Ahtisaari
May 19, 2004	State of civil emergency in Aceh
September 20, 2004	Presidential elections in Indonesia
December 2004	Invitation to parties for negotiations in Finland
December 26, 2004	Tsunami hits Indian Ocean
Late December 2004	Informal halt of hostilities in Aceh
January 27–29, 2005	First round of negotiations in Finland
January 29, 2005	Finland sends COREU; Ahtisaari informs Solana
February–April 2005	Ahtisaari negotiates funding with Commission
February 21–23, 2005	Second round of negotiations
February 2005	Oksanen meets Moschini, Feith, and planners
March 9–12, 2005	Commissioner Ferrero-Waldner visits Indonesia
April 12–16, 2005	Third round of negotiations
April 21, 2005	Ahtisaari briefs PSC
May 26–31, 2005	Fourth round of negotiations; Feith briefs parties
June 24– July 2, 2005	EU fact-finding mission to Aceh
July 11, 2005	Feith briefs parties on the fact-finding mission
July 12–17, 2005	Fifth and final round of negotiations
July 18, 2005	Council is, in principle, prepared to send observers
July 19, 2005	Disagreement over financing in PSC
July 26, 2005	Solana/Ahtisaari address PSC
July 29, 2005	PSC accepts IMP
July 30–31, 2005	EU mission to Aceh
August 1–14, 2005	EU/ASEAN technical assessment mission to Aceh
August 15, 2005	Memorandum of Understanding
August 15, 2005	IMP
August 16, 2005	CONOPS
August 17, 31, 2005	Release of prisoners by Government of Indonesia
August 30, 2005	OPLAN
September 9, 2005	Joint Action
September 15, 2005	Start of AMM
September–December	Decommissioning and withdrawal of troops
March 15, 2006	First extension of the mission
June 7, 2006	Second extension of the mission
September 7, 2006	Third extension of the mission
December 11, 2006	Local elections
December 15, 2006	Termination of AMM

It is again necessary to understand that this second round of talks did not take place in a vacuum. Shortly before the second round, the representatives from the GAM and the Indonesian government met with the bilateral ambassadors of Australia, Japan, Malaysia, Singapore, Sweden, the

UK, and the US (Kingsbury 2006). These ambassadors had a rather strong message for the negotiating parties: "they wanted to see a negotiated end to the Aceh conflict preserving the territorial integrity of Indonesia" (ibid.: 34). In the eyes of the political advisor to the GAM, Damian Kingsbury, this was a key communication to the Indonesian government that reconstruction had to go ahead. The potential blame for possible failure and reductions in development aid gave the Indonesian government an incentive to work with Ahtisaari. As for the GAM, this meeting made them realize that they were politically isolated and that they could no longer hope that the international community would support their cause for independence. The GAM paid considerable attention.

In addition to keeping Solana informed, Ahtisaari also sent Jaakko Oksanen to Brussels after the second round of negotiations. Oksanen was a Finnish general whom Ahtisaari had met during a UN mission in Iraq. He became the military advisor to the CMI. In Brussels he met the chairman of the EUMC, General Mosca Moschini, as well as Pieter Feith, the deputy DG E of the Council Secretariat (and later Head of Mission), and 10 of his staff members (Merikallio 2008). Ahtisaari himself, at an earlier stage, had already contacted Feith, whom he had known since the 1970s. During the Brussels trip, Feith and his staff members showed an interest in a possible mission, but, as Oksanen recalled, it was "problematic for the EU to see how an unarmed monitoring mission [what Oksanen was proposing] could actually disarm GAM" (quoted in ibid.: 82). Feith said that the EU would see how the third round of negotiations would go before they would get involved. Interesting, however, EU planners were involved at a far earlier stage than, for example, the planning team of the Finnish (!) Ministry of Foreign Affairs, which only got involved in July (interview national official).

During the third round of talks on April 12–16, 2005, Oksanen briefed both parties on the possible external monitoring mechanisms. Yet while the CMI had its scenario ready, the parties were not willing to close the deal. The Government of Indonesia was still reluctant to have international governmental monitors and was thinking in the proportions of one hundred monitors. The GAM asked for thousands of peacekeepers rather than monitors (which the EU was unlikely to provide) (Kingsbury 2006). Ahtisaari maintained that any peace agreement should in principle be self-enforcing and that the monitors were only there to build trust. He thus supported a low number of monitors. He also introduced the idea of monitors coming from regional organizations rather than from the UN, colonial powers, or even the US. In a press statement, he said that "both parties welcome the possible involvement of regional organizations in monitoring the commitments."

Shortly after the third round of talks, Ahtisaari and Oksanen left for Brussels to brief the member states in the PSC (April 21). Ahtisaari gave a short presentation on the state of affairs and stated that he thought the situation favorable (Merikallio 2008). He furthermore outlined how the EU could help in the event of a peace agreement and he noted that he had been in earlier contact with Solana, who supported his vision (ibid.). While the initial reception was positive (with France, The Netherlands, Portugal, and the Nordic States supporting Ahtisaari), Germany quickly pointed to the limited budgetary means of the EU. Many member states were also worried about the security situation. In fact, the EU ambassadors in Jakarta had been critical about a possible EU monitoring mission (ibid.; interview Commission official). When the PSC returned to the issue in May, they decided not yet to take an official stance, but to send observers to the negotiations in Helsinki and to have a fact-finding mission. Ahtisaari once more returned to Brussels before the fifth round of negotiations to keep the member states up-to-date and discuss with them his monitoring plans.

During the fourth round of talks on May 26–31, 2005, the CMI invited Commission and CSDP experts as observers. The presence of Commission officials was mostly symbolic and gave the talks a higher status. This was important for the GAM (interview participant in negotiations). The attendance of the CSDP officials was more substantive. Feith stressed that if the EU were to get involved, failure was not an option. He demanded security guarantees, primarily from the Indonesian government, which was the only party that the EU actually recognized. He furthermore stressed that he wanted to have a single contact person for both parties with sufficient authority. Feith also discussed with Oksanen the possibility of an interim presence between the signing of a peace agreement and the formal launch of the AMM (Merikallio 2008) (see further below). Finally, the parties agreed on an EU fact-finding mission – formally called assessment mission – to the region (June 24–July 2, 2005). This mission included Feith, Oksanen, Christiansen, four EU officials, and ASEAN representatives.

Prior to the fifth round of negotiations on July 12–17, 2005, Feith briefed the parties on the assessment mission (July 11). He stated that he had been impressed by the "seriousness and determination" of both the Indonesian President Yudhoyono and Vice-President Kalla (Kingsbury 2006). He gave an outline of the mission consisting of approximately 200 foreign monitors from EU and ASEAN member states. The main tasks of the AMM were limited to security questions only – taking care of the decommissioning of GAM weapons and monitoring the pullout of Indonesian troops and police – thus limiting the possible risks of failure. These arrangements were presented to the parties as a *fait accompli* and they were accepted. The fifth round of negotiations ended with the initialization of the Memorandum of Understanding (July 17). The formal signing would take place in Helsinki on August 15. The next day the Council of the EU Ministers met and put the AMM on the agenda by agreeing that "the EU was prepared, in principle, to provide observers to monitor implementation of the [Memorandum of Understanding]."

Decision-making

During the negotiations on the Memorandum of Understanding, there was a preference among the participants that the monitoring mission would commence on the day of the signing of the peace agreement in order to avoid any escalation. Yet it was clear that the EU would not be able to launch a fully fledged monitoring mission within a month during the summer holidays.[2] It was therefore decided in the PSC that the formal mission would commence on September 15 (one month after the signing of the Memorandum of Understanding). For the period until September 14, there would be an IMP consisting of bilateral missions of EU and ASEAN member states to Indonesia. Over the summer, there were thus two parallel processes going on. Several officials of the EU and the member states went on a technical mission, set up the IMP and drafted locally most of the content for the planning documents establishing the AMM. In addition, the EU bureaucracies and the member states in Brussels sorted out the institutional and financial aspects of the mission. This chapter discusses first the decision-making procedure in Brussels and then discusses the parallel processes on the ground.

One day after the formal "go-ahead" from the Council, the member states met in the PSC, where they discussed the Crisis Management Concept and an "information note" of the Commission on the financing of the mission (July 19, 2005). The Crisis Management Concept had been written, on the insistence of the British Presidency, by the Civil-Military Cell of the Military Staff in close cooperation with the DG E IX. The CSDP officials thus had the lead. The Commission's information note had been drafted in close cooperation with the CSDP officials as well. While it was not an official Commission position, it reflected "work in progress by Commission services and guidance from the Commissioner for External Relations" (Grevi 2005: 24). The information note led to a strong debate between the Commission, the Council's legal service and several member states on the legality of the Commission financing second pillar activities.

The background to the debate was the following. At the time that civilian crisis management was established, it was foreseen that the CFSP budget would cover the expenses of civilian missions. When the AMM came up, however, the budget was very small (€62 million for 2005) and most of it had already been spent. Since the Commission could not go back to the European Parliament to increase the budget ceiling, the relevant desk officers started inventing creative ways of paying for the operation. The Commission's information note came down to the idea that development money would be made available for the mission. One of the member states (i.e. Finland) would then apply for these funds and act as a framework nation, which would hire monitors from the other member states and the ASEAN countries. The framework nation would report to the Commission, which in turn had to report to the member states. The Commission's proposal differed little from the financing of twinning projects, where the Commission pays for civil servants from the member states to support officials in developing and transition countries. It was also not so different from the Commission entering into a contract with the Head of Mission, as happens during civilian CSDP missions (interview Commission official).

During the meeting of the PSC on July 19, 2005 many of the member states were sympathetic to the proposal. Given the lack of funds in the CFSP budget, first pillar funding was a good way out. Some of the member states, and particularly the legal service of the Council, however, made clear that this was not the way that civilian CSDP had to be organized. Quite apart from the fact that first pillar funding should not be used for foreign policy objectives, the legal service objected to the idea of the Commission having a formal role in the mission. Following this discussion over funding, the Commission backed down and the Presidency, together with officials from the Council Secretariat, started looking for alternative ways of paying for the operation. They proposed using €9 million from the CFSP budget and asking individual member states to contribute the remaining €6 million in cash or kind. The proposal was put to the member states in the PSC on July 26, 2005. It was accompanied by personal interventions from Solana and Ahtisaari, who quite simply stated that the EU had to find a way of paying for the mission. The member states accepted this solution, but at least 10 of them noted that it did not constitute a precedent for funding (Grevi 2005).

The overall lack of support of the member states for the mission is interesting. Giovanni Grevi (2005) identified only four member states that were fully in favor. France naturally saw the mission as a good opportunity to portray the EU as a global actor. The Netherlands had a colonial past in the region. Finland supported its former president and Sweden hosted the Aceh government-in-exile. The very limited support of the member states was reflected in the bilateral financial contributions. Sweden significantly contributed €4 million, but the other member states together only made €1 million available. The final million euros were contributed by Norway and Switzerland, which are not EU members. The whole question of funding was thus rather embarrassing for the EU. It formed a major input for the European Council in Hampton Court on October 27–28, 2005, where Javier Solana successfully lobbied for a (much) higher CFSP budget in light of the future civilian CSDP missions in Afghanistan and Kosovo (see also Chapter 3).

After the financing proposals had been accepted, the planning of the remainder of the mission was relatively straightforward. On July 29, the PSC accepted the Initial Monitoring Presence, which concept had been drafted by EU officials based on an OSCE precedent in Kosovo (interview AMM official). In the days that followed, the mission leadership and several CSDP planners went to Aceh (see also below). From the ground, they wrote the CONOPS. While this is normally done in Brussels, Feith had taken most of the planners with him, so there was no one left to do the job. The CONOPS was accepted by the member states on August 16. Two weeks later, they accepted the Joint Action, which was adopted by the Council on September 9. It allowed the AMM on September 15.

Implementation

The AMM informally started with a mission of its future leadership – Feith, the Head of Mission, Oksanen, one of the deputy Heads of Mission, and Christiansen, the political advisor – to the province of Aceh in order to make contact with the GAM commanders on the ground (July 30–31, 2005). For the EU it was critical to know whether the GAM negotiators in Helsinki, most of whom had been in exile for decades, actually had authority among the local combatants. Meeting their field commander, Tengku Ubit, was not an easy task, however. He was still on the most-wanted list, with a 100,000 dollar reward on his head (Merikallio 2008). Only during a second attempt on July 31 did they finally meet him. Feith had a discussion with him that lasted an hour and a half, during which he said that "he had received instructions from Stockholm" (ibid.: 121) and that he would comply with the

Memorandum of Understanding. The fact that communication between the leaders-in-exile and the rebels on the ground was apparently good strengthened Feith's trust in the GAM. On this basis he recommended Brussels to move forward.

Back in Jakarta, Feith, Oksanen, and Christiansen met with the CSDP planners and ASEAN officials (August 1–2). Kalle Liesinen, the Chief of Decommissioning seconded by the Finnish ministry, had also arrived in Indonesia. After this meeting some of the EU staff members (including Feith) went back to Brussels to arrange things at headquarters. Most of the civil servants of what was called the Technical Assessment Mission decided, exceptionally, to stay in order to start preparing for the arrival of the monitors taking part in the IMP (August 15–September 14). This preparatory mission on the ground was led by an EU official, Justin Davies, who would become the chief of staff of the AMM. It also included Oksanen and a colonel from the Presidency as well as most of the CSDP planners. The reason why the Technical Assessment Mission stayed on the ground had everything to do with time pressures. It put EU officials in the leadership of the operation, as most member states were not capable of seconding personnel on such short notice.

From August 3–14, several problems became apparent. As the Council had not provided a mandate for the Technical Assessment Mission (or for the IMP), none of the EU staff members was supposed to be in Aceh. One official taking part in the assessment mission recalled that "we were there as tourists or as representatives of our respective member states at best" (interview AMM official). Apart from drafting the necessary documents and making the first contacts with the local parties, the Technical Assessment Mission also arranged some practical matters, such as renting offices, accommodation, computers, and cars in the provincial capital Banda Aceh. Initially Liesinen and Christiansen were the only ones with money to pay for such expenditures. They were formally seconded by the Finnish foreign ministry and had been given a personal budget. They soon found out that ATMs have a maximum amount per withdrawal (ibid.; interview national official). Within days, however, the Finnish, Swedish, and UK embassies in Jakarta started transferring money. Many bilateral embassies also provided personnel and support in kind. Such unilateral support was crucial for the successful preparation of the mission (e.g. Kirwan 2008; Schulze 2007). The deputy Head of Mission, Lt. General Nipat Thonglek from Thailand, joined halfway the Technical Assessment Mission and Feith came back to Aceh on August 14.

The Initial Monitoring Presence started on August 15. Within days many monitors and other staff members from various EU and ASEAN member states arrived, increasing the number of officials from 25 to 82 (interview AMM official). The Finnish and Swedish ministries, in particular, had already at an early stage identified potential staff members, which gave these countries the possibility of putting them on the plane at a short notice (interview national official). Finland furthermore provided the majority of the core of the decommissioning team at an early stage, which was important as the first decommissioning exercise would take place straight away on day one of the AMM (i.e. September 15; see below). The team started drafting the decommissioning procedures, but also had to negotiate with the two parties, for example, about what constituted a "firearm." In the Memorandum of Understanding the GAM had agreed to hand over 840 arms (Article 4(3)) and it was for the decommissioning team to decide which arms could be counted towards that number (Liesinen and Lahdensuo 2008; interview AMM official).[3]

To give an idea of the speed with which the process of force generation took place: one official flew in directly from Bosnia; another official had just returned from Sri Lanka; and yet another had to arrange a leave of absence from a university (interviews AMM officials). In terms of force generation, there is strong evidence that people became members of the monitoring mission because they happened to know people rather than through a thorough selection process (interview AMM official). It was the holiday period in the capitals and the time pressure was very high. The moment that potential monitors were available they were sent to Aceh. Some arrived during the IMP. Most of the monitors arrived towards the end of the IMP (September 10–12). The monitors were trained in the city of Medan on the Island of Sumatra just outside the Province of Aceh (September 12–14). During their training the monitors were allocated to one of the 11 District Offices and afterwards they were helicoptered in (Kirwan 2008; interview AMM official). They started work on September 15.

In terms of the backgrounds of the personnel, half of the officials from EU member states had a civilian background, while the ASEAN officials were drawn from the military. ASEAN countries organized their own force generation. As a member of the Technical Assessment Mission recalls, "they turned up quickly. They were funded by the Indonesian government. They got there in time for the IMP and they came equipped with 4-by-4s and sorted their own accommodation" (quoted in Schulze 2007: 6). Despite this parallel process, EU and ASEAN monitors were integrated during the operational phase. While the recruitment of monitors was relatively swift in most member states (interview national official), there were some minor problems with getting monitors for the decommissioning teams at district level. The AMM was the first mission of the EU to include Disarmament, Demobilization, and Reintegration and most member states did not have experience in this field. The team therefore consisted of many Finnish and ASEAN officials. Only a limited number of officials from the other member states were involved (France, Netherlands, Belgium, Ireland, Norway).

The conduct of the operation

One of the major conditions of the Memorandum of Understanding was the amnesty of "all persons who [had] participated in GAM activities ... not later than within 15 days" of the signing of the memorandum (Article 3(1)(1)). On August 17, to celebrate Indonesia's Independence Day, some 300 persons were released. On August 31, another 1400+ GAM prisoners were released. The numbers were considerably higher than the AMM and the GAM had expected. It thus served as a confidence-building measure at the beginning of the process (Schulze 2007; Merikallio 2008). While many former fighters were released in the days after the signing of the Memorandum of Understanding, the Government of Indonesia kept some hundred rebels in prison on charges of "ordinary crimes." The legal advisor of the AMM served as a mediator between the Government of Indonesia and the GAM in discussing these remaining cases. The process was, however, slow (ibid.).

After the amnesty of the large majority of former GAM fighters, the next thing on the agenda was the decommissioning of weapons and the withdrawal of troops. During the four subsequent months, 210 arms of the GAM had to be destroyed after which the Government of Indonesia had 10 days to withdraw 8,000 troops from the province of Aceh. The atmosphere before the first decommissioning exercise was tense. For the unarmed EU monitors, it was a nightmare scenario to be caught in an escalating situation between the armed forces of the Government of Indonesia and the GAM (Kirwan 2008). The former GAM rebels, on the other hand, feared that they would be registered or even arrested by the Indonesian army once they had handed over their weapons. The local leader of the GAM, Jusuf Irwandi, had therefore initially demanded a secret site for decommissioning by his own choice. On the day of the weapons decommissioning, however, he led the decommissioning team and members of the world press to a public central square in Banda Aceh, right in front of the house of the highest military commander of the Government of Indonesia (Merikallio 2008). This created transparency and trust between the parties.

Several days after the first successful decommissioning exercise, the Indonesian army removed its troops as planned. This parallel process of decommissioning and withdrawal of troops continued in the months of October, November, and December. Towards the end, it remained in question whether the GAM could indeed hand over its 840 weapons, as the tsunami had destroyed many of the houses in which these weapons were hidden (interview AMM official). They eventually succeeded. On December 20, 2005, the decommissioning team held a final ceremony to formally mark the end of the period of weapon collection. Approximately half of its 45 members became monitors of the AMM. The other half left shortly after Christmas. The Chief of Decommissioning, Kalle Liesinen left on December 29, after handing a full report on decommissioning, listing every single weapon, to the Indonesian President Yudhoyono (December 27), who was in Banda Aceh for the commemoration of the tsunami one year earlier.

Decommissioning was a Finnish-led exercise, but Feith initiated at the same time a process of "pro-active monitoring" through the creation of the Commission on Security Arrangements (COSA). The COSA was a model that he copied from his time in Bosnia, where NATO ran similar arrangements. The idea was that representatives of the GAM and the Government of Indonesia would meet on a regular basis, chaired by Feith himself, to discuss all incidents that had taken place. It also discussed other urgent questions, such as the definition of a firearm (see also above). The meetings took place initially twice per week, but at later stages once every 14 days and even monthly (Kirwan 2008). Before the meetings, Feith generally had his staff investigate the incidents that had taken place (Barron and Burke 2008). This allowed him to put this information forward and blame one of the parties from an impartial point of view. The meetings thus took place with "complete directness, evenhandedness and openness" (Feith quoted in Marikallio 2008: 165). The COSA meetings at the central level were copied at the district level for issues of lesser importance. Most people involved stressed the importance of these meetings (Kirwan 2008; Schulze 2007; interviews AMM officials).

The Memorandum of Understanding also gave Feith the authority to make binding decisions, in dialog with the parties, in the event of disputes regarding the implementation of the Memorandum (Article 6(1)). This arrangement closely resembled the executive powers of the United Nations High Representative in Bosnia-Herzegovina (and the International Civilian Representative in Kosovo (ICR), which would be the next position in Feith's career, see Chapters 5 and 8).

In the event of any problems remaining unsolved, President Ahtisaari would make a final ruling. The fact that such a ruling was never necessary shows the added value of the COSA meetings and the personal weight and competence of Feith himself.

Then there was the active monitoring in the field. On a daily basis, the monitors in the District Offices left in the early morning to drive through the villages and to talk to the local population. The number of incidents varied significantly per district, but it was the task of the monitors to find out what had happened and to report on these incidents to the headquarters in Banda Aceh. Most incidents were generally not too serious, but some could potentially escalate. The extortion of civilians was a regular returning practice. People were also being arrested and detained by police without being told why. The monitors tried to give the local police some basic training, which was later done more professionally by the International Organization for Migration (interview AMM official). The division of labor in these District Offices was informal. Both EU and ASEAN monitors worked side-by-side, with six of the 11 offices led by a monitor from ASEAN and the other five by a EU monitor. The ASEAN monitors were generally more familiar with the local security situation and the integration of teams was considered as mutually beneficial.

Finally, the work of the AMM was supported through accompanying measures by the Commission. DG RELEX and the EuropeAid office had put together a package (see Table 6.2). This support was important and necessary. The former combatants, for example, had to be reintegrated into society and the Commission provided them with some funding. The Commission also tried to improve the local administration, the police, and judiciary services, and it played an important role with regard to human rights. Finally, it financially supported and observed the local elections in 2006. The necessity of these activities can only be underlined by the fact that the AMM had a limited mandate, focusing solely on security questions, and that it was rather short (Schulze 2007; Barron and Burke 2008; Aspinall 2008). The Commission thus took care of many tasks that the member states were not willing to do for political reasons. This gave the Commission some influence, allowing it to sit at the table. The AMM did not take directions from the Commission (interview Commission official).

Prolongation and termination

From the beginning Ahtisaari thought that the initial mandate of initial six months was too short (interview in Accord 2008). It gave the

Table 6.2 Commission's accompanying measures for AMM

Project description	Implementing authority	Amount
Aceh Peace Process Negotiations	CMI	€269,000
Facilitating Aceh Peace Agreement Dispute Settlement	CMI	€115,000
Demobilization and Reintegration of former Combatants and Detainees in Aceh	International Organization for Migration	€4,000,000
Support to Conflict Affected Communities receiving former Political Prisoners and Combatants	International Organization for Migration	€1,460,000
Support to the Aceh Reintegration Agency (BRA) and Peace Building in Aceh	EC/United Nations Development Programme	€3,000,000
Support to the organization of local elections in Aceh	United Nations Development Programme	€750,000
Capacity building to support local police reorganization, with particular emphasis on respect for human rights	International Organization for Migration	€6,000,000
Support to the civil judicial system and access to justice with particular regard to respect for human rights	United Nations Development Programme	€4,400,000
Enhancement of local public administration	Deutsche Gessellschaft fur Technische Zusammenarbeit	€4,400,000
EU Election Observation Mission		€2,400,000
TOTAL		€27,094,000

AMM just enough time to carry out the decommissioning exercise and to ensure that the soldiers of the Indonesian army actually withdrew. This would leave the EU the option to claim success and provide for a smooth exit in March 2006 rather than staying committed in Aceh possibly indefinitely (Barron and Burke 2008; Aspinall 2008). In particular, if the situation had been worse than it turned out, having an exit strategy was convenient. The short period and the mandate focusing only on security issues led Kristen Schulze (2007) to conclude that the mission was "not so impossible." It furthermore needs to be said that having a continuous foreign presence also limits the possibilities for local ownership. So it was important to leave at a certain point. Finally, the mission was expensive. The member states had to pay the salaries of the monitors.

When the issue of termination and possible prolongation came up towards the end of the six months, there was a considerable lack of clarity about the future role of the mission. Most security issues had been dealt with and there were not many serious security incidents to speak of (Barron and Burke 2008). On the other hand, several other issues in the Memorandum of Understanding had not yet been dealt with and were still awaiting implementation. The critical Law on the Governing of Aceh was months behind schedule, some 60 prisoners were still detained, reintegration of former combatants was problematic and little had been done in the field of human rights (ibid.). It was felt by all parties involved that if these underlying issues were not addressed the process could still derail in the long run. Yet paradoxically these were some of the issues that the AMM had actually tried to avoid through its limited mandate. On February 27, however, the Council decided to prolong the mission by three months until June 15, 2006. It amended the objectives of the mission in order to address the outstanding points (2006/202/CFSP).

The first extension of the mission thus took place on March 15. Two days earlier, some hundred monitors had already returned home, leaving the mission with approximately 85 monitors in the District Offices (Barron and Burke 2008). At the political level, the Law on the Governing of Aceh became a focal point. Its creation was a necessary condition for local elections, yet passing this law through the Indonesian parliament required constitutional amendments. It needs to be said, in this respect, that parts of the Indonesian parliament had been critical about the peace negotiations over Aceh. Passing the Law on the Governing of Aceh was thus not an easy task. The Indonesian government informed the parties that it could not be done before June 15. On April 29, somewhat optimistically as it turned out, Pieter Feith stated during a COSA meeting that, following a request from the Government of Indonesia with the support of the GAM for an extension until August 15, he would make a positive recommendation to the EU and ASEAN, as the "elections [are] in sight" (AMM 2006a).

From Brussels came a favorable consideration by the PSC on the extension after a briefing by Solana on May 11, 2006. The AMM was to be extended until the elections (to be held on September 15 at the latest), yet the PSC also stressed that the parties must understand that "this extension must be the last one" (AMM 2006b). The extension was finalized on June 7 (2006/407/CFSP). The additional operational expenditures (non-salaries) for these three months were €300,000, paid for by the CFSP budget. The Government of Indonesia, however, failed again to finalize the procedures on time, with the result that during the summer the issue of extension came up once more. On July 21, the Government, with the support of the GAM, invited the AMM to stay until December 15. After another briefing of Solana in the Political Security Committee (July 28), the member states decided to extend the mission (2006/607/CFSP). An additional €1,530,000 was found in the CFSP budget to cover the expenses (interview Commission official).

Despite these prolongations, the AMM was already terminating most of its activities over the summer of 2006 due to a lack of local security incidents. The District Offices were closed and staff remained only at the headquarters in Banda Aceh. Most monitors left before September 15, with just 36 monitors staying until December. Four places were kept open in the province of Aceh where monitors could stay overnight (interview AMM official). The relevance of these monitoring activities was no more than their symbolic presence. The number of COSA meetings was also reduced in order to prepare for the final handover of authority to the parties themselves. On December 11, the local elections were held in Aceh and the GAM contact person won by a landslide. The elections were observed by the EU Election Observation Mission, which was paid for and implemented by the Commission. On December 15, the AMM was terminated during a final closing ceremony.

Overview of the findings

This chapter has so far discussed the role of the EU officials during the phases of the policy process of the AMM. As in the previous chapter, this concluding part of the chapter will turn to their influence. In the introduction of this book, a yardstick was presented to compare influence across the observations. It defined a high level of influence as EU officials playing a leadership role during a particular phase of the policy process (in cooperation with one/two member states). For a medium amount of influence, they need to be a necessary condition in explaining the outcome of a particular phase of the policy process. Low influence means that the EU officials participated actively in the discussions, but that they did not have a major impact on the course of the operation. Finally, they have no influence if they do not take part in the discussions.

Solana and his officials played a major role in the *agenda-setting* of the AMM. For Ahtisaari it was clear from the beginning of the negotiations that a governmental rather than an NGO would have to be in charge of monitoring. He understood that the EU would be the main candidate to take the lead. Therefore he contacted Solana and Feith at a very early stage. While Solana and Feith obviously could not decide for the member states, they encouraged Ahtisaari to continue, which gave him room to negotiate with both parties. If Ahtisaari had not been given the green light at that stage, he would have encountered problems in the negotiations. The eventual involvement of the EU gave the process credibility, which was particularly important to the GAM. Moreover, Feith and his team started with the planning process far earlier than other member states. Initial discussions took place in February 2005, while most of the member states did not get actively involved before July. Feith also briefed the negotiating parties on the various options in May. This created expectations. The same goes for the fact-finding mission in June/July. The extensive involvement of the EU officials in the negotiations made it impossible for the member states to say no. Their influence during the agenda-setting phase was thus high.

The *negotiations* about the AMM focused on the financial aspects. As the CFSP budget was insufficient, the Commission creatively found ways to finance the mission using development instruments. This would also imply a stronger role for the Commission in this specific CSDP mission. The Commission's proposal immediately ran into objections from some of the member states and the Council's legal service. Following its rejection, the Presidency and officials of the Council Secretariat became actively involved in finding possible ways of paying for the mission. They suggested using the remaining funds of the CFSP budget and bilateral contributions of member states. In the week of July 19–26, 2005, there were many discussions about this proposal, which effectively came to an end when Solana and Ahtisaari addressed the PSC about the need to resolve the problem. In spite of this intervention, most of the member states remained against the operation and accordingly were unwilling to make contributions. In the end, the bulk of the funding was provided by Sweden, Switzerland and Norway. Solana and the EU officials thus played a leadership role in convincing the member states to accept their plans for financing, but they were still dependent on a number of member states to make funding available. Their influence was therefore medium.

During the *implementation* of the operation, the role of the EU officials was significant. Pieter Feith, supported by some Finnish officials, made contact with the local GAM commanders during the Technical Assessment Mission. When Feith left for Brussels, Justin Davies (a CSDP official) took charge of establishing the operation. During the IMP, the majority of the monitors consisted of officials of the EU, Finland, and Sweden. Yet despite this leadership role, the EU officials lacked sufficient budgetary means. During the month of August, the mission relied extensively on bilateral support from the member states and particularly from the Finnish, Swedish, and UK embassies in Jakarta. This created constraints on the autonomous actions of the EU officials. During the conduct of the AMM, the EU officials did play an important coordinating role, while Finnish officials were in charge of decommissioning. The COSA meetings and the notion of pro-active monitoring, for example, were an initiative of Feith and not foreseen in the Memorandum of Understanding or in the Joint Action. The EU officials furthermore knew their way around in Brussels and kept people in Brussels informed.

In discussions over prolongation and termination, EU officials briefed the member states in Brussels. However, they had hardly any impact on whether the Indonesian parliament passed its legislation. They could not therefore affect the timing of the termination. Eventual prolongations very much followed the schedule of the local elections, and this roadmap was not set by the EU, despite its pressure. The decisions on prolongation and eventual termination were thus in the hands of the member states, who had to decide whether they wanted to stay longer and to put more resources into the mission. When looking at the launching of the mission, its conduct, and the termination phase, there are instances where the EU officials played a leadership role and there are cases where they could only facilitate the process. Its overall influence during the implementation phase was thus medium. All these results are summarized in Table 6.3 below.

From a counterfactual point of view, it is worth stating that the majority of member states would not have accepted this operation if the EU officials had not pushed so hard for it. There was thus a clear conflict in preferences. Furthermore, it is necessary to point at the asymmetry in bureaucratic resources. The EU officials used international networks,

Table 6.3 Influence of EU officials in the AMM

Agenda-setting	High
Decision-making	Medium
Implementation	Medium

their central position in policy-making, content expertise, and time pressures to make the mission a reality and to get the mandate that they wanted. The negotiating parties and the member states were played against each other. The control mechanisms of the member states were not, in this respect, sufficient. This counted not only for the decision phase, but also for actual implementation. From Brussels, it was very difficult to get a grip on a mission on the other side of the globe.

7
Military Operation in Chad

In January 2008, the EU launched its most ambitious autonomous military operation to date. Almost 3,700 troops contributed to a "safe and secure environment" in eastern Chad and the Central African Republic. This was to the benefit of internally displaced people and refugees from the Darfur region, as well as local personnel from humanitarian organizations and the UN. The operation lasted exactly one year. The EU troops operated in a political minefield and overcame tremendous logistical problems. After the mandate expired, the EU handed over the operation and the infrastructure to the UN Mission in the Central African Republic and Chad (MINURCAT). In spite of some problems in the planning process, the EUFOR Tchad/RCA operation was eventually successful from a military perspective. However, given the lack of participation of some member states in the operation, the tense relations between the EU and the UN at a political level, and the questionable impact on the ground, this type of bridging operation – where the EU prepares the ground for the UN – is unlikely to be repeated in the near future (see also Dijkstra 2010b).

As with the preceding chapters, this chapter traces the influence of the EU officials during the policy process. It will discuss how EUFOR came on the agenda leading up to a Council Secretariat-Commission joint options paper (fall 2006–July 13, 2007). The chapter subsequently analyzes the decision-making phase from the moment that planning authority was delegated until the adoption of the Joint Action (July 13–October 15, 2007). It then looks at the role of the EU officials during the implementation and the eventual handover to the UN (October 15, 2007–March 15, 2009). In the conclusion, the chapter gives an overview of the influence of the EU officials.

Agenda-setting

The Darfur conflict in Sudan started early 2003. The US formally called it genocide in 2004, but the international community initially did little to stop it. One of the reasons for inaction was that Sudan objected to interference in what it saw as an internal conflict. With China, as one of its business partners, in the UNSC, it was extremely effective in undermining any international response. Under international pressure, however, Sudan accepted a 7,000-strong peacekeeping force of the African Union Mission in Sudan (AMIS) within its territories in 2005. When it turned out that the African Union was not able to deal with the situation on its own, Sudan finally agreed to a joint United Nations–African Union peacekeeping operation (UNAMID), consisting of 26,000 troops, in July 2007. As with most peacekeeping missions, UNAMID suffers from a lack of military capabilities.

The conflict in Darfur resulted in a high number of people seeking refuge in bordering countries. About 250,000 refugees left for eastern Chad. In the same region, there were some 185,000 internally displaced people (International Crisis Group 2008). The border between Darfur and eastern Chad is porous, which meant that there was no safe environment in these refugee camps. It was in this context that the UN Department of Peacekeeping Operations (DPKO) started to look into improving the situation. It suggested that the UN should carry out a number of humanitarian functions inside the refugee camps, train local police to provide some security within the camps, and have a military component to create a secure environment outside the camps. The planning of this operation was at an advanced stage (February 2007) when the Chadian President, Idriss Déby, made clear that the UN military component would not be welcome in his country (see United Nations 2007a). MINURCAT was allowed to train local police and carry out humanitarian tasks, but it had to operate without military protection.

With hindsight, the solution to this problem and the EU involvement might seem obvious. At the time it was not. After the French elections on May 5–6, 2007, President-elect Sarkozy appointed Bernard Kouchner as foreign minister. Kouchner directly noted that the Darfur conflict would be on his priority list (Agence France-Presse, AFP 2007a). On his second day in office, he convened a meeting about the situation with his senior diplomats and representatives of the *Urgence Darfour* initiative, with which he was associated himself (May 19) (Liberation 2007). One diplomat noted about this meeting that "Kouchner is, admittedly, an idealist, but he is also a realist who deals with the concrete. We did not discuss the possibility of parachuting troops into Darfur" (ibid.). Kouchner advocated humanitarian corridors, no-fly zones, putting pressure on the Chinese, and looking into securing the border regions in Chad and the Central African Republic. France also sent a COREU to the EU partners on May 21, requesting an options paper before the next Council meeting (interview Council Secretariat official; Mattelaer 2008). One observer recalled the COREU as a "vague document."

While Kouchner was creating momentum, it is necessary to pay some attention to longer-standing French interests. France, after all, had a significant bilateral military presence in Chad (Operation *Epervier*) and a presence in the Central African Republic. These troops had several objectives, including the protection of French nationals, but also to support the incumbent regime of President Déby against various rebels. It is likely that France was continuously engaged in monitoring the situation in Chad and in advance planning of all sorts. When the UN Security Council, under French pressure, started discussing a potential military presence, advance planning, it is reasonable to assume, must have been intensified. The main point thus is that while Kouchner probably had humanitarian concerns on his mind, there was also an interest in stabilizing Chad (Charbonneau 2010; Mattelaer 2008). This was more systemic than the event of the election of Sarkozy and the subsequent appointment of Kouchner.

Following the COREU, a delegation of EU officials was invited to the French headquarters in Paris (*Centre de planification et de conduite des opérations*, CPCO) at the end of May. The purpose of this meeting, as one of the participants recalled, was to come up with a real comprehensive approach and a plan. None of the other states knew about this meeting and the EU officials were told not to discuss it with anybody else. While the content of this meeting was preliminary, it helped to focus attention on Chad rather than on Darfur. Furthermore, it again shows that, as in the previous case studies, EU officials got involved at an early stage in the process. The PSC, by comparison, only became involved in the discussions mid-July. Most member states, in fact, started paying real attention when troop contributions were on the agenda in September/October.[1] The reasons for France to invite EU officials merit some attention. If France was to do anything militarily in the EU, it would have a natural ally in the EU bureaucracies, which were equally ambitious in terms of getting CSDP operations started. DG E VIII, in particular, was at the time a French "fiefdom" consisting of a high number of French nationals that could get things moving.

The French plan did not take off immediately. The German Presidency was unenthusiastic and kept EUFOR off the agenda (Berg 2009). Kouchner nonetheless went ahead. On June 10, he met with President Déby in the Chadian capital. At the time, there was a delegation from the UN Security Council on the ground to clarify the options. The delegation was told that "following discussions with Mr. Kouchner the President had agreed, in principle, to the deployment of an international military presence in eastern Chad composed of French and other European Union forces" (United Nations 2007a, Article 25). The UN delegation also learnt from Chadian officials that "a United Nations military presence was not favored by the Chadian Government, although it could eventually be discussed as a second phase of a United Nations deployment" (ibid., Article 23). Thus, the idea of a bridging operation where the EU would prepare the ground for the UN gradually took shape already at that early stage.

In contrast to the German Presidency, the incoming Portuguese Presidency had made Africa one of its priorities. During its term in office, the process started moving again at EU level. The French and the EU officials, in particular, put pressure on the other member states. In an early document on the timeframe of the planning of the operation, the CSDP planners made clear that the Crisis Management Concept could be accepted on July 23 and that the Council could approve the Operations Plan – thus effectively launching the operation – during its meeting in October 2007 (interview national official). The other member states were in less of a hurry. They tasked the Council Secretariat and the Commission to draft a joint options paper for the Council in July.

The options paper of July 13, 2007, was a truly joint Council Secretariat–Commission document with civil servants on both sides being very positive about the cooperation (interviews Commission and Council Secretariat officials). For the EU officials, it was an opportunity, in the words of one official, to "[kill] the stupid ideas" (Mattelaer 2008: 14; interview Council Secretariat official) put forward by Kouchner, such as no-fly zones and humanitarian corridors in Darfur. These were non-starters, because the Sudanese President would not let the UN Security Council pass such initiatives. The humanitarian community, in addition, was strongly opposed to these corridors (Berg 2009). The only thing remaining for the EU was to "close the two backdoors in order to avoid spillover in Chad and the Central African Republic" (interview national official). During the agenda-setting phase, the focus thus shifted from Darfur back to eastern Chad and the northern part of the Central African Republic. This was not the only result of the options

Table 7.1 Chronology of EUFOR Tchad/RCA

February 2003	Start of conflict in Darfur, Sudan
April 2005	African Union Mission in Sudan (AMIS)
June 4–10, 2006	Security Council visits Chad and Sudan
August 31, 2006	UNSC Resolution 1706 mentions Chad-Sudan border
February 23, 2007	UNSG Report on possible UN presence in Chad/CAR
February/March 2007	Chadian government rejects UN military presence
May 5–6, 2007	French presidential elections
May 16, 2007	Sarkozy becomes president
May 19, 2007	Meeting at Quai d'Orsay on Darfur
May 21, 2007	French COREU to EU member states
May 2007	Visit Council Secretariat/Commission officials to Paris
June 10, 2007	Visit Kouchner to Chad
July 13, 2007	Council Secretariat/Commission options paper
July 31, 2007	UNSC approves UN-AU Mission in Darfur (UNAMID)
August 25–September 1	EU fact-finding mission to Chad/CAR
Early September 2007	Visit Carl Bildt to Chad
September 3, 2007	Pre-activation of Mont Valérien as OHQ
September 10, 2007	PSC gives planning authority to Mont Valérien
September 12, 2007	Adoption Crisis Management Concept
September 15, 2007	Council Secretariat sends liaison to Mont Valérien
September 24, 2007	Indicative force generation conference
September 25, 2007	UNSC Resolution 1778 on EUFOR/MINURCAT
September 28–29, 2007	Meeting of defense ministers in Évora, Portugal
October 4, 2007	Adoption Military Strategic Options
October 15, 2007	Adoption Joint Action
October 21–24, 2007	Reconnaissance mission by Operations Commander
November 12, 2007	Adoption Concept of Operations
November/January	Force generation conferences
January 14, 2008	Operations Plan released by OHQ
January 28, 2008	Launch of the operation
February 1–2, 2008	Assault on Chadian capital by the rebels
March 13, 2008	Initial Operational Capability
June 18–24, 2008	EU-UN mission to prepare mid-mandate review
September 17, 2008	Full Operational Capability
September 24, 2008	UNSC Resolution 1834 on starting handover process
October 28, 2008	Arrival of first 29 (!) local police officers
November 26, 2008	Meeting UNSG with Chadian President
December 4, 2008	UNSG Report on handover
December 8, 2008	Arrival of four Russian helicopters
January 14, 2009	UNSC Resolution 1861 on handover
March 15, 2009	Handover between from EU to UN

Source: See further Mattelaer (2008) and Seibert (2010).

paper. The French, after all, had an interest in the stability of Chad, and had long been promoting UN action. Based on the options paper, the Council gave the planning authority to the EU (July 23).

Decision-making

The options paper marked the start of a lengthy decision-making process in Brussels that would eventually lead to the adoption of the Joint Action on October 15, 2007. One of the great paradoxes of this process – and the mission as a whole – was that two of the most vocal member states on the crisis in Darfur, the UK and Germany, did not participate. They made clear from the beginning that while they would not obstruct the process, they would not make a contribution to the Chad operation due to military commitments elsewhere (e.g. Afghanistan, Iraq, Lebanon, Kosovo). France, as the initiator of the operation and as the only remaining large member state, would thus have to carry a substantial proportion of the burden itself. Yet, given its own bilateral role in Chad, it thus had to search for contributions of the other member states to make it a genuine European endeavor. During the decision-making phase this led to discussions over the mandate, the relations with the UN, and the financing of the operation.

Mandate, humanitarian principles, and coordination

The main reason why the member states were so reluctant to support the EUFOR operation was the strong perception of French bias. It was clear from the outset that the EU could only make a meaningful humanitarian contribution if EUFOR was to be perceived as an impartial actor in internal Chadian politics. Yet this was problematic due to the French bilateral military presence supporting the government. EUFOR thus had to be distinct from the French contingent, and few member states saw how this was going to happen if France provided the bulk of the troops and the leadership roles. It took some time for France to convince other member states that EUFOR could be an impartial actor in the region and that it would not interfere in internal politics. Looking back, it turned out that the fear that EUFOR would be perceived as partial was unfounded (interview Commission official).[2]

Another reason why the decision-making phase took so long was that – apart from Germany and the UK – member states were also hesitant to sponsor a French pet project. It was felt, as Mattelaer (2008: 16) notes, "that however well intentioned the operation, in the end it would serve French interests the most." To put it a bit bluntly, Chadian infrastructure (such as airports and roads) would be upgraded with EU money, while the EU would not stay engaged in Chad for the long-term. It was only a one-year bridging operation. In terms of financial investment, the other member states would get little return. The resulting argument was that France would have to pay for the operation. This was at odds, however, with the objective of Europeanizing the operation. France continually stressed that it only wanted to make up some 40% of the eventual force. As a result of questions over France's true intentions, few member states were fully enthusiastic about the operation.

The concept of a bridging operation with a clear end-date was nonetheless appealing. This made things much easier for other member states. Without an end-date, EUFOR would not have been launched. In addition, various interviewees stressed that they were excited about the fact that EUFOR was to be part of an international multidimensional presence, in which MINURCAT would take care of police training and humanitarian functions (interviews national officials). It was felt that this was the sort of things that the EU should be doing. It would be a typical example of the so-called comprehensive approach, with the Commission providing humanitarian aid and development. The military operation would create a secure environment in which the UN could operate. This fitted well with the EU's preference for multilateralism. The temporary nature and the multidimensional presence explain why the member states eventually endorsed the French initiative.

The comprehensive approach meant intensive coordination between the officials of the Commission and the Council Secretariat. Following the invitation of the Commission in May and the joint options paper, the Commission now got involved in detailed planning. The role of the CRCT, in which civil servants of the Commission and the Council Secretariat met on a weekly basis, has to be noted in this respect. Reviving this mechanism was regarded on an institutional level as a major achievement, particularly compared to Operation Althea (see Chapter 5). In this respect, one observer calls the participation of the Commission in EUFOR a break with the past. Through the CRCT, the Commission communicated its preferences and ideas. While the CSDP planners in the Council Secretariat remained officially in charge of planning, the involvement of the Commission affected the outcomes in two ways. First, it resulted in proper accompanying measures on the order of €35 million. Second, the Commission gave the CSDP planners insight into humanitarian principles and contact with the NGO community.

152 *Policy-Making in EU Security and Defense*

The comprehensive approach went beyond Brussels. From August 25 to September 1, 2007, EU and UN officials went on an EU-led fact-finding mission to the region under the leadership of General Leakey (interview UN official). From the Council Secretariat's side, this mission included the usual officers (e.g. policy, planner, logistics, intelligence). The UN sent four similar officers, who briefed the Council Secretariat personnel on the work that had been done so far. Furthermore, the future Force Commander, the French B. General Jean Philippe Ganascia became involved at this stage as well. Finally, since General Leakey had place left in his helicopter, he invited officials from the Commission to come along (interview Council Secretariat official). Despite this coincidental nature of the Commission's involvement, it was lauded by the Commission as another sign of good cooperation. The fact-finding mission eventually led to the adoption of the Crisis Management Concept by the Council on September 12, 2007.

Finally, a word on the EU–UN relationship during the early stages of the planning is important. Despite the involvement of the UN, the EU felt the need not to rely overly on the UN. Throughout the planning and implementation this was not always clear to both sides. One UN official stated that "the military is supposed to provide some sort of security umbrella" to protect their policing activities. An interviewee from the Council Secretariat, however, noted that "some people said about the operation that we were providing the security umbrella for the UN to perform ... on the UN side they also had too high expectations of us, for example that we would provide them with escorts. But this was not our role, we were not their drivers" (cf. seminar Brussels 2010). With regard to the planning of the operation, one observer (interview Council Secretariat official) recalled that "because they had done the planning, they thought that we would do exactly the same. They wanted us to do the military part and they would do all the rest. It took us some time to explain to them that we would do it differently." The UN interviewee, on the other hand, noted "for political reasons ... there was a need to re-do kind of the major concept ... but the main goals were definitely shared."

United Nations Security Council Resolution 1778

After the Crisis Management Concept was adopted, EUFOR required a UNSCR to proceed. Looking back with the benefit of hindsight, this turned out to be one of the most important documents for the entire operation. It arranged the details of the military handover to MINURCAT. There were two competing agendas. For the EU, it had to be absolutely clear that MINURCAT would take over after exactly one year. The Chadian government, on the other hand, was still reluctant to accept UN peacekeepers, even if this was only during the second phase of a UN deployment. Complete clarity about the handover in the UNSCR would thus lead to delays in the launching of the operation.

Within the EU, these competing agendas led to a split. For France and the CSDP officials in the Council Secretariat absolute guarantees on the handover were less important than for the other member states. A problem for the other member states was that, as force generation would only start at a later stage, they were in a rather weak position to make demands. France, which actually put its soldiers on the line, quite understandably led the negotiations. Within the UN Security Council, it was eventually decided to postpone the final decision on the handover to the Mid-Mandate Review, which would take place six months after the start of the operation. The precise wording of the paragraph was the following:

> [The Security Council] requests the Secretary-General to report to it ... six months from the date [that initial operating capability is declared by the EU] on the arrangements for following up the intended European Union operation which has been authorized for a one-year period, including a possible United Nations operation, depending on the developments in the situation. (UNSCR 1778, paragraph 10)

Anyone capable of reading UN-speak notices that this paragraph actually promises very little in terms of the handover. Even amongst the national interviewees there was considerable difference in the interpretation of the Security Council Resolution. Some noted that the bridging operation was agreed from the start, while others stated that nothing had been agreed. This difference partially resulted from the fact that in internal EU documents, the handover by MINURCAT was explicitly spelled out. These were much clearer than the Security Council Resolution (interview Council Secretariat official). The clear language in the internal documents was to convince several member states about the commitment of France to the end-date concept. Despite the obvious ambiguity in the Security Council Resolution, a civil servant from the Council Secretariat noted that "we were happy with the results ... we got exactly what we wanted." The careful phrasing of the Resolution was enough to get the operation going. This was very much in the interests of France and the CSDP officials. It would, however, lead to major political problems with the UN later on.

Joint Action and finances

Parallel to the discussions over the UNSCR, the member states discussed the Military Strategic Options. The Military Staff presented the member states with four options (Mattelaer 2008; interview national official). Option one was for the EU to train Chadian military forces and have them provide security in eastern Chad. This was quite different from the plans of the UN and from what had earlier been discussed in the EU, but it was a possible option. After all, the MINURCAT was doing the same with regard to the local police forces. The big advantage of this military option was that it would not cost the EU much and that the EU would not be dragged into a difficult conflict. The problem was that it fitted badly with the impartiality requirement of the Crisis Management Concept. By training the local military forces, the EU was indirectly interfering in domestic politics. This option was therefore not discussed as a serious alternative.

Option two was to deploy three battalions gradually over eastern Chad, while the third option was to deploy four battalions immediately. The gradual approach would ease the logistical burden of the operation. It also had the political advantage of simply sending fewer troops. The major disadvantage was that the rainy season in eastern Chad would start at the end of May/beginning of June. If the operation were not to be in place before this period, it would lead to considerable extra logistical problems. From a military perspective option two was thus unlikely. Finally, option four suggested a gradual deployment with an emphasis on the Central African Republic. The UK, however, opposed such focus (interview national official) and France had also a clear preference for Chad. This fourth option was thus neither considered seriously. The member states eventually chose October 4 for strategic option three.

The step from the Crisis Management Concept, the UNSCR and the Military Strategic Options to the Joint Action is normally straightforward. It generally only implies codification. This was a little different in the case of EUFOR due to the financial implications. In the period between the Military Strategic Options and the Joint Action (only 11 days), it turned out that there was a difference in the reference amount of the common costs estimated by the people who drafted the Military Strategic Options and those responsible for the implementation of the Joint Action. This was the result of the division of labor between the RELEX counselors and the officials of the Athena mechanism. Put simply, the CSDP planners from the Council Secretariat had underestimated the common costs when presenting the Military Strategic Options to the Council. Now that the member states were presented with the reference amounts mentioned in the draft Joint Action, they wanted to know why this was possible. Their ministers had signed off on the lower budget (interview Council Secretariat official).

During the negotiations over the Joint Action, the RELEX counselors managed to decrease the reference amount of common costs from €120 million to €99.2 million (only for it to increase again in the budget of the Operations Commander to €120 million). There were also a few discussions on the scope of the common costs – what is exactly common and what is not. This ended up on the COREPER agenda (interview Council Secretariat official). The ambassadors, however, quickly decided that common costs were to be defined in a minimalistic sense. On this basis, the Joint Action was finally accepted on October 15. The differences over financing can be attributed to the fact that the amounts mentioned in the Military Strategic Options are very preliminary (interview national official) and that EUFOR was the first operation with a substantial budget for common costs (interview Council Secretariat official). It is, however, difficult to escape the impression that the Council Secretariat tried everything to make the operation more palatable for the member states – bureaucratic influence as a case in point.

Implementation

Military planning and getting to the theater

On September 3, 2007, the OHQ in Mont Valérien was pre-activated. This was almost six weeks before the member states adopted the Joint Action, which formally appointed the Operations Commander and the Headquarters. One week later (September 10), the PSC gave planning authority to Mont Valérien. Despite the early activation, it took in total some three months before the Headquarters was completely up and running. The delay was caused by the *augmentees* of the other member states arriving late (interview Council Secretariat official). In the absence of the Operation Commander, who still had to wait for the Joint Action to be adopted, the OHQ started working on a Mission Analysis Brief. Its activities were supported by the Military Staff, which had sent a liaison officer to Paris on September 15. Moreover, several French liaison officers joined the EUMS in Brussels to improve communication (interview Council Secretariat official).

Before discussing how the Mission Analysis Brief led to the CONOPS and other planning documents, it is necessary to say a few words about the appointment of the Operation Commander. From an early stage, it was clear that the force generation process would present problems.

This is why France initially thought of using the Nordic battle group (1,500–2,000 troops) led by Sweden. The battle group concept, which focuses on rapid deployment for a short period of time, was not the optimal scenario for the operation in Chad (also because the Nordic battle group would only be operational on January 2008, while the operation was to start in October 2007). Yet for France its deployment would kill two birds with one stone. Apart from the substantial contribution in terms of forces, it would be the first time for the battle group concept to be used. Given that troops had been on permanent standby since 2007, this was about time. Because France was so eager to get Sweden on board, it offered the post of Operations Commander. It would imply that a foreign national would be in charge of the French headquarters leading an operation consisting in majority of French troops.

To ask Sweden was also a logical choice. Foreign minister Carl Bildt had been one of the most outspoken politicians on Darfur. Yet it turned out that Sweden was not ready to take on the leadership of EUFOR. Sweden rather preferred to participate as part of the broader UNAMID operation in Darfur under UN command (AFP 2007b). When the Sudanese president rejected western participation in the UNAMID operation, the focus shifted back to EUFOR. In particular, Finland, which was part of the Nordic battle group, made clear that it wanted to participate as part of a Swedish contingent (Helsingin Sanomat 2007). Sweden, however, refused to take the lead. After Bildt had visited Chad to see the situation for himself in early September 2007, it became clear that Sweden would not play a leadership role in this operation. One national interviewee noted, in this respect, that France and the CSDP planners in the Council Secretariat had seriously misread the Swedish intentions. The saga nonetheless promoted the idea that the member state that would make a large contribution, besides France, would get the leadership post.

With Sweden rejecting leadership, the process of force generation continued. On September 24 there was an indicative force generation conference to get an idea of which of the member states would be interested in contributing to EUFOR. This conference was perceived as a "disaster" (Mattelaer 2008: 17), as few substantial contributions were made. As a result, France started looking intensively for contributions. During the informal defense ministers meeting in Évora, Portugal on September 28–29, they contacted Ireland and offered the Operations Commander post (interview national official). A couple of days later, Lt. General Pat Nash was called back from his golfing holiday in South Africa to take command. He was, at the time, the Deputy Chief of Staff of the Irish

Defense Forces and he had left for holiday on the day of the adoption of the Security Council Resolution. Ireland was at that moment not in the picture for EUFOR (interview EUFOR official). After the informal defense meeting, things moved quickly. On October 11, 2007, staff from the OHQ and the Council Secretariat flew to Dublin to brief General Nash on the political context and on the work done so far (interview EUFOR official). General Nash arrived in Paris on the day of the adoption of the Joint Action (October 15).

General Nash was not pleased with the preparatory work presented to him by the French officers at the Headquarters. He insisted on having another look at it and on going on a reconnaissance mission to Chad (from October 21–24) (interview EUFOR official). General Nash eventually made quite a number of changes relating to the content of the operation (interviews EUFOR and Council Secretariat officials). Two stand out. First, following the agreed Military Strategic Option Three, the EUFOR required four battalions. Nash thought that this was too heavy an engagement in terms of organization. He thus decreased the number to three battalions (interview EUFOR official). Second, the Chadian government argued that, for sovereignty reasons, the location of the Force Headquarters should be in eastern Chad – in the area of operations – rather than in the capital in western Chad. General Nash accepted this argument, but it implied building an extra camp at additional costs.[3] On this basis, the Headquarters wrote the CONOPS and the PSOR. These documents went for consultation to the EUMS and were eventually adopted by the member states on November 12.

The CONOPS marked the start of the formal Force Generation process, but most member states had already been considering their possible contribution for some time. They made them available at the first force generation conference in November. These contributions included many of the "ground troops" by the three leading states (France, Ireland, and Poland) and many smaller contributors (interview national officials). A problem existed, however, with a number of specific enablers for the EUFOR operation. The requirements for these enablers became clear only with the publication of the CONOPS (interviews EUFOR and Council Secretariat officials). Given that the operational theater was of tremendous size, that there were no paved roads and that the rainy season would make life difficult, EUFOR required substantial tactical air transport (i.e. helicopters and small planes). In addition, EUFOR had to be able to transport any seriously injured soldier within two hours to a Role 2 Hospital (basic surgery). Finally, there was a need for many logistical enablers to provide everything from food to fuel.

158 *Policy-Making in EU Security and Defense*

These specific assets were in short supply. The result was a lack of progress during the force generation conferences at the end of 2007. One EUFOR official recalls about the fourth conference in December that it "resulted in a very negative feeling. We felt a break/make moment then." At that point in time, General Nash decided not to send his OPLAN to the PSC, but rather to wait for additional commitments and thus to postpone the start of the operation (interview Council Secretariat official). During the final force generation conference in January 2008, France announced that it would cover all gaps in logistical enablers by becoming the logistical framework nation. This added 520 troops to the operation. France also decided to provide air assets. Italy provided the Role 2 Medical Facilities. There remained, however, a substantial shortfall in tactical air transport. General Nash allegedly noted that "it was not a luxury plan" (interview EUFOR official). One other observer states that "[Nash] had to take a risk ... if you are waiting for all ducks to be lined up in the pond, it would never happen." General Nash, nonetheless, decided, on the basis of what had been committed, to release his draft OPLAN (January 14). On January 28, the Council formally launched the operation.

On the substantive side of the military planning, the OHQ kept officials from the EUMS and the Commission involved. This went beyond liaison officers and several POLADs. The Military Staff had more experience with previous CSDP operations, which was very helpful in the beginning when setting up the OHQ (interview Council Secretariat official). The CONOPS and the OPLAN were furthermore sent to the Military Staff for continuous informal consultation before they were released to the member states for formal approval. In this respect, one interviewee noted that it was sometimes difficult to get the Military Staff off the back of the OHQ. General Leakey had, after all, been involved in the fact-finding mission and he was sometimes overly involved in the military planning at the OHQ. Officials from the Commission also visited the Headquarters to make sure that the points they had made earlier were included in the planning documents. They also stressed that EUFOR should not engage in Quick Impact Projects (e.g. drilling water wells) (interview Commission official). These were the tasks of the humanitarian community.

The deployment of EUFOR was by no means easy. Björn Seibert (2007) has provided an overview of the tremendous logistical challenges that the member states had to undertake to transfer their troops to a theater 4,000 km away from Brussels and some 2,000 km from the nearest available port in Cameroon. It is still good to give some figures.

In the period January–June 2008, between the launch of the operation and the beginning of the rainy season, EUFOR used 530 airlift flights, 140 road convoys, and 21 rail convoys, and it shipped 2,400 containers (interview EUFOR official). Eventually, and despite some delays with logistics (interview national official), most of the troops arrived on the ground on time, where they had to build their own infrastructure: five camps, including the Force Headquarters. This had to take place in a well-ordered manner so that there was enough security for incoming supplies as well as for the protection of the troops. Furthermore, there had to be sufficient medical facilities from the beginning. That EUFOR managed to do all these things is a major achievement.

The biggest (political) challenge during the start of the operation was, however, the assault of the rebels on the capital (February 1–2, 2008). While interviewees of various member states did not see why this incident would make a difference for EUFOR, an interviewee from the mission noted that "it was a very difficult week for us." It was not a coincidence that the rebels launched their attack on the same day that EUFOR started launching its operation from Brussels. The rebels hoped to create confusion in the EU, which could potentially undermine the operation. After all, EUFOR would create stability and thus informally protect the *status quo*, which was not in the rebels' interest. The main problem with this attack was that it was nearly successful. The rebels reached as far as the Presidential Palace. On his wedding day, the French President Sarkozy reportedly called President Déby to ask whether he should send a helicopter to get him out (The Independent 2008). If the rebels had been successful, this would have raised several major questions on a political and tactical level. EUFOR, after all, had signed its SOFA with President Déby. Moreover, some personnel were already on the ground and force protection was at its weakest (interview EUFOR official). In the end, Déby managed to resist the assault. Overall, the operation was delayed two weeks. On March 15, 2008, EUFOR declared IOC, which meant that its mandate of one year had formally started.

The conduct of the operation

It is important to note that the objectives of the EU were modest. This was to be expected given that EUFOR was only in Chad for a one-year period, that it had only 1,400 troops available to ensure a safe and secure environment, that it never had enough tactical airlift, and that its area of operations was nearly 350,000 km^2 (somewhat larger than Poland).[4] With such limited ambitions, it is difficult to assess success. Oxfam (2008) noted in an early report that it "believes that EUFOR has made many civilians feel safer through its activities, which include patrolling known dangerous routes, destroying unexploded ordnance, making contact with local leaders, and positioning itself defensively around civilians during rebel and government fighting" (p. 13). In addition, EUFOR de-escalated a number of conflicts through robust engagement (interviews EUFOR officials). Patrick Berg (2009) is, however, much more critical, pointing out that EUFOR was unable to protect the refugees, internally displaced people, and humanitarian workers as a result of its lack of capabilities.

One of the problems of EUFOR during the implementation phase was undoubtedly the lack of tactical air transport. The problem could partially be mitigated by building up larger inventories of supplies in the camps via ground transport before the rainy season. This took some pressure off the air assets (interview national official). However, it also required many *ad hoc* arrangements and lobbying member states for short-term usage. Another major issue for the operation was the absence of the police element of the MINURCAT operation. MINURCAT was supposed to deploy police trainers, who would train local police. However, it had problems in its own force generation. As a result the first 29 (!) local police officers were only deployed to the refugee camps on October 24, 2008 (United Nations 2008a, paragraph 22). By March 27, 2009, which was two weeks after the termination of EUFOR, 667 local police officers had been deployed to eastern Chad (United Nations 2009, paragraph 31). This still fell short of the 850 target. In other words, there was no local police presence of any noticeable size operating in parallel to EUFOR.

On a military-strategic level, the absence of local police was problematic. After all, it had been a planning assumption from the start that local police would provide security within the camps and that EUFOR would deal with the security outside the camps. The result of the absence of the police force was that security problems, such as banditry, inside the camps continued and that people expected EUFOR – as the only security actor present – to deal with it. Yet EUFOR was not prepared for this. It had planned for armed confrontations with gangs of 100–200 people. Such confrontations did not take place due to the robust nature of EUFOR and its technical advantages. When these gangs split themselves into small groups of two–four people and started committing lower level criminality and human rights violations within the camps, EUFOR had to adapt itself in the absence of the local police forces (interview EUFOR official). This problem was made public by the Force Commander General Ganascia already on June 16, 2008 in *Le Figaro*. EUFOR could not solve this problem with the means available, but it made some adaptations. The increased number of lower level crimes, which had a large impact on the refugees and internally displaced people, is considered by some observers as evidence of failure on the side of EUFOR. Yet it clearly needs to be underlined that EUFOR was not prepared for police tasks.

In terms of the organization of EUFOR, it is worth noting that contacts between the Force Commander, the Operations Commander, and the Brussels-based decision-making bodies were intense. While General Nash tried not to micro-manage the Force Commander, they were in contact regularly: from several times per day to minimally several times per week (interview EUFOR official). The Operations Commander furthermore went to Chad some 10 times during the course of the operation and the Force Commander regularly came to Paris for intensive two-day discussions. The same holds true for the relations with Brussels. From the moment that General Nash was appointed as Operations Commander to his financial report on the budget at the end of September 2009, he attended 47 formal briefings in Brussels, primarily for the PSC and the EUMC. In addition, he had to go to the briefings in the various capitals, for example for the incoming EU Presidencies.

The Commission made available a substantial amount of money for accompanying measures through the Instrument for Stability and the European Development Fund. Probably most important for EUFOR was the immediate one-time contribution of €10 million to the trust fund of MINURCAT in support of the police training. This contribution arrived in New York before the end of 2007 and was the major initial contribution to MINURCAT (United Nations 2007b, paragraph 21). It also contributed more than €13 million for several development projects in eastern Chad and the Central African Republic to improve medium-term stability. It contributed another €11.5 million to support the electoral process reform in Chad and to support Security System Reform in the Central African Republic. These donations were also geared towards the medium term. As part of the tenth European Development Fund, the Commission has made substantial longer-term commitments beyond EUFOR. All these accompanying measures were on top of the €30 million in humanitarian aid the Commission had been giving per year since 2003 (see Table 7.2).

Termination and handover

Already, before EUFOR could declare Full Operating Capability on September 17, 2008, it started the Mid-Mandate Review process, which would lead to the termination of the operation and the handover to

162 Policy-Making in EU Security and Defense

Table 7.2 Commission's accompanying measures for EUFOR Tchad/RCA

Support for police training MINURCAT	Instrument for stability	€10 million
Support for electoral process Chad	Instrument for stability	€5 million
Security System Reform in the Central African Republic	Instrument for stability	€6.5 million
Programme d'Accompagnement à la Stabilisation Chad	European Development Fund	€10.1 million
Programme d'Accompagnement à la Stabilisation Central African Republic	European Development Fund	€3 million
Humanitarian assistance (2003–date)	DG ECHO	€30 million/year

MINURCAT.[5] This process was carried out jointly by the EU and the UN during a mission to the region (June 18–24, 2008) (United Nations 2008b). During this trip officials from both institutions discussed the terms of reference for the Mid-Mandate Review and subsequently wrote separate reports – one by Javier Solana to the Secretary-General of the United Nations and one by the Secretary-General of the United Nations to the Security Council (interview Council Secretariat official). These reports were discussed in the UNSC on September 24, 2008, on the occasion of the adoption of Security Council Resolution 1834, which started the handover process. It is worth noting that for the adoption of Resolution 1834, Javier Solana, Bernard Kouchner, and the Belgian foreign minister Karel de Gucht attended the meeting of the Security Council. Such high-level presence was quite remarkable. The message that the EU would leave after one year had to be clearly communicated to the UN.

Security Council Resolution 1834 asked for a new report of the UN Secretary-General by November 15 on "the planning and conducting preparations ... of the proposed UN military presence in the northeastern Central African Republic to take over EUFOR's presence" and a final decision on that matter on December 15. With less than six months to the eventual handover, there was very little time for the UN to do the planning and to raise enough forces for its operation. Almost immediately, however, it sent a Technical Assessment Mission to the region (October 2008). Déby remained reluctant to allow UN peacekeepers. The UN dispatched its Under-Secretary-General for Peacekeeping Operations to N'Djamena for consultations. Yet only after a meeting between the

Secretary-General Ban Ki-Moon on November 26 did Déby agreed to a smaller than foreseen UN military presence (United Nations 2008c).

The report of the Secretary-General came in on December 4, thus three weeks too late. As a result, the Security Council could only adopt Resolution 1861, deciding on the handover, on January 14. This was two months before the handover had to take place. It is worth noting that it was not only the Chadian government that was reluctant to receive a UN Peacekeeping Operation. Also within the UN Department of Peacekeeping Operations, there was internal resistance against a takeover from the EU. One observer notes they "did not have an appetite to do the operation." An interviewee from the Council Secretariat similarly noted:

> The transition itself was difficult. The UN spent all its time trying not to take over the operation. We tried, on the other hand, to make it effective on the day as scheduled. It was really difficult to get the UN involved. We used all the levers, with the Solana report, with [the Under-Secretary-General of Peacekeeping operations] coming to Brussels.

The resistance from the UN was quite understandable given the tremendous difficulties with force generation during other peacekeeping missions. They were not keen on the EU launching a mission for a short period and to have to clean up the remaining mess. Given that nothing had been formally put on paper in the initial Security Council Resolution 1778 about the handover, the UN was in a comfortable position. When it appeared over time that it would not be ready for the handover, the message that came across from New York was that it was the EU's problem. This "blackmail" (interview Council Secretariat official) was not accepted. As one observer notes, the "French effectively forced them ... they forced DPKO to get in. It also came at the cost of good relations." The handover was considered a "nightmare" (ibid.). The same observer stated that "the Security Council Resolution was only there in January 2009 and everyone was very nervous." This was, according to one of the interviewees (EUFOR official) "too short, too problematic and a big problem for us."

There were three reasons why the handover did take place on time. First, several member states of EUFOR were persuaded to re-hat some of their troops to be part of the MINURCAT operation, at least for a short period of time. On the day of the handover more than 2,000 troops thus moved from EUFOR to MINURCAT. In addition, EUFOR continued to provide logistical support to MINURCAT in the beginning of the mission. Third, one observer notes that since "there was a panic about the transition," EUFOR decided to hand over all the infrastructure and assets to the Chadian authorities, in line with the SOFA, rather than to MINURCAT. This created a point of no return, because without infrastructure EUFOR could no longer fulfill its mandate. Thus it then had to leave. The Chadian Government, in turn, had to give the infrastructure to MINURCAT. It was, in the words of the same observer "the safest way to ensure that [EUFOR] could leave" on March 15, 2009, as planned.

Handing the infrastructure to Chad created a specific problem. As part of a gentlemen's agreement, the EU had negotiated with the UN that the latter would pay part of the costs of upgrading the local infrastructure. This was €70 million in total. In the confusion surrounding the takeover, the Chadian government refused to pay the EU for the assets, as there was nothing stipulated in the SOFA. It did, however, charge the UN for the infrastructure. The UN subsequently refused to pay the EU. Eventually, it paid for 20% of the €70 million (interview Council Secretariat official). The episode was rather embarrassing: as it concerned the common costs of the operation, Germany had to pay the largest share.

Overview of the findings

This chapter has so far given an overview of the policy process of EUFOR. Special emphasis has been paid to the role of the CSDP officials working in the Council Secretariat. The remainder of this chapter will discuss the influence of these officials during the various phases of the policy process. As with the previous cases, it will use the yardstick presented in the introduction of this book. For the EU officials to have a high level of influence, it should play a leadership role during a particular phase in the policy process. For them to have a medium level of influence, they should constitute a necessary condition in explaining the outcome during a particular phase of the policy process. For them to have a low amount of influence it is necessary for them to be involved. If they were not involved, they did not have any influence. Compared to the previous two chapters, measuring the influence of EU officials in this military operation is very difficult. Its interests throughout the process were much in line with those of France and it is sometimes difficult to distinguish between France and CSDP officials. The contribution of EU officials was in facilitating the process and helping France to Europeanize the mission.

The EU officials were present from the very beginning of the process. Only a couple of days after the *agenda-setting* of France via a COREU, officials from the Council Secretariat were invited to the French military headquarters. They were thus involved in the process at least four months before most of the other member states started to consider the operation. They then helped France to get it as a priority high on the European agenda by means of publishing a very ambitious timeline. CSDP officials helped to narrow the options through the joint options paper, which they wrote with Commission officials. While all these activities were not necessarily in conflict with French interests, they did make matters easier for France at a time that the German Presidency was not cooperative. It also helped that many of the involved Council Secretariat officials were French nationals. EU officials were not in the lead during the agenda-setting phase, but their influence can be regarded as medium. They teamed up with their French counterparts and, as such, played an important role.

During the *decision-making phase* of EUFOR, many "member state issues" were discussed, such as the difference between impartiality and neutrality, and how the mission would guarantee it. The same goes for the financing of the operation and whether it was acceptable to upgrade the French backyard with EU money. On these topics, EU officials had little to contribute. In the decision-making phase, there were, however, three points where the officials from the Council Secretariat made an important difference. First, in preparing the Crisis Management Concept, the CSDP officials were clearly in the lead. It was General Leakey who led the EU fact-finding mission. The report of the fact-finding mission resulted in the Crisis Management Concept. Second, the Council Secretariat played under French leadership a role in the drafting of Security Council Resolution 1778, the precise wording of which made the operation possible. Third, the Military Staff drafted the Military Options. They pointed the member states in a particular direction and they underestimated the common costs of the operation. In other words, the CSDP officials clearly pushed for the operation and this had an effect during the decision-making phase. Its influence is therefore medium.

During the *implementation phase* one of the challenges was force generation. The CSDP officials in the Council Secretariat did not play a meaningful role in this process. It was clearly a member state issue. Behind the scenes, President Sarkozy called his Irish and Polish counterparts to ask for contributions. Where civil servants of the Council Secretariat played a role was in helping the OHQ with the planning documents. Various civil servants from the Council Secretariat were posted at the OHQ. This was beneficial during the setting up of the Headquarters. The

Table 7.3 Influence of the EU officials in EUFOR Tchad/RCA

Agenda-setting	Medium
Decision-making	Medium
Implementation	Low

conduct of the operation was characterized by the lack of tactical airlift and the absence of MINURCAT. Both were issues where EU officials could make little difference. During the termination phase, France took the lead in forcefully pushing the UN to do their follow-on planning. Overall, the influence of the CSDP officials in the Council Secretariat was therefore low during the implementation phase.

When looking at the overall dynamics of EUFOR, it is once again not too difficult to identify the goal conflicts between the EU officials and the member states. France and the EU officials wanted to establish the operation, whereas most of the other member states were much more reluctant. Once again, EU officials made strategic use of resources. Their pivotal position in policy-making was important, just as the process and negotiating expertise and the strategic use of time. Skeptical member states were kept out of the loop, external expectations were raised, and budgets were underestimated. With the regard to the actual implementation of the operation, the influence of EU officials was lower. Standard military procedures played an important role and the individual member states had, of course, almost full control during force generation.

8
Rule of Law Mission in Kosovo

The EULEX, consisting of approximately 2,000 international and a 1,000 local staff members, is the largest civilian operation to date.[1] Apart from its size, it differs from many other civilian missions in terms of mandate. EULEX carries out traditional "monitoring, mentoring and advising" tasks at the central governmental level, but is also co-located at each police station, courthouse, correctional facility, and customs service. Moreover, international policemen, judges, and prosecutors are in charge of a restricted number of executive tasks in areas of the fight against organized crime, high-level political corruption, and war crimes. EULEX judges sit on the Mitrovica District Court in Northern Kosovo, a region dominated by Serbian minorities. EULEX customs officers keep an eye on the border between Serbia and Kosovo. Finally, Integrated Police Units provide a so-called "second response" when the Kosovo Police is unable to handle civil disturbance. EULEX is therefore an ambitious mission. Its planning took a long time and the handover from the UNMIK, which had previously been in charge of civil administration and the rule of law, was very problematic.

As with the previous case studies, this chapter traces, in detail, the role of the EU officials in the different phases policy process. It discusses how EULEX Kosovo came on the EU agenda (March 2004–December 2005). Subsequently, it analyzes the lengthy decision-making phase from the deployment of the EU Planning Team until the adoption of the Joint Action just before the unilateral declaration of independence by the Kosovo Assembly on February 17, 2008. The chapter finally takes a look at the implementation of EULEX from its launch in 2008 until the tensions in Northern Kosovo in the fall of 2011. As the operation is still ongoing, this chapter will naturally not discuss the termination of the mission. In the conclusion, it gives an overview of the influence of EU officials during the phases of the policy process.

Agenda-setting

Following the NATO air campaign (March 24–June 10, 1999), the Kosovo war came to an end with the adoption of UNSCR 1244. This resolution mandated an international security presence and an international civilian presence in the Serbian province. The 60,000-strong KFOR of the North Atlantic Alliance was put in charge of the security aspects, while the UN led the civilian presence through its Mission in Kosovo. Under its auspices, a number of tasks were further contracted to the United Nations High Commissioner for Refugees (UNHCR) (humanitarian affairs), the OSCE (democratization and institution building), and the EU (reconstruction and economic development). UNMIK remained in charge of the rule of law and civil administration. It was led by the Special Representative of the UN Secretary-General (SRSG). The first office holder was Bernard Kouchner. He was also in charge of facilitating the political process on the future status of Kosovo – a not insignificant detail, on which Resolution 1244 remained inconclusive.

During the first years of UNMIK, various tasks were handed over to the local institutions. Yet following the formation of the first Kosovo government in 2002, there was a renewed demand for a political process on future status. SRSG Michael Steiner, however, noted in front of the UNSC that "Kosovo society and institutions will have to show that they are ready for this process ... we must make clear what is expected of them" (quoted in Weller 2008: 18). Thus, the UN established a series of benchmarks for Kosovo before the status talks could commence. This "standards before status" policy conveniently bypassed the fact that there was disagreement in the Security Council among the five permanent members on status. In March 2004, however, it became clear that the UN's way of doing business was unattainable when large-scale riots broke out (United Nations 2004; King and Mason 2006). Following these events, Secretary-General Kofi Annan asked for a review process under the leadership of the Norwegian ambassador Kai Eide. Eide noted that status should be addressed. His work resulted in the Comprehensive Review of the Situation in Kosovo of October 2005, on which basis Annan appointed former Finnish President Ahtisaari as his Special Envoy in charge of the future status process for Kosovo.

The EU had always been a key actor with regard to Kosovo. Through various channels, it had spent some €2 billion in different projects on the ground (e.g. Pond 2008; Koeth 2010). The UK, Germany, France, and Italy were furthermore part of the Contact Group for the Western Balkans, which also included the US and Russia, and the informal Quint (same five without Russia). EU officials were also involved, particularly the Western Balkans Director Stefan Lehne (interview Council Secretariat official). It is therefore not surprising that the EU followed the events in Kosovo closely and that the Council strongly condemned the riots by stating that "Kosovo's leaders and the [Provisional Institutions of Self-Government] must be aware that what is at stake is their credibility, the future of Kosovo and its European perspective. They must act accordingly" (Council 2004: 5). The member states expressed their full support for the UN's efforts, but decided to send Javier Solana to the region nonetheless. He did so two days later on March 24, 2004.

Local politicians did not unambiguously denounce the riots. NATO and UNMIK were also blamed for letting things run out of control (King and Mason 2006; Ker-Lindsay 2009; Perritt 2010). SRSG Harri Holkeri took responsibility and resigned in May 2004, some two months before the end of his mandate. He noted on departure that "someone [had] to become the scapegoat" (Guardian 2004). The main point was that the position became vacant. Solana quickly seized the initiative in terms of the appointment of the future office holder. He met with Søren Jessen-Petersen, the EUSR in Macedonia (March 30). After Jessen-Petersen's appointment in August 2004 he took his staff of seconded EU officials with him to lead UNMIK.

The impression of SRSG Petersen was that "there was a complete lack of confidence amongst the national elite about the United Nations" (interview UN official). The riots had taken place because the status process was not moving. During the UN years, the Kosovo dossier had slipped from the agenda, but the riots created renewed momentum. As a UN interviewee stated, "there was actually optimism about the possibility of having a new Security Council resolution." At the end of 2004, Petersen launched a series of informal discussions on the future arrangements of Kosovo with the UN, EU, NATO, and OSCE. There was a clear agreement among these actors that "the UN had to reduce its presence, that NATO and OSCE were staying and that the European Union should raise its profile" (interview UN official). UNMIK would hand over most tasks in the area of rule of law to the local authorities. The EU would take over some of the residual tasks in this field. These discussions were useful, "because it became over time conventional wisdom that the European Union would go in. It started to send experts to meetings to see what was necessary" (ibid.).

As part of this review process, Petersen naturally visited the Council for an exchange of views with the member states (February 21, 2005). The ministers noted that since the Thessaloniki European Council of June 2003 had reaffirmed the "European perspective" of the Western Balkans, the EU would have to play a major role in any discussion concerning status. They "invited the [High Representative] and the Commission ... to examine with the United Nations and other relevant players what might be the future contribution of the European Union to the efforts of the international community in Kosovo" (Presidency Conclusions: 12). On June 13, 2005, Solana and Enlargement Commissioner Olli Rehn released a joint report on the *Future EU Role and Contribution in Kosovo*.[2] The main strength of this report was in the process. The Commission and the Council Secretariat had a common vision on the future of Kosovo. This made it difficult for the member states to disagree. It created a precedent, although one Commission official noted that "Rehn co-signed the papers ... the political drive was from the Council Secretariat."

The report included some fairly standard internationally agreed language – such as the leadership of the UN in the status negotiations, Kosovo as an multi-ethnic entity, and no change in borders. These were also the guiding parameters with which Ahtisaari had to work. The Solana–Rehn report made, however, three innovative points with a view to a future EU role in Kosovo. First, it stated that "the future international civilian presence could take the form of an international office with an important EU component but cannot be EUMIK." The role of UNMIK had been compromised and the EU wanted to make a fresh start. Second, it was not willing to take over the all-encompassing mandate of UNMIK, but rather wanted to focus on a few specific tasks. Thus the report argued, second, that "core areas will be the protection of minorities and the rule of law (police and justice)." This was in line with the earlier informal discussions under Petersen, but it was the first time that Solana formally stated that he thought of a rule of law mission. Third, the report noted that there were financial implications and that "resources may have to be provided from both the Community budget and from the EU Member States' budgets." Solana would repeat this point at the informal European Council at Hampton Court (October 27, 2005).

The process on the future status of Kosovo formally started after the UNSC had endorsed the Comprehensive Review of Eide and had appointed President Ahtisaari as Special Envoy (October 24, 2005). The work of Ahtisaari was not concluded until March 2007, but the large member states and the EU bureaucracies would stay involved in the

Table 8.1 Chronology of EULEX Kosovo

March 24, 1999	Start NATO air campaign
June 10, 1999	UNSC Resolution 1244 on Kosovo
March 17–18, 2004	Riots between Kosovo Albanians and Serbs
March 24, 2004	Solana visits Kosovo
August 15, 2004	Søren Jessen-Petersen arrives in Kosovo as SRSG
February 21, 2005	SRSG Peterson briefs EU member states
June 13, 2005	First Solana–Rehn report on EU contribution in Kosovo
October 7, 2005	Kai Eide report presented to UNSC
October 24, 2005	Appointment of President Ahtisaari
October 27, 2005	European Council in Hampton Court, United Kingdom
December 6, 2005	Second Solana–Rehn report
February 19–27, 2006	Fact-finding mission to Kosovo
May 2006	EU Planning Team in Kosovo
September 26, 2006	EU Planning Team options paper
December 11, 2006	Crisis Management Concept adopted
January 26, 2007	CONOPS released
March 26, 2007	Ahtisaari plan for Kosovo
March 29, 2007	Third Solana–Rehn report
August–December 2007	Troika negotiations
December 10, 2007	Troika negotiations lead to no result
December 14, 2007	European Council states that negotiations are exhausted
February 4, 2008	Joint Action and CONOPS adopted; Feith appointed
February 16, 2008	Operations Plan adopted
February 17, 2008	Unilateral Declaration of Independence
June 12, 2008	UNSG proposes six-points plan on UNMIK/EULEX
June–November 2008	Negotiations over UNMIK/EULEX in New York
November 26, 2008	Agreement in UNSC over UNMIK/EULEX
December 9, 2008	Initial Operational Capability
April 6, 2009	Full Operational Capability
June 30, 2009	Serbian policemen return to work
August 2009	EULEX signs police protocol, which leads to riots
August 26, 2009	Riots in Kroi i Vitakut (Northern Kosovo)
November 15, 2009	Local elections in Kosovo
May 30, 2010	Local elections in northern Kosovo leads to riots
July 22, 2010	Ruling of International Court of Justice
October 13, 2010	UN General Assembly Resolution 64/298
March 8–9, 2011	Facilitated Dialogue starts
February 22–23, 2012	Facilitated Dialogue major agreement
February 28, 2012	General Affairs Council grants Serbia candidate-status

Source: See further King and Mason (2006) and Ker-Lindsay (2009).

whole process. On December 6, 2005, for example, Solana and Rehn published a second joint report on the future EU role and contribution in Kosovo. This report reiterated that, regardless of its future status, Kosovo was in need of some international presence and that the EU would play a leading role. It stated again that the future international civilian presence would not be European Union Mission in Kosovo (EUMIK). In line with the previous report, police and rule of law were highlighted as priority areas. They would require both the support of Community instruments and CSDP measures. Therefore, "contingency planning for a possible ESDP [i.e. CSDP] mission on police and rule of law should start" (Solana and Rehn 2005: 2).

The member states agreed and mandated an EU-led fact-finding mission (February 19–27, 2006). The main conclusion of this mission was that the EU engagement in Kosovo would be a challenging endeavor that needed to be carefully planned and executed in a complicated political environment. It advised the member states to set up a permanent EU Planning Team in Kosovo to "ensure that EU decision-making could be based on a solid and well analysed basis that is in step with the future status process" (2006/304/CFSP, preambular paragraph 10). The Planning Team saw the light of day with the adoption of a Council Joint Action on April 10, 2006. About a month later, it was established on the ground. Its legal basis carefully noted that the EU Planning Team would not prejudge any subsequent decision by the Union to launch a CSDP mission.

Decision-making

The status of Kosovo was very divisive amongst the member states; the idea that the EU should step up its efforts on the ground less so. On the planning and the content of the rule of law mission there was not too much disagreement. First, because Kosovo was a divisive dossier, the member states preferred not to talk about it in their committees, particularly not in the PSC. Instead, they let EU officials figure out the details. This became clear when they tried to adopt all the planning documents quickly in the days before the declaration of independence (February 17, 2008). It would not be possible to agree on EULEX after the changed circumstances on the ground. Second, it was quite simply in everyone's interest, regardless of status, to have a rule of law mission supporting local authorities in their fight against organized crime and corruption. To avoid endless discussions over status among the member states, EULEX became a technical, "status neutral," operation. The main question during the decision-making phase was how to agree to the deployment of EULEX without an agreement on status.

The status discussions had a major impact on the planning of the EULEX mission. The key planning assumption, for instance, was that

Serbia and the Kosovo authorities would reach a settlement in the political dialogue led by President Ahtisaari (interviews with Council Secretariat and EULEX officials; Grevi 2009). Such an agreement, it was then assumed, would lead to a new Security Council Resolution replacing 1244. It was for political reasons irrelevant whether this was a realistic assumption. The EU could not plan or adopt documents on the basis of a political disagreement. It therefore did not have a Plan B for a very long time in the event of no new resolution. The fact that it did not have such contingency plans created tremendous problems during the launch of the mission. One UN official cynically noted that "you hope for the best and plan for the worst." This planning assumption, however, allowed the EU officials to move forward.

The EU Planning Team, which consisted initially of 12 staff members, was deployed to Pristina in May 2006. At that point in time, it expected the Ahtisaari negotiations to conclude in late 2006/early 2007 (Grevi 2009). This meant that the EU would deploy its mission in the summer of 2007 (interview EULEX official). The Planning Team initially did a lot of "mind-clearing" about what it was going to do (interview EULEX official). On July 17, 2006, it sent a first assessment report to the member states noting that it had established itself and on what it was going to do (interview EULEX official). Over the summer, specialists in the field of police, justice, and customs – the future three components of the mission – arrived, bringing the total number of staff members up to 35. They started the planning process, on which they presented an options paper in September. In Brussels, the structures remained small. In the DG E IX, one desk officer and two police officers worked on the Kosovo dossier.

Mandate and chain of command

In addition to the assumption of settlement, many of the parameters had already been spelled out. Ahtisaari's deputy, Albert Rohan, for example, noted that the future international civilian presence in Kosovo should be "as light as possible and as robust as necessary" (UN Office of the Special Representative for Kosovo UNOSEK 2006). This was in line with the Solana–Rehn reports, which clearly stated that the future EU contribution should not resemble UNMIK. The Planning Team thus looked particularly at options with a light footprint. In the options paper of September 26, 2006, it made clear that the EU should take over a number of specific tasks in the field of rule of law. Many other tasks in the area of rule of law could be delegated to the local authorities. Moreover, the Planning Team stated that EU should not take over tasks in civil administration, as crisis management operations are not the right tool for such a purpose (interviews EULEX and Council Secretariat officials). Support for customs services was included, as levies made up 60–70% of the Kosovo government's budget. Without revenues, police services and the judiciary could not be paid. Thus it was seen as an area of vital importance for future stability. On this basis, the Planning Team presented three options (light, medium, robust).

The light option was the preferred one. The EU would deploy 800–850 international staff members and engage mainly in monitoring, mentoring, and advising of the local authorities. The total number would break down to 100–150 officials at the headquarters, 300–350 police officers engaged in non-executive functions, about 60–80 executive police officers working on a limited number of tasks, 200–225 police officers as part of the Integrated Police Units dealing with riot control and civil disturbance, some 30 judges and prosecutors in total and 15 customs officers (interview EULEX official). An interviewee noted with regard to the light footprint that the "initial idea was to change the UNMIK vehicle into a Smart. UNMIK had been omnipresent; there was a need for discretion" (interview UN official). It needs to be stressed though that this light option was only possible given the assumption of settlement. The number of customs officers, for example, was clearly not enough in the event of disagreement over the border between Serbia and Kosovo.

When it became clear over time that there would not be an agreement on status, this light option was no longer credible. Member states started to beef up the mission (interview EULEX and UN officials). They wanted to see more riot control capabilities. The medium option was thus discussed, which foresaw that EULEX would take over the Polish and Romanian Integrated Police Units from UNMIK, in addition to the French and Italian ones (bringing the total up to 450). This option also included a competence for EULEX to deal with property-related law suits, which meant the need for civil judges, more prosecutors, and more legal officers. Finally, however, the member states accepted the robust option, which included a much stronger customs presence at the borders (up to 60 staff members), an increase in the number of executive police tasks, and a higher number of judges, prosecutors, and legal officers (total 300). This brought the total authorized strength of the EULEX mission to about 1,800 international staff members. For the member states an increase in numbers seemed the best way to guarantee stability. A number of interviewees, however, argued that EULEX is doing too much.

It is important to note that these increases were accepted over time, as the political process continued. At an early stage, the Planning Team sent a Crisis Management Concept to Brussels, which was adopted by the Council on December 11, 2006. On this basis the EU officials issued the CONOPS on January, 24 2007. In partially declassified minutes of a CIVCOM meeting "it was stressed that a final CONOPS cannot be adopted until after the UNSC Resolution, but that it was important to proceed as far as possible at this time" (Council 2007). These discussions over the CONOPS continued during February and March and the final staff numbers were left blank. This allowed for them to be adjusted at a later stage. With regard to the formal planning process, it is also important to note that the member states were already working on the CONOPS long before the Joint Action was adopted in February 2008.

An innovation was that the member states designated Lt. General (r) Yves de Kermabon as the future Head of Mission on May 4, 2007 (which is normally done through the Joint Action). His salary was paid for through a so-called preparatory measure. De Kermabon was a retired French general who had previously been KFOR Commander (2004–2005). He thus brought with him great experience on how to deal with command and control. He was furthermore familiar with the local politicians. The French government provided him with two assistants. They supported the CSDP planners. De Kermabon remained in Brussels until the launch of EULEX in the summer of 2008. He became based in Pristina only from November 2008. He was thus not part of the Planning Team. Instead, he started working on the OPLAN from Brussels. At this point there were 17 people within the EU bureaucracies planning the Kosovo mission. They were supported by a number of officers from the Military Staff (interview Council Secretariat official).

One of the discussions, which took place parallel to the planning process, was the command and control of civilian missions. Following the Cologne European Council (1999), the member states had set up military structures with a chain of command running from the Force Headquarters to the OHQ to the political bodies in Brussels. Civilian structures remained underdeveloped for a long time, with an *ad hoc* chain of command going through the CSDP bureaucracies (see Chapters 3 and 4). However, with the Kosovo mission in mind, the member states wanted to professionalize civilian crisis management structures as part of the post-Hampton Court Reforms (2005-onwards). Solana also particularly insisted on this point. The idea was to create a fully fledged Civilian OHQ under a Civilian Operations Commander, who would have final operational authority. This civilian structure was created in 2007, albeit under a slightly obscure name – the CPCC.

Figuring out this new structure took much time. The national diplomats in CIVCOM were naturally reluctant to delegate responsibilities, partially as a result of a lack of expertise. A Council Secretariat interviewee noted that "we were not there in front of the Military Committee of the EU. We were in front of the civilian committee ... the diplomats that were around the table were probably not the best people in the world prepared to talk about the chain of command." In the case of EULEX, it was also clear that there would not be a single command structure. It was unlikely that judges or prosecutors would take direct orders from policemen given their supposed autonomy. It was thus decided to give the position of Civilian Operations Commander to a diplomat instead. Pieter Feith became the first office holder. When Feith left for Kosovo, Kees Klompenhouwer was appointed (May 2008). The idea was that the Civilian Operations Commander would deal with the political bodies in Brussels, so that the Head of Mission on the ground could put all his attention into the day-to-day management of the operation.

The main point about the planning process was that lower-level EU officials had to invent civilian crisis management along the way. They received precious little support from the member states. This was because member states did not want to deal with the Kosovo dossier and because the diplomats in CIVCOM did not have adequate expertise to plan such a major operation. A Council Secretariat official (ibid.) recalls that:

> Most of the time [the PSC] did not want to hear it. They did not want to take up the subject, they did not want to have Kosovo on the agenda, because they knew they would be divided ... That is the way it works in committees, you tend to prefer to talk about subjects where you agree and not about subjects you disagree. So they were avoiding their responsibility ... they were looking forward to have someone in charge ... [the PSC] could not have Kosovo on the agenda every week, so they decided that CIVCOM should have it on the agenda every week. But if you look at the level of CIVCOM people, they are pretty young, they are officials that have not been charge of departments in their countries, so they were also afraid to make decisions. So we went in circles all the time, because everybody was avoiding responsibility.

On many topics, the EU officials had to make their own decisions. The member states only played a significant role regarding the total authorized strength. The mission thus eventually did not become the light type of operation that the EU officials had envisaged.

Money issues with the European Commission

Deploying the largest civilian mission had financial consequences. While the member states pay the salaries of their seconded personnel, almost all other costs, including *per diems*, salaries of contract staff, infrastructure, travel expenses, and vehicles fall under the CFSP budget, administered by the Commission. The CFSP budget was, for a long period, insufficient. During the Aceh mission (see Chapter 6), it turned out that several member states had to complete the bill to make the mission possible. This problem was already on the minds of the EU officials when they started planning the Kosovo mission. Solana, for example, asked the Heads of State and Government at the Hampton Court European Council for an increase in the CFSP budget (fall 2005).

The member states are, however, not the only ones to decide on the CFSP budget. It is part of the larger Community budget and thus requires the approval of the European Parliament. Since this was the only CFSP issue (pre-Lisbon) where the Parliament had a say, getting an increase in the budget was not a simple exercise. The budget negotiations were conducted by the Commission, and substantial new funding was eventually secured in April 2006 (up to €250 million /year for 2007–2013). The problem with funding was that, with the budget ceiling established, the mission had to be planned accordingly (rather than the other way around). One Commission interviewee made it very clear that there was no way for the Commission to go back to the Parliament and to ask for more money. There was, however, some flexibility between the budgetary years. It was, for example, decided to bring 2009 money forward to 2008.

Getting an overall increase in the CFSP budget was one thing; allocating it to the Kosovo mission another. Eventually €140 million was reserved for 2008, including for the work done in the context of the Planning Team. An additional €65 million was allocated for 2009. Within these reference amounts, the CSDP officials had to negotiate with the Commission about the details (for example on the ratio of vehicles/staff members or the maximum price of four-wheel drives) (interview Commission official). One of the problems for the CSDP officials was with the length of tendering procedures and the lack of flexibility. For this purpose, Feith regularly had to make noise in the PSC in order to get things moving (interview national official). While interinstitutional cooperation in terms of financing worked better than during the infamous Police Mission in Afghanistan, this period is equally remembered by CSDP officials as a nightmare.

The interesting thing is that the Commission did not seem to use its position as financial administrator to gain leverage during the planning phase. Actually, one Commission interviewee stated that the Planning Team "reported occasionally, but not too often." In addition, there were no coordination meetings, in which the Commission was involved during the planning of the operation. DG Enlargement only appointed a desk officer in the field of freedom, justice, and security in January 2009 (previously there was only a political desk officer). What is interesting is that people from DG Enlargement and DG Freedom, Justice, and Security actually tried to steer clear of the financial discussions with the CSDP officials (interview Commission official). They did not want to compromise their own relations and they were simply not interested in the financial details.

Kosovo status endgame

President Ahtisaari concluded his work on March 26, 2007. He suggested "supervised independence" given the exceptional historical circumstances. This would allow Kosovo to part from Serbia. The international community, he stated, should remain involved through the creation of an International Civilian Representative (ICR) with strong "corrective powers," the international military presence of NATO, the OSCE mission and EULEX. It was also proposed that the ICR would be the same person as the EUSR in a double-hatting agreement. Not surprisingly, Serbia rejected the "Ahtisaari package." The discussions continued at the UN, where Russia rejected several draft Security Council resolutions (July 2007). Solana then proposed continuing negotiations in the context of the Contact Group in what became known as the Troika talks. The EU was represented by Wolfgang Ischinger, who reported directly to Solana.

With Russia blocking the process in the UNSC, it became increasingly clear that there would not be a resolution. The EU Planning Team therefore started working internally on contingency planning from the summer of 2007 onwards. It circulated a timeline mid-September, which gave an overview of the subsequent steps to be taken in case of no new resolution. Following this timeline, the EU would prepare EULEX before the unilateral declaration of independence. After the declaration, the UN Secretary-General would decide to withdraw UNMIK "due to exceptional circumstances." This would allow for the EULEX deployment (interview EULEX official). This timeline was discussed with the UN Department of Peacekeeping Operations. Looking back with hindsight, it went almost exactly as planned, although with more delay than anticipated.

The Troika negotiations bought the international community (particularly the EU) time to plan its subsequent steps. Its work was concluded without result on December 10. The European Council noted four days later "that the negotiating process facilitated by the Troika between the parties on Kosovo's future status has been exhausted" (Presidency Conclusions, paragraph 66). This allowed for the final unilateral declaration of independence and it gave the EU officials the green light that planning had to move ahead. At the end of January 2008, the EU officials issued the Joint Action and the CONOPS, which had been prepared before. These were adopted by the Council on February 4. In parallel, the Council appointed Feith as the EUSR to Kosovo. Four days later, the EU officials issued the OPLAN, which was adopted by silence procedure on February 16, 2008. Now that the EU had agreed on EULEX, the local authorities were free to declare their independence. The Kosovo Assembly did so the next day (February 17).

The key point was that the member states finished the complete planning process before the unilateral declaration of independence. It was felt that the member states would not be able to agree on status-related details after the declaration of independence. This proved exactly right. While the US and the four EU members of the Contract Group (UK, France, Germany, and Italy) directly recognized Kosovo, in a concerted action, a notable number of member states (Cyprus, Greece, Romania, Slovakia, and Spain) did not. Yet the EULEX mission was status neutral and it was supported by all the member states.[3] A last detail of the problems surrounding status was that the EU could not sign a Status of Mission Agreement with the local authorities. Instead, the Kosovo authorities and UNMIK (being the legitimate authority under Resolution 1244) unilaterally stated that all the personnel of EULEX would receive diplomatic immunities.

Implementation

The member states decided already in December 2006 that the EU Planning Team would become the core of the future CSDP operation. Joint Action 2006/918/CFSP authorized the Planning Team to start recruiting personnel "in view of [EULEX's] rapid deployment," for which purpose it was asked to issue a deployment plan (Article 2(5)). Until mid-2008, the Planning Team remained the core around which the mission was built. Many officials of the Planning Team eventually joined the mission, often as deputies to the newly recruited heads of components. As such, much expertise of the Planning Team remained in the mission. The Planning Team grew from the initial 12 staff members to about 120 officials at the time of the unilateral declaration of independence in February 2008. One reason why the Planning Team became so large was that the CFSP budget could only pay for operational expenditure. It could pay salaries in Pristina and not in Brussels (interview Council Secretariat official). Many functions that were normally done in Brussels were therefore moved to Pristina.

Gradually establishing the mission through increasing the personnel was one thing; the political conundrum around status quite another. As mentioned above, the Planning Team had worked out a scenario and timeline in case there would not be a new resolution on the future of Kosovo. The plan stated that UNMIK would withdraw "due to exceptional circumstances." It was the expectation in the EU that because it was supported by New York, it was supported on the ground as well. It turned out that the UN (a) could not leave Kosovo and (b) that the staff did not want to leave Kosovo. The first point was political. Following the declaration of independence, Secretary-General Ban Ki-Moon wrote – according to plan – to members of the Security Council that "the United Nations is confronting a new reality in Kosovo, with operational implications for UNMIK that it must take into account" (United Nations 2008d, paragraph 10) (June 12, 2008). He also noted that "Serbia and the Kosovo Serbs have indicated that they would find an enhanced operational role for the European Union in the area of the rule of law acceptable, provided that such activities would be undertaken under the overall status-neutral authority of the United Nations" (paragraph 12).

Yet this was precisely the problem. The Kosovo Albanians no longer recognized the authority of UNMIK. The EU was not going to report to the UNSC. In the following months, there was intensive consultation. Ban Ki-Moon made various proposals to the relevant parties (interview UN official). It took the UNSC eventually until November 2008 to come to a workable compromise. UNMIK would keep a large presence in Kosovo focusing on more political tasks. EULEX would then be in charge of rule of law. It would send a short quarterly report to the UN Secretary-General, which would be included as an annex in his report to the Security Council. These negotiations in New York, needless to say, created problems with the deployment of EULEX. In the summer of 2008, there were sincere doubts as to whether EULEX would indeed continue, and the recruitment of new personnel was temporarily put on hold (interviews EULEX and UN officials).

The second problem was that many UNMIK staff members did not want to leave. It meant the end of their contracts. One UN interviewee noted that "people were trying to hold on to their unit. [The leadership of UNMIK] asked all units [well in advance] which tasks they could hand over to the local authorities in terms of the transition. Several units came with good overviews, but many units refused to hand over any tasks. They were apparently indispensable." An interviewee from the Council Secretariat similarly recalls that:

> We had the feeling, and that was ... a major planning error, ... that because the General Secretariat of the UN had told us that they wanted to withdraw ... we took it for granted that they wanted to go. We discovered in fact that UN missions are pretty much autonomous structures and the people on the ground in Kosovo, they really did not want to go away. The only option for them to keep a UN job was to go to Sudan and they said that it is much better to do nothing in Kosovo than to go and live in Sudan.

One national interviewee was even more outspoken:

> The problem with UNMIK is that it is still full of Russians, who are systematically sabotaging the whole project, including through not answering their mail. They are doing difficult on the instruction of Moscow. The relationship with the United Nations is good at the higher level ... the problem is really at the lower level ... it is the tyranny of the low-grade civil servant.

The political problem combined with the local issue created tremendous logistical difficulties for the deployment of EULEX. To save costs, it had been agreed in advance that EULEX would take over many vehicles and buildings from UNMIK. Now that UNMIK would continue to have a presence in Kosovo, it could no longer hand over all these assets. As a result, the EU had to start lengthy procurement procedures for cars and find new buildings, which were in short supply in Pristina. One senior EULEX interviewee noted that he became "Kosovo's leading expert on how to get hold of second hand cars and four-wheel drives." A Council Secretariat interviewee recalled spending one week per month in New York during the summer of 2008 negotiating with UN officials over lists of cars and then finding out that the UNMIK people on the ground had different preferences. "That was nightmarish." These logistical issues had also financial consequences. After all, the EU had budgeted on the basis that EULEX would buy used cars. This was cheaper than buying new cars. EULEX thus also ran into trouble with the Commission.

Finally, there was a recruitment problem. As there were long delays in the deployment, many of the identified staff members had already moved on to new jobs and were no longer available. Their posts thus had to be filled again. This issue was particularly urgent with the judiciary. While it has become common practice to send policemen on international missions, it does not fit into the career paths of judges and prosecutors to go abroad. EULEX has to recruit senior judges, because the cases are generally complicated and politically sensitive. Life as a judge in Kosovo is, as a result of the high security restrictions, not particularly pleasant either. This is the reason why there continues to be a shortage of judges and prosecutors among EULEX staff.

Agreement was reached in the Security Council on November 26, 2008 on the reconfiguration of UNMIK. The Serbian foreign minister gave the green light stating that EULEX could deploy all over Kosovo (interview UN official). Three weeks later, after intense preparations, UNMIK handed over the control to EULEX. EULEX declared IOC on December 9, 2008. It immediately started its operations through deploying police agents to all local police stations. During the 120-day transition period, EULEX overcame many of the logistical challenges, which resulted from the fact that UNMIK did not fully withdraw. It was capable of declaring its FOC on time on April 6, 2009.

Monitoring, mentoring, advising, and executing

The emphasis of EULEX is on "monitoring, mentoring and advising" local police, judiciary, and customs services. For this function, the mission has developed the so-called "programmatic approach," which entails a whole range of benchmarks, action points, and fiches to measure the progress of the Kosovo authorities (interview EULEX official). Each EULEX official has his own set of benchmarks to work with. It needs to be said that this approach is mostly geared towards the (central) governmental level, ensuring that all the laws and protocols are in place. With regard to these non-executive tasks, EULEX has been most active in the field of the police, where it could build on a longer UNMIK tradition. An early highlight was the return to work of almost all police agents from Serbian minorities in June 2009. They had refused to perform their tasks for the 16 months following the declaration of independence (Reuters 2009).

In the field of police, EULEX also made its first major mistake. For the purpose of effective policing, it is essential to exchange information with the neighboring states. Organized crime, after all, typically does not respect borders. Serbia and Kosovo jointly have a stake in tackling this problem. Because both countries cannot do business with one another due to the recognition issues, EULEX had to negotiate the practical details with the Serbs in the context of a police protocol. These negotiations were badly communicated to the population, which led to nationalist upheaval and claims that the territorial integrity of Kosovo was not respected. The end of the episode was that EULEX lost much credits and that it had to postpone similar protocols on justice and customs. Within the EU, it led to confusion. The Swedish Presidency in Brussels, for example, was taken off guard by the events (interview national official).

On the executive policing front, the developments have been mixed. Following the protocol, the local Kosovo Police provides the first response to riots and civil disturbance. If they are unable to handle the situation, EULEX police provides a second response. When civil disturbance gets out of hand and turns into para-military violence, NATO stands ready as the third responder. Initially there were very few cases for EULEX, but the Integrated Police Units intervened successfully (interview EULEX official). More recently, and in particular during the summer/fall of 2011, riots broke out in the Serbian-populated North of Kosovo, after the Pristina authorities tried to take over the border posts. This led to significant violence and NATO intervention. As the Kosovo Police is increasingly well trained, there is less need for the Integrated Police Units. Three out of the four have therefore already been withdrawn.

Apart from civil disturbance, EULEX police also has a role in other executive functions, such as the fight against organized crime, witness protection, and war crimes. Over time, it wants to hand over these tasks to the Kosovo Police. It has already done so in the field of counter-terrorism. The local police are willing to take over more tasks, which they see a sign of confidence, but EULEX has been reluctant so far when it comes to organized crime and high-level corruption. In particular, witness protection remains an important concern (interview EEAS official). In September 2011, a witness in a high-level case under EULEX protection committed suicide in Germany. The ability for EULEX to handle important political cases has been specifically criticized.

While the executive tasks in the area of police are rather specific, they are wider in scope in the judiciary. In sensitive cases, EULEX judges are sitting in mixed panels with local judges. One of the major problems that EULEX encountered in the judiciary was the enormous backlog of 1,800 open cases left by UNMIK, many going back to 1999/2000 (interview with EULEX official). EULEX immediately decided to close 400 cases due to a lack of evidence and little chance of positive future developments. Of the remaining cases, which were ready for trial, EULEX managed to bring most of them up to date within the first year of operations. This was a major achievement. Finally, EULEX made incremental progress by putting its own judges on the Mitrovica District Court in northern Kosovo after it had been ransacked by local gangs.

As customs have to do with borders, this was always the most politically sensitive area. This was only emphasized by the fact that Serbian minorities burned down the two gate houses between Serbia and Kosovo directly following the declaration of independence. EULEX did deploy its customs officers to these gates shortly after declaring its IOC. Initially they did nothing. In the summer of 2009, EULEX started copying the commercial documents of truck drivers, with the result that customs revenues went up by 80%. The situation got out of hand when the Kosovo authorities in Pristina decided without much consultation to send their own officers to the gate houses in the north in 2011. This resulted in continuous riots, road blockages, and repeated NATO interventions. A possible way out has been the agreement on integrated border management that Kosovo and Serbia reached in the context of the Facilitated Dialogue mediated by the EU.

Command and control in practice

The command and control structure of EULEX Kosovo is different from many of the earlier civilian CSDP missions. Specially for EULEX, after all, the supporting structures in Brussels were improved through the creation of the post of Civilian Operations Commander and the CPCC (see also above). In theory, this would put a stronger emphasis on Brussels and a tighter leash on the Head of Mission. In practice, it is certainly the case that the Brussels arena is much more closely involved with the conduct of EULEX than with many earlier civilian crisis management missions. This is for a different reason. EULEX (together with the Police Mission in Afghanistan) is simply the biggest and most important civilian operation. It is thus hardly surprising that it is, on average, discussed in the PSC once per month and in CIVCOM every two weeks (interview Council Secretariat official).

On a daily basis, however, EULEX remains a rather autonomous entity. The three officials working in the CPCC are no match for the hundreds of staff members working at the local headquarters. It performs, in this respect, mostly mission support functions rather than giving instructions. The Head of Mission generally talks to the Civilian Operations Commander twice a week for an hour on the phone (interview EULEX official). This is less, for example, than the contacts between the Commanders of EUFOR Tchad/RCA, though considerably more than in the case of EUFOR Althea (see Chapters 5 and 7). Needless to say, the position of Civilian Operations Commander was not completely modeled after the military equivalent. He is furthermore in charge of almost a dozen civilian missions. This makes it an impossible job to really assume daily command of all of them.

One of the key functions of the CPCC is to protect EULEX from all sorts of member state interference in Brussels, so that it can focus on its day-to-day work. It has been fairly effective in this regard. Not only does it have to follow all civilian missions, the diplomats in CIVCOM have to do this as well. The result is that CIVCOM has become completely overloaded with information. One national interviewee explicitly pointed at this problem: "[the people in the CPCC] are the real experts on this, they only have to deal with Kosovo. You have to take into account, I am dealing with nine missions, so it is a bit more difficult to have an in-depth picture of all things." As part of the formal dialogue with the member states, EULEX issues a weekly, monthly, and six-monthly report. In addition, there are incident reports, all sorts of informal contacts, and parallel reporting by the local embassies. In the six-monthly report, EULEX makes recommendations on the course of the mission. This report is orally presented to the PSC by the Head of Mission (interview EULEX official). Inter-institutional coordination in Brussels takes place through the weekly Kosovo Coordination Meeting.

Rule of law and the European Commission

One of the problems of EULEX is that it does not have money for projects to support the local rule of law authorities. For example, if a courthouse needs to be built or if the customs services need a new computer system, it cannot pay for it. On a daily basis, EULEX works with the local rule of law institutions, and their lack of proper assets thus limits the progress of the EU. For project money, the local institutions have to go to the Commission, which has a large liaison office in Pristina (or the member states). This gives the Commission an important role, because it spends substantial amounts on projects in the field of rule of law (€57 million through the Instrument for Pre-Accession 2007–2009). The role of EULEX is ambiguous in this respect. Since it has officers in all police stations and judges in every courthouse, it naturally has a good overview of the needs of the local rule of law institutions. Yet Commission funding is based on the principle of ownership, which requires the local institutions to apply for funding. The Commission procedures are not one-off affairs, which often leads EULEX, the Commission and the local institutions to draft proposals together (interview Commission official).

186 *Policy-Making in EU Security and Defense*

Table 8.2 Projects under the Instrument for Pre-Accession

2009	Support to Civil Registration Agency and unified address system
	Legal translators/interpreters and legal linguists
	Adequate working facilities for the Public Prosecution
	Improved education in the Public Safety and Security Sector
	Integrated Ballistics Identification System
	Equipment for the Ministry of Internal Affairs
	Support to Juvenile Justice System in Kosovo
2008	Legal Education Reform
	Standards for the Ministry of Justice
	Asylum/Migration/Readmission
	Equipment for the Kosovo Border and Boundary Police
	Improvement of the Penitentiary System – High-security prison
	Upgrade of the Infrastructure – Palace of Justice Building

Source: Commission (2009).

EULEX is not only dependent on the Commission for the project money. Most of the other carrots come from the Commission as well. Of importance are the annual progress reports on Kosovo's European perspective. Before the Commission publishes its report, EULEX gives input (interview Commission official). This is a good way for it to point the attention of the local authorities to pressing concerns in the rule of law sector. Through its progress reports, the Commission can be exceptionally frank with the local authorities in a way that EULEX never could, given its day-to-day cooperation. Another carrot in the hands of the Commission is visa liberalization. This is formally a technical process, but something that is in high demand by the authorities in Kosovo (particularly after the visa liberalization of Serbia in 2009). Since the Commission has access to these carrots, EULEX has become somewhat dependent on the Commission.

Finally, it is worth noting that the EU also has a shared competence in the area of freedom, security, and justice. This gives the Commission potentially a say over the contents of EU policy in this area. The involvement of the Commission has been limited to the Stabilization and Association Process Dialogue (a recent upgrade from the Stabilization and Association Process Tracking Mechanism) so far. There is potential overlap between this dialogue and the advising activities from EULEX. The Commission and EULEX have therefore created a number of coordination mechanisms in Pristina and Brussels to make sure that everything is cleared. On the ground, for example, EULEX has a permanent contact, who keeps in touch with the Commission. In Brussels, the relevant desk officers from both DG Enlargement and DG Freedom, Security and Justice attend the weekly Kosovo Coordination meetings. Because the numbers on the side of the Commission are relatively small, good personal contacts have avoided inter-institutional tensions (interview Commission official).

Overview of the findings

This chapter has provided an analysis of the policy process of the EULEX. Special emphasis has been paid to the role of EU officials. The remainder of this chapter will discuss their influence during the phases of the policy process. It will do so by measuring their influence against the yardstick presented in the introduction of this book. To briefly repeat the indicators: for EU officials to have a high amount of influence, they should play a leadership role (together with one/two member states) during a particular phase of the policy process. For them to have a medium level of influence, they should constitute a necessary condition in explaining the outcome of a particular phase of the policy process. For them to have a low amount of influence, they should be actively involved in the deliberations. If they were not involved at all, they did not have any influence.

With regard to the *agenda-setting phase*, it is difficult to miss the personal involvement of Solana. Kosovo has always been close to his heart. He was NATO Secretary-General during the air campaign (1999). His first official trip abroad as the High Representative of the EU was to Kosovo (interview with Council Secretariat official). After the riots in March 2004, Solana played a role in getting Søren Jessen-Petersen appointed as the United Nations SRSG. Petersen took with him EU officials and clear instructions from Solana. There was more. Solana's contacts with President Ahtisaari undoubtedly gave him access to the political process on the status of Kosovo. On a day-to-day basis, Solana was represented by his Western Balkans Director, Stefan Lehne. He thus had people at the heart of the UN machinery. Finally, as a Spanish national, he tried to keep the Kosovo negotiations going even after President Ahtisaari failed to come to an agreement.

Within the EU, Solana was also building up support over time to get things done. Getting the Council in February 2005 to invite him to draft a report on the future of Kosovo was not very difficult. Teaming up with Commissioner Rehn, however, was smart, because it created a unified front towards the member states. Solana was far ahead in starting the planning for Kosovo. He foresaw the problems with financing and he brought this to the attention of the European Council in Hampton Court (2005). On the basis of the Solana–Rehn report of December 2005, the member states decided to send a fact-finding mission to Kosovo. They eventually ended up with a Planning Team that would stay there for more than two years. At that point in time, Solana had already set the most important parameters for the operation. It would focus on rule of law and it would be much smaller than UNMIK. As a result of Solana's leadership, the EU influence during the agenda-setting phase was high.

During the *decision-making phase*, EU officials in Brussels and the Planning Team played a crucial role. They drafted all planning documents and prepared the operation on the ground. As noted before, the member states preferred not to discuss the sensitive Kosovo dossier in committee and the EU officials were thus very much left alone while they struggled to get the job done. It also needs to be said that the EULEX mission was not the most sensitive amongst the member states. The main issues in the planning of this operation were with the UN and with the Commission. Despite the EU officials shaping the EULEX mission to a large extent, they were in the end not in control. As the political dialogue on status became more difficult between the parties, the member states started to beef up the mission. As a result, EULEX did not become the light footprint that Solana and his civil servants had once imagined. In the end it actually became very heavy and to some observers it resembled UNMIK II. This was not the intention of the EU officials, but they could do little about it. Therefore their influence during this phase of the policy process was medium.

The *implementation* phase has been a long process. It started with launching EULEX after the unilateral declaration of independence. This was one of the mission's most difficult moments. In the end it came down to power politics by the permanent members of the Security Council and Serbia. The Planning Team had prepared a timeline for the case that there would not be a new resolution. Solana and his officials were heavily involved in attempts to get UNMIK out of Kosovo. Yet they could try as hard as they wanted and put pressure on the UN institutions, but as long as Serbia and Russia were blocking the political process and the logistical handover of assets, it made little difference. The daily work of the EU officials in preparing the handover was definitely necessary, but it could not make the difference.

As for the conduct of the operation, the EU officials are well placed to influence the mission with the CPCC and the Civilian Operations Commander. In reality, however, their options are more limited. They

Table 8.3 Influence of the EU officials in EULEX Kosovo

Agenda-setting	High
Decision-making	Medium
Implementation	Medium

do not possess sufficient expertise, and the role of Civilian Operations Commander is different from that of the military commanders. EULEX also faces extensive scrutiny on the ground due to the presence of many bilateral embassies and liaison offices, and it is on the radar screen of everyone in Brussels. Finally, the EULEX headquarters consists of a lot of personnel who do not have an EU background. They have often worked in international missions for other organizations (e.g. UNMIK, OSCE, NATO, United Nations), but they have no strong links with the EU bureaucracies (cf. AMM). The European Commission plays an important role through its financial instruments. The influence of the EU officials on the implementation of the mission itself is medium. All results are summarized in Table 8.3.

During the planning of the EULEX mission, conflicting preferences between the EU officials on the one hand and the member states on the other were perhaps not always as clear in some of the other cases. The real issue with EULEX were the conflicting interests among the member states themselves. The fact that the Union eventually still came up with this mission can be credited to a large extent to Solana and the EU officials. They acted with considerable foresight and continuity, and used their international networks, content, and process expertise, as well as time pressures. Through depoliticizing the negotiations and at the same time trying to step over member states' differences, they contributed tremendously to the final result. The divisions amongst the member states clearly made it difficult to control the agent, but the complexity and innovative nature of EULEX also played a clear role and gave EU officials opportunities for influence.

9
Conclusion

The dynamic relationship between the member states and the EU institutions is a major topic in the study of European integration. Ever since the *Uniting of Europe* of Ernst Haas (1958), scholars have been intrigued by the role of the European Commission and later the Court of Justice and Parliament. There is good reason for such interest. If the EU institutions "matter" – and most observers think they do – they potentially challenge a centuries-long tradition in which states were the key actors in international relations. Within the context of this broader debate, this book has tried to make a contribution. It is one of the first attempts to discuss CSDP policy-making from an institutionalist perspective by addressing the role of the EU bureaucracies. It has done so by means of a distinctive analytical framework using insights from rational choice institutionalism. It is based on detailed empirical sources gathered through extensive fieldwork. Importantly, the findings have relevance beyond the specific topic during the period under analysis. They tell us something about European integration, EU foreign policy, and the institutional design of international organizations.

In conceptualizing the relations between the member states and the EU bureaucracies in terms of principals and agents, the previous chapters have answered two research questions. The first one concerned *delegation*. Why do the EU member states delegate functions in the area of security and defense? It has been noted before that studying the process of delegation is important, as it determines the context in which the member states and the EU bureaucracies operate and the resources the latter have at their disposal. The second research question dealt with the all-important consequences of delegation – the *agency* of the EU bureaucracies. Under which conditions did EU officials exercise influence in the area of security and defense? Both questions have been tackled in the preceding chapters. Chapter 2 provided an argument for delegation and agency in the EU security and defense. Chapter 3 empirically analyzed the most important instances of (non-)delegation. Chapters 5 to 8 looked at four case studies in the CSDP in order to assess the influence of the EU officials.

This concluding chapter discusses the argument in light of the empirical evidence. It brings all the findings together. The chapter consists of three parts. First, it analyzes the instances of (non-)delegation. It shows that during different periods in the history of EU foreign and security policy, various facets of the principal–agent model usefully explain the delegation decisions of the member states. Member states carefully weighed efficiency gains against sovereignty costs. Due to uncertainty about sovereignty costs, member states often delegated too few functions. As the potential efficiency gains increased and member states started to understand the consequences of delegation, they delegated more tasks. During these intentional decisions agent selection was a recurring theme. Second, the chapter compares the observations of influence across the case studies. In line with the principal–agent model, they confirm the importance of bureaucratic resources. They show that variation in resources indeed affects influence. The EU officials exerted, for instance, influence during the agenda-setting phase due to their pivotal position in CSDP policy-making. Moreover, they had more influence in civilian than in military operations resulting from a relative advantage *vis-à-vis* the member states in terms of expertise.

Third, the possible contribution of alternative explanations is discussed. The introduction of this book identified constructivist approaches as potentially being able to challenge and complement the rationalist argument. With regard to the first research question, it will be argued that constructivism provides a better answer than the rationalist explanation in a few isolated instances of delegation. As an alternative explanation, constructivist approaches do a much better job in explaining agency. They can also account for variation across the case studies. The section on alternative explanations should, however, be read as a proposal for further research rather than a definite conclusion in itself. The book has evaluated rationalist theories and should be judged on those terms.

Delegation in EU security and defense

This book has employed rational choice institutionalism to analyze why the member states, in the sensitive area of security and defense, have delegated functions to the EU bureaucracies. It has argued that the prime rationale for delegation is that the EU bureaucracies can lower the transaction costs of cooperation. In the CSDP, these include negotiation, information, coordination, and implementation costs. Credible commitments play a less important role (Wagner 2003). In their delegation decisions member states are likely to make cost–benefit analyzes, weighing efficiency gains against sovereignty loss. Given the anticipated problems of unintended consequences and sanctioning under multiple principals, the member states generally delegate fewer tasks than is functionally optimal. As they do not fully understand the consequences, they are likely to be wary of delegation. Delegation is not a one-off affair, but it takes place over subsequent delegation rounds, which allows for feedback loops. Finally, the book has made the point of agent selection. The member states prefer agents with similar preferences, over which they can exert control.

How does this argument live up to the evidence? In this book, all major instances of (non-)delegation have been analyzed. They have been sub-divided into four historical periods: the establishing of cooperation (1970–1999), the Amsterdam Treaty (1999), the CSDP (1998–2009), and the Lisbon Treaty (2009). In all these periods, in spite of variation in the scope of EU foreign policy, the argument provides convincing explanations for the delegation of functions. In the first period, there was a conscious trade-off between the gains from outsourcing administrative support and the loss of sovereignty. Member states kept tasks in-house by delegating them initially to the Presidency and later to the Council Secretariat – a clear case of agent selection. In the Treaty of Amsterdam, the member states delegated information and implementation functions to the Council Secretariat following the EU failures during the Yugoslavian wars, while deliberately by-passing the Commission. For the CSDP, institutional demands increased due to the desire of the EU to send uniformed personnel abroad. This led to significant delegation. Member states, however, remained reluctant to delegate, with the result that there is, for example, still no standing military OHQ. Coordination costs were an important rationale for the Treaty of Lisbon, but agent selection continued as well.

During the initial establishment of cooperation (1970–1999) the member states were mainly concerned with creating a platform where they could discuss foreign policy matters. For this purpose, they required little institutional support. In fact, they could comfortably keep the strong EU bureaucracies at arm's length. The functional demands were low. They involved negotiation, coordination, and administration costs.

Through a number of delegation rounds, these costs were addressed by delegating functions first to the Presidency and later to the EPC and Council Secretariat. Most important about this period, however, was the non-delegation. Member states weighed efficiency gains against sovereignty loss and they came – time and again – to the conclusion that delegation was not worth it. This was most notable in discussions regarding the role of the Commission. The integrationist member states wanted the Commission to play a role equal to that in the internal market. Intergovernmental-orientated member states resisted such tasks. This contest became most apparent on "Black Monday" (September 30, 1991), when the integrationist blueprint for the EU was finally buried.

The Maastricht Treaty had still to be ratified when the conflict in former Yugoslavia went from bad to worse. In the years that followed, the member states failed to bring the civil war to an end. The institutional innovation in the Amsterdam Treaty should be seen in this context. The member states addressed both the information and implementation costs of foreign policy. They established the Policy Unit for the purpose of information processing and the position of High Representative to make EU foreign policy more coherent, visible, and effective. They codified the Special Representatives as tools for implementation. In general terms, the member states felt that the need for efficient foreign policy-making had increased, which allowed them to delegate more functions. It is important to note that, even though the international context had made delegation possible, the member states did not lose their rationality on the spur of the moment. This book has paid much attention to the Report of the Reflection Group (1995) highlighting the cost–benefit analyses. In particular, the discussion about agent selection is fascinating. The member states intentionally chose the Council Secretariat, over which they had more control.

The third period under analysis was the creation of the CSDP (1998–2009). Following the war in Kosovo, the EU decided to establish a capacity for autonomous action. The desire to send troops abroad immediately raised new functional demands. This was recognized in the initial St Malo Declaration. CSDP operations require planning capabilities and command and control structures. These demands were quickly addressed by delegating military planning functions to the EU bureaucracies and by establishing intergovernmental control bodies, such as the PSC. Sovereignty costs once again continued to play a role. Equivalent civilian planning bodies were, for example, kept understaffed. Member states had little experience in sending policemen and judges abroad. Being well aware of the possible unintended consequences, they therefore preferred to keep these functions in-house. Only when more challenging civilian operations came on the agenda (e.g. EULEX Kosovo), did member states delegate further tasks. Moreover, they refused on a number of occasions to equip the EU with a military headquarters. Instead, military operations rely on NATO or national assets, which are known to be suboptimal. This is again a case of agent selection.

The Treaty of Lisbon is the latest instance of delegation. This delegation decision was in fact a rather lengthy process that started with the Laeken Declaration. The emphasis in terms of foreign and security policy was on making the EU a more effective and coherent actor following feedback from previous delegation rounds. During the European Convention various options were discussed concerning the merger of the positions of the High Representative and the Commissioner for External Relations. A compromise was made to balance efficiency gains with sovereignty loss. The Treaty furthermore established the EEAS, which merged the relevant foreign policy services of the Commission and Council Secretariat and complemented these services by national diplomats. While the EEAS is bringing EU foreign policy forward, it is by no means a further integrative step. Indeed, agent selection was critically important and the Commission had to hand back significant external relations competences. Finally, the member states decided to make more efficient use of the various delegations in third countries by giving them a political function.

Looking at these four periods of delegation, one can conclude that the rationalist argument, as presented in this book, provides a solid explanation of delegation. While the periods were different in terms of the scope of EU foreign and security policy, there are several constants in the delegation decisions of the member states. First, delegation is usefully framed in terms of demand and supply. Cooperation involves a number of costs and they can be addressed through delegation to the EU bureaucracies. If the scope of cooperation changes, functional demands may change accordingly. This can trigger new rounds of delegation. Second, the balance between anticipated efficiency gains and sovereignty costs provides a convincing explanation. In most instances of (non-)delegation, the trade-off between efficiency and sovereignty is almost explicitly mentioned in the official documents leading up to delegation decisions. Efficiency reasons in themselves cannot explain the limits on delegation, while sovereignty costs cannot explain why there is delegation. Together they make for a powerful argument.

Third, non-delegation or too little delegation plays an important role. In many cases, the functional alternative chosen was not the optimal scenario. In delegation rounds, where various proposals were circulated, it has not been difficult to identify better functional options than the ones that were chosen. It is interesting that member states in several cases knowingly opted for inefficiency. They are wary about unintended consequences or the difficulty of sanctioning. They therefore delegated less. Fourth, agent selection has turned out to be very significant. In the initial instances the rotating Presidency was preferred. In later cases, the Council Secretariat and the EEAS were chosen above the Commission due to their preferences and limited bureaucratic resources. NATO and national military assets were preferred to a permanent military headquarters. Finally, the absence of credible commitments is noteworthy (cf. Wagner 2003). While this is the main rationale for delegation in the internal market (Moravcsik 1998; Pollack 2003), it hardly plays any role in foreign and security policy. Even after member states have collectively approved a CSDP mission, they still have to individually decide on their contribution.

As a final note, it is important to reiterate that rational choice institutionalism constitutes a middle-range theory. It does not have the objective of explaining everything, and in terms of principal–agent relations is solely interested in the relations between member states and the EU bureaucracies. This is important, as there are a considerable number of factors beyond the control of member states that have had an impact on the development of the EU bureaucracies. The end of the Cold War is an obvious systemic factor and there have been multiple other events. Moreover, third actors, such as the US, have had a considerable influence on the extent to which the member states could build up their foreign policy cooperation and by extension delegate functions to EU bureaucracies. Such factors, which often condition the opportunities for delegation, have been outside the scope of the internal relationship between member states and EU bureaucracies.

Agency in EU security and defense

In order to address the transaction costs of cooperation, the member states have equipped the EU bureaucracies with considerable bureaucratic resources. This naturally triggers the question of agency. The EU officials may not have strong formal powers, but they hold several advantages over the member states. They are likely to accumulate institutional memory, process and negotiation expertise, and international networks. The EU officials have continuity and occupy central posts in the policy-making web. They may have content expertise and they can play with time to limit the information-processing capabilities of the member states. They use these resources to further their preferences. The EU officials have an interest in "more" Europe and in tilting the inter-institutional balance in their favor. The member states are, however, not powerless and can apply a range of control mechanisms. The drawback of such mechanisms is that they are costly and undo some of the gains of delegation. Some degree of discretion is thus inevitable.

The second part of the book has empirically analyzed instances of agency. By studying in depth the phases of the policy process of four CSDP operations, it has tried to make explicit the processes that lead to influence for EU officials. As influence is notoriously difficult to measure, the book has provided a yardstick, which allows us to compare relative influence across the case studies (see Table 1.1). To briefly summarize the criteria, a high level of political influence has been defined as the EU officials performing a leadership function (together with one/two member states) during a specific phase of the policy process. A medium amount of influence requires them to be a necessary condition in explaining the outcome of a particular phase of the policy process. Low influence indicates that EU officials were actively part of the discussions, but that their contributions were not reflected in the outcome. No influence means that they were not involved in the phase of the policy process. In the preceding chapters, the empirical findings of the case studies have already been summarized. This concluding chapter brings these findings together and tries to explain variation on the basis of the theoretical argument.

Looking at the findings of the case studies, two main conclusions can be drawn (see Table 9.1). First, EU officials are important CSDP agenda-setters. They have been at the forefront of promoting all four operations, often against the preferences of the majority of member states. During the agenda-setting of military operations, their influence was medium, while during civil missions it was high. Second, EU officials had more influence during civilian (Aceh/Kosovo) than military operations (Bosnia/Chad). Such variation between the phases of the policy process and between the nature of CSDP missions is in need of an explanation.

Table 9.1 Influence of EU officials in the CSDP

	Bosnia (mil)	Chad (mil)	Aceh (civ)	Kosovo (civ)
Agenda-setting	Medium	Medium	High	High
Decision-making	Low	Medium	Medium	Medium
Implementation	Low	Low	Medium	Medium

This book has noted that agenda-setting essentially relates to the ability of EU officials to pick and choose issues that further their interests, to put them high on the agenda, and to keep them there. In terms of strategy, there are political and administrative routes to agenda-setting and it can pay off for actors to alternate between these venues. By testing venues, actors come across opportunities where they can raise their issues. To be a successful agenda-setter, continuity is a valuable asset. The same goes for the ability to coordinate between the political and administrative level, and having an informational surplus concerning the state of play in order to detect policy windows. In light of these conditions, EU officials are well placed to affect the foreign policy agenda. They have continuity *vis-à-vis* the member states, superior information on the state of play resulting from its pivotal position in the policy-making web, and one of their functions is to coordinate policy.

This theoretical argument has strong internal validity. One of the most interesting findings of this book is the major advantage of EU officials in terms of time. In all cases, EU officials were involved much earlier in the CSDP operations than the large majority of member states. Due to their position in the policy-making process (Mérand et al. 2010, 2011), they started the initial planning process at a very early stage. Most member states, on the other hand, only seriously started to consider a mission when they were asked to make a military or financial contribution. At that point the operation was often a *fait accompli*. EU officials had cleverly raised the expectations of external actors about EU involvement through their preparatory activities. For the majority of member states, there was no way back. They did not want to be accused of undermining the Aceh peace agreement, leaving the refugees in Chad to their own fate, or refusing to carry part of the burden in the Western Balkans. Increased expectations by third parties made missions difficult to reject. The head start of EU officials in the missions in Aceh and Chad was at least four months compared to the majority of the member states. In the cases of Bosnia and Kosovo, the time lag was even longer. Given that CSDP is characterized by rapid decision-making, with member states generally deciding within weeks, four months is significant.

The finding that EU officials had more influence in civilian than in military operations is at least as interesting. Given that the EU bureaucracies were initially understaffed in civilian crisis management, this presents a paradox. What cannot be stressed enough, in this respect, is the importance of *relative* resources. In relative terms, the resources of EU officials for civilian missions were significant compared with those of the member states. First, the member states have only one control body for civilian missions (CIVCOM) compared with three control bodies for military operations (Military Committee, EUMC working group, PMG). Second, these military bodies normally deal with one or two operations in parallel; CIVCOM was at times handling a dozen civilian operations. This made it very difficult for the national diplomats to remain informed of all developments. Third, the Military Committee consists of two- and three-star national generals at the end of their careers; CIVCOM is made up of early- and mid-career diplomats (Cross 2010). The CSDP planners (at colonel-level) thus have a different relationship to the member states than their civilian counterparts, for whom seniority and hierarchy are less relevant. Fourth, expertise in civilian crisis management in the capitals is limited and scattered (e.g. Vanhoonacker and Jacobs 2010). This hardly provides for quality instructions.

The innovative character of civilian crisis management also needs to be mentioned. The member states have limited experience with sending policemen abroad – let alone judges and prosecutors. Consequentially, there is not much civilian doctrine and there are few standard operating procedures (Benner and Bossong 2010). This allows for more entrepreneurship by the EU officials. During the rule of law mission in Kosovo and the AMM, they were at times inventing the practice of civilian crisis management along the way. Suggestions from Javier Solana to focus on the fight against corruption in Bosnia, in contrast, were immediately blocked by the generals, who noted that these were not military tasks. When the Force Commander followed Solana's instructions nonetheless, the member states reacted by reducing their troops. Finally, the command and control structures of civilian and military crisis management differ. While EU officials have operational control over the civilian missions, military operations rely on NATO or national assets. The civilian missions thus have a higher degree of "Brusselization," which also has the effect that expertise in the capitals remains more limited.

One of the important questions is whether the member states have reacted to these instances of (excessive) agency by the EU officials. The principal–agent model, after all, predicts that principals learn and that they make the necessary adjustments. While this book has not provided conclusive answers, it is noteworthy that the number of CSDP missions has decreased over time. This is indirect evidence that the EU officials have recently been less successful in furthering their interest of "more missions." At the time of writing, the member states were in no mood to sponsor pet projects, which made entrepreneurship difficult. Needless to say, international affairs are volatile, which can lead to new demands for CSDP missions. Of importance is also the question of why the member states have not yet strengthened their civilian control bodies. They can establish a working group for CIVCOM, appoint senior diplomats, or organize domestic coordination more effectively. One reason why this has not happened may be disagreement among the member states. Several member states tend to think that civilian crisis management is a distraction. They may not be very keen on increasing its stature. Another reason is the lack of willingness of national interior ministries to invest in civilian crisis management. These explanations remain, however, tentative and require further research.

The agency of EU bureaucracies is an important topic of debate among scholars. When it comes to the influence of EU officials in the area of foreign policy, this book has found interesting variation across issues areas and phases of the policy process. Such variation can be explained by the bureaucratic resources of the EU officials *vis-à-vis* the member states. These strongly relate, in turn, to the rationale for delegation. It has been noted before that a certain loss of agency is inevitable when delegating tasks ("no pain, no gain," Lake and McCubbins 2006: 343). The question thus remains whether some instances of influence by EU officials can be labeled as excessive. Some instances of agenda-setting certainly were. Given that agenda control constitutes an important power, such cases were significant. Various member states ended up having troops and monitors in places where they would otherwise not have been. EU officials arguably also exerted excessive influence in civilian crisis management. In the other cases, the member states held the bureaucracies on a short leash.

Alternative explanations

The rationalist principal–agent model has provided the framework for this book. Questions of delegation and agency – two *loci* of the model – have been discussed theoretically and empirically. The introduction of this book, however, has already made clear that several theories deal with the role of EU bureaucracies in policy-making. Constructivism, in particular, potentially provides a number of alternative and complementary explanations for delegation and agency. When delegating tasks, this theory argues, the member states do not make cost–benefit analyses to achieve efficiency gains. rather, they apply best practices and use models of institutional design, which seem appropriate and normatively legitimate. Agency does not result, according to constructivist approaches, from the strategic use of bureaucratic resources. It depends on the actor's authority in the negotiations. This section of the chapter shows that constructivism can complement rationalist accounts of delegation. In addition, it provides a useful alternative explanation of supranational influence.

Delegation, according to constructivist approaches, does not result from rationalist cost–benefit analyses or the search for efficiency. In making delegation decisions, policy-makers use best practices and models they consider as legitimate rather than the most efficient models. The effect is that institutional structures do not fit purpose. This leads to inefficiency or, at best, efficiency that is historically or culturally grounded (McNamara 2002). Popular with non-rationalist scholars is the incrementalism and path dependence argument. It effectively states that a seemingly unimportant instance of delegation can become significant over time. Small steps add up, and by going in one direction, switching costs increase and increasing returns endogenously start to affect the actor's preferences. Does this provide a convincing explanation for the delegation of functions in EU foreign policy? Several observers think so. Thomas Christiansen and Sophie Vanhoonacker (2008), for instance, use historical institutionalism to explain the institutional development of the Council Secretariat. They state that "the role of the [Council Secretariat] has changed over time ... What there has not been, however, is a formal reform of the institution, either recently or indeed at any point in its history" (p. 751). Johan Olsen (2010: 63) similarly writes that "key choices were made when the secretariat was set up. Since then, there has been change without formal reform, following mergers, new tasks, and the new institutional balance after Maastricht."

This book has shown that delegation has been less automatic than these scholars claim. It is not, however, necessary to repeat the rationalist argument. What is interesting is to point at instances where the rationalist explanation is not necessarily the most convincing. An anomaly, for example, is the frequent references to the European Parliament in the context of the Treaty of Maastricht. While this treaty did not eventually delegate important functions to the Parliament, these references do testify to the fact that some of the member states were considering the legitimacy of EU foreign policy-making. The appointment of Solana as High Representative following the Amsterdam Treaty is a second example where the rationality of the member states can be questioned. One can argue that the decision was only rational in the specific historical context of the ongoing NATO air campaign. Had it occurred three months earlier or later, the decision might have been different. Thirdly, several observers argue that the EU used NATO best practices when setting up the CSDP. While this brushes somewhat too quickly over the specificities of the CSDP (e.g. civil–military character, lack of headquarters), the EU definitely used some of the models. In such instances, constructivist approaches potentially provide a better explanation of delegation than the theory advanced in this book. These cases therefore require further analysis.

What about alternative accounts of agency? Constructivist approaches argue that member states and the EU officials are not intentionally competing for power and/or influence. Civil servants and diplomats try instead, by means of deliberation, to persuade others of their "better" arguments in order to come to mutually acceptable outcomes. Negotiations are about problem-solving and not about tough bargaining (e.g. Joerges and Neyer 1997a, b; Lewis 1998, 2005). What counts, in this respect, is not the size of the member states, formal rules, or veto points, but the claim of actors to authority. It is interesting that constructivists rely on information and expertise as well. These resources are not, however, strategically used. Instead they structurally determine which of the actors holds authority and is able to put forward persuasive arguments. While this argument of agency is better developed than the sociological theory of delegation, there continues to exist disagreement on how persuasion relates to power (e.g. Risse 2000). The absence of power in most accounts is a major weakness.

When looking at the four case studies, there is certainly a case to be made that EU action was "appropriate." Given the EU's legacy in the Western Balkans, it was considered "normal" for the EU to increase its presence on the ground and take responsibility for its own "backyard." The idea of burden-sharing with the US, which made clear that it had priorities elsewhere, also fits the argument. As a result, it became "logical" that the EU took over the military operation in Bosnia from NATO and the civilian rule of law mission in Kosovo from the UN. In institutional terms, EU officials undoubtedly contributed to this discourse. By being involved so early in the process, they could frame the discussions, which then led to these follow-on missions. A similar argument can be made for the cases of Aceh and Chad. A lot of the discourse surrounding the monitoring mission in Aceh was that the EU could make a meaningful contribution. Despite the fact that most member states had their doubts, EU officials persuaded them of the merits and feasibility of this endeavor. The military operation in Chad was framed in humanitarian terms – to do "something" about the situation in Darfur. Contributing to a safe and secure environment in this part of the world hardly fitted with the EU's strategic interests. EU officials convincingly explained to skeptical member states that it was not (or was more than) a French pet project.

When it comes to variation in agency, constructivism provides several explanations. The influence of the EU officials in agenda-setting fits in with the ideational accounts of European integration (Parsons 2002; Schimmelfennig 2001). By framing operations in line with prominent discourses, it contributes to putting some issues high on the agenda. Constructivist approaches also argue that it is logical for EU officials to have a bigger say in civilian than military operations. The national defense ministries and the generals in the Military Committee have authority when it comes to military affairs. The EU officers do not have the same levels of authority. In civilian crisis management, as has been established, however, member states do not have similar expertise and experience. EU officials can thus more easily compete with the member states in terms of authority. Together with the experts in CIVCOM it can search for solutions in crisis management and jointly establish civilian operational doctrine and standard operating procedures. Since EU officials draft the planning documents, they naturally have some authority.

To conclude the discussion of alternative explanations, constructivist accounts of delegation provide a complementary explanation to some cases of delegation and their use can enrich the analysis. These approaches, however, potentially have more to say about the agency of EU officials following the delegation of tasks. Constructivism provides an alternative explanation of why the EU has launched missions, and it can also explain variation in the influence of the EU officials. While these alternative explanations are competing on several levels with the principal–agent framework analyzed in this book, it is hardly fair to declare a "winner." Making a good case for constructivist approaches is beyond the scope of this book and requires further research.

Conclusion

This book started off with the remarkable institutional developments in the area of EU foreign and security policy at the turn of the 21st century. In the space of few years, the member states established a plethora of bureaucratic bodies. The CMPD, EUMS, CPCC, INTCEN, and EEAS are now household names for people working in Brussels on issues of security and defense. It has not always been like this. The book has indeed shown how member states hesitantly build up their foreign policy cooperation since the 1970s. Uncertainty about the consequences of delegation resulted in them keeping foreign and security functions firmly in-house. It was only after the wars in former Yugoslavia, where EU absence was deplorable, that the member states accepted the costs of having professional Brussels-based EU bureaucracies for security matters.

The relations between the member states and the EU bureaucracies and their officials have been the subject of this book. It has tried to put the rapid institutionalization of the late-1990s and early 2000s in a wider perspective by systematically studying why the member states delegate functions to the EU bureaucracies in foreign and security policy. The dilemma between the prospects of efficiency gains and sovereignty costs helps us to understand many of the instances of (non-)delegation. Importantly, sovereignty concerns have resulted not only in non-delegation, but have also affected agent selection and the extent to which the member states have delegated functions. In most cases, the member states took great care in deciding whom to empower. In many cases, the delegation of functions also fell short of what would be functionally efficient.

Debates over delegation continue. The question of whether the CSDP should have its own dedicate civil–military headquarters, for example, remains on the agenda and unanswered. In many ways it epitomizes the overall debate over security and defense cooperation in the EU. Most serious observers agree that it is a functional necessity if the CSDP is to further develop in the 21st century. It is, however, unclear that all member states accept this direction and are willing to face the consequences that such an additional round of delegation means. Setting up crisis management in the EU has real consequences and affects the way in which member states make policy.

This is indeed where the second research question comes in. By studying the conditions for influence of EU officials, this book has made a real attempt to analyze the effects of delegation. Questions of political influence are, needless to say, hard to answer, and it has required four case studies and many interviews. Still the answer is nuanced. In many cases, the member states have managed more or less to stay on top of the dossiers. The military crisis management operations show, in particular, that excessive influence by the Brussels-based bureaucracies was limited. However, in a number of instances – relating to agenda-setting and civilian crisis management – EU officials have crossed their mandates. Some of the smaller member states eventually ended up sending staff members on missions that they did not really support in the first place.

The number of new CSDP operations has decreased in recent years. One can convincingly argue that this has limited the relevance of EU officials in the CSDP. Moreover, it can be seen as evidence of increased control by the member states. Various international crises (Congo,

Kenya, Sri Lanka, Libya) have passed the EU agenda without having resulted in much CSDP action. It also needs to be said, however, that since the beginning of 2012 the CSDP has found some momentum again with the deployment of several smaller operations. The EU Training Mission in Mali is, in this respect, the most promising one. Much of this renewed emphasis on the CSDP seems to have come from a handful of member states and strategically operating EU officials. The institutionalist perspective on CSDP policy-making helps to explain it.

Notes

1 Introduction

1. In addition to giving EU officials CSDP functions, the member states also strengthened the role of EU bureaucracy in the area of foreign policy (see Chapter 3).
2. This book prefers the terminology of "bureaucracy" over "institution" or "organization" in line with recent international relations literature. This also circumvents the Brussels' problem that the Commission is considered an "institution," the EEAS a "service" and the Council Secretariat a "secretariat" serving an "institution" (i.e. the Council).
3. Burley and Mattli (1993) put neofunctionalism squarely in the rationalist camp. Haas (2004: xv) argues *post hoc* that the ontology is "'soft' rational choice." Needless to say, neofunctionalism does contain a number of constructivist elements by stressing value-derived interest and its transformative nature (Haas 2001; Schmitter 2004; Rosamond 2005; Pollack 2005).

2 Delegation and Agency in International Relations

1. Many scholars argue that a secretariat is part of the definition of international organizations (e.g. Young 1986; Ruggie 1992).
2. The Prisoner's Dilemma is an often-used game-theoretical example.
3. Arguably sovereignty has always been an implicit part of the analysis. International political economy, as some would argue, was established to get away from the dominance of security (and the related dominance of self-help and sovereignty) in international relations. In international delegation theory, however, the conceptual and theoretical consequences of sovereignty costs are hardly ever spelled out.
4. Needless to say, this is only one element of the multi-dimensional concept of sovereignty.
5. Influence is defined as EU officials getting one member state to do something it otherwise would not have done. It is, however, perfectly possible that the costs of such instances are still lower than the overall benefit of delegation.
6. While rationality and efficiency are important explanations for delegation in the principal–agent model, one of the first models already pointed at suboptimal outcomes (Spence and Zeckhauser 1971; cf. Miller 2005). It argued that own risk in insurance schemes may limit moral hazard, but that it is suboptimal, as clients remain partially exposed to risks and companies receive lower premiums.
7. It should not fully affect the payoffs, because then the action becomes indirectly observable (Arrow 1985).

3 Institutional Development in EU Security and Defense

1. This book only refers to the source of official documents when it is not obvious (such as in the case of Treaties, Council Decisions or the formal Reports that formed the basis of EPC). CVCE stands for *Centre Virtuel de la Connaissance sur l'Europe* <www.cvce.eu> and AEI for the Archive of European Integration <aei.pitt.edu>.
2. Quoted in "A Secretariat for European Political Cooperation" (September 1985) by the Secretariat of the European Parliament (AEI).
3. Annexed in "A Secretariat for European Political Cooperation" (September 1985) by the Secretariat of the European Parliament (AEI).
4. There was considerable confusion about the outcome of the European Council. During the press conference a journalist raised the question "Prime Minister, the intergovernmental conference will also discuss a new treaty on foreign policy and ...," to which Thatcher answered "No, no, no, no!"
5. The Western European Union is a European collective defense organization (cf. NATO), which has never been really active, and which was partially integrated into the European Union (1993–2002).
6. CSDP was called European Security and Defence Policy (ESDP) until the Treaty of Lisbon.
7. The European Union prides itself on its comprehensive approach to crisis management, which brings together civil and military instruments.
8. Before the referendums in France, The Netherlands (both 2005), and Ireland (2008), the member states had already started negotiating the details of the EEAS. These negotiations were twice put on hold.
9. The Commission admittedly keeps the desks in DG Enlargement and some of the member states also had to made concessions regarding the military services.

4 Policy-Making in EU Security and Defense

1. These were often cleverly engineered by France.
2. Before the Treaty of Lisbon, there existed the Crisis Response Coordination Teams (CRCTs), which had a similar coordination role (Council 2003).
3. The Political-Military Group, consisting of Defense Counselors, advises the PSC on the political dimension of military operations.
4. The Council Secretariat circulates a proposal. If none of the member states reacts before the deadline, the proposal is automatically accepted.
5. There is some flexibility in the scope of the common costs. This is subject to agreement by the member states.
6. The only exception concerns the financing of military operations. The ATHENA mechanism in the Council Secretariat administers the budget.
7. 146 officers in EUFOR RD Congo (2006) (Major 2009) and 141 officers in EUFOR Chad (2008) (Seibert 2010).
8. Needless to say, much of the planning process also differs in practice between those operations. In the case of follow-on operations, the planning documents are often based on planning documents by the previous operation.
9. The Force Commander is appointed together with the Operations Commander in the Council Decision. He/she has responsibility on the ground.

10. 173 officers in EUFOR Chad (Seibert 2010) and 122 officers in EUFOR RD Congo (Major 2009).
11. The Head of Mission is the equivalent of the Force Commander.
12. The exception is integrated police units.
13. At the time the CPCC with the Civilian Operations Commander had not yet been established (see above). Feith continued his function as Deputy Director General during his time in Aceh, so in practical terms he "was" the Council Secretariat. Needless to say, this was not an optimal command and control structure.
14. The only notable exception is the financial rules and procurement procedures of the Commission in civilian crisis management.

5 Military Operation in Bosnia

1. The position of EUSR was decoupled from the position of High Representative in 2011.
2. FT stands for *Financial Times*; IHT for *International Herald Tribune*.
3. Thomas Bertin was one of General Leakey's three political advisors (POLADs).

6 Monitoring Mission in Aceh

1. The United Nations was not acceptable due to the situation in East Timor.
2. There was no Council meeting in August to approve the Joint Action.
3. The number of weapons that the GAM had to hand in was extremely low, but as one Council Secretariat interviewee noted this was irrelevant given that the Government of Indonesia had agreed to this number.

7 Military Operation in Chad

1. Apart from France, only Sweden was to a reasonable extent involved in the planning at the early stages of the process (interview national official).
2. Critics argue that EUFOR was not impartial because it gave the government the possibility to re-group (Charbonneau 2009; Berg 2009).
3. There was a need for a camp close to the capital in any case to coordinate the logistics (airport/seaport).
4. Of the 3,700 troops, only 1,400 could perform active functions in the area of operations ("EUFOR Tchad/RCA in Retrospect" 2010).
5. EUFOR never reached Full Operating Capability, because the Force Generation process was never completed as a result of a lack of helicopters. Instead it declared the elements deployed as fully operational ("EUFOR Tchad/RCA in Retrospect" 2010).

8 Rule of Law Mission in Kosovo

1. EULEX is consistently understaffed and has on average between 1,500 and 1,600 international officials.
2. This report and subsequent reports by Solana and Rehn are not publicly available. Summaries can be found online at http://www.consilium.europa.eu.
3. Cyprus abstained from voting on the Joint Action establishing EULEX.

References

Abbott, K. and D. Snidal (1998) "Why States Act through Formal International Organizations," *Journal of Conflict Resolution* 42(1): 3–32.

Abbott, K. and D. Snidal (2000) "Hard and Soft Law in International Governance," *International Organization* 54(3): 421–456.

Abbott, K. et al. (2000) "The Concept of Legalization," *International Organization* 54(3): 401–419.

Accord (2008) *Delivering Peace for Aceh: An interview with President Martti Ahtisaari* [online] available at: http://www.c-r.org/our-work/accord/aceh/ahtisaari.php (last accessed: April 17, 2009).

Aceh Monitoring Mission (2006a) *Website Archive*, 29 April [online] available at: http://www.aceh-mm.org/english/info_menu/archive.htm (last accessed: December 19, 2010).

Aceh Monitoring Mission (2006b) *Press Release on Extension*, 12 May [online] available at: http://www.aceh-mm.org/download/english/AMM extension HoM.pdf (last accessed: April 22, 2009).

Adebahr, C. (2011) "From Competitors to Deputies: How the EU Special Representatives Integrated into the Solana System," in G. Mueller-Brandeck-Bocquet and C. Rueger (eds), *The High Representative for the EU Foreign and Security Policy: Review and Prospects*, Baden-Baden: Nomos.

Agence France-Presse (2007a) *Darfur to top agenda for French FM Kouchner*, 18 May.

Agence France-Presse (2007b) *Sweden, Norway mull joining Darfur force*, 1 August.

Moravcsik (eds), *Power, Interdependence, and Nonstate Actors in World Politics*, Princeton: Princeton University Press.

Ahtisaari, M. (2008) "Lessons of the Aceh Peace Talks," *Asia Europe Journal* 6(1): 9–14.

Alter, K. (2009) *The European Court's Political Power: Selected Essays*, Oxford: Oxford University Press.

Arrow, K. (1985) "The Economics of Agency," in J. Pratt and R. Zechhauser (eds) *Principals and Agents: The Structure of Business*, Cambridge: Harvard University Press.

Ashdown, P. (2007) *Swords and Ploughshares: Bringing Peace in the 21st Century*, London: Weidenfeld and Nicolson.

Aspinall, E. (2005) "The Helsinki Agreement: A More Promising Basis for Peace in Aceh?" *Policy Studies* 20, Washington: East-West Center.

Aspinall, E. (2008) *Peace without Justice? The Helsinki Peace Process in Aceh*, Geneva: Centre for Humanitarian Dialogue.

Bachrach, P. and M. Baratz (1962) "Two Faces of Power," *American Political Science Review* 56(4): 947–952.

Barnett, M. and M. Finnemore (1999) "The Politics, Power, and Pathologies of International Organizations," *International Organization* 53(4): 699–732.

Barnett, M. and M. Finnemore (2004) *Rules for the World: International Organizations in Global Politics*, Ithaca: Cornell University Press.

Barron, P. and A. Burke (2008) "Supporting Peace in Aceh: Development Agency and International Involvement," *Policy Studies* 47, Washington: East-West Center.
Bauer, S. (2006) "Does Bureaucracy Really Matter? The Authority of Intergovernmental Treaty Secretariats in Global Environmental Politics," *Global Environmental Politics* 6(1): 23–49.
Baumgartner, F. and B. Jones (1991) "Agenda Dynamics and Policy Subsystems," *Journal of Politics* 53(4): 1044–1074.
Bawn, K. (1995) "Political Control versus Expertise: Congressional Choices about Administrative Procedures," *American Political Science Review* 89(1): 62–73.
Beach, D. (2004) "The Unseen Hand in Treaty Reform Negotiations: The Role and Influence of the Council Secretariat," *Journal of European Public Policy* 11(3): 408–439.
Beach, D. (2005) *The Dynamics of European Integration: Why and When EU Institutions Matter*, Basingstoke: Palgrave Macmillan.
Bendor, J., S. Taylor, and R. Van Gaalen (1985) "Bureaucratic Expertise versus Legislative Authority: A Model of Deception and Monitoring in Budgeting," *American Political Science Review* 79(4): 1041–1060.
Bengtsson, R. and D. Allen (2011) "Exploring a Triangular Drama: The High Representative, the Council Presidency and the Commission," in G. Mueller-Brandeck-Bocquet and C. Rueger (eds), *The High Representative for the EU Foreign and Security Policy: Review and Prospects*, Baden-Baden: Nomos.
Benner, T. and R. Bossong (2010) "The Case for a Public Administration Turn in the Study of EU Civilian Crisis Management," *Journal of European Public Policy* 17(7): 1074–1086.
Berg, P. (2009) "EUFOR Tchad/RCA: The EU Serving French Interests," in M. Asseburg and R. Kempin (eds), *The EU as a Strategic Actor in the Realm of Security and Defence*, Berlin: Stiftung Wissenschaft und Politik.
Bertin, T. (2008) "The EU Military Operation in Bosnia," in M. Merlingen and R. Ostrauskaite (eds), *The European Security and Defence Policy: An Implementation Perspective*, London: Routledge.
Biermann, F. and B. Siebenhuener (eds) (2009) *Managers of Global Change: The Influence of International Environmental Bureaucracies*, Cambridge: MIT University Press.
Björkdahl, A. (2008) "Norm Advocacy: A Small State Strategy to Influence the EU," *Journal of European Public Policy* 15(1): 135–154.
Bonvicini, G. (1988) "Mechanisms and Procedures of EPC: More than Traditional Diplomacy?" in A. Pijpers, E. Regelsberger, and W. Wessels (eds), *European Political Cooperation in the 1980s: A Common Foreign Policy for Western Europe?* Dordrecht: Martinus Nijhoff Publishers.
Bradley, C. and J. Kelley (2008) "The Concept of International Delegation," *Law and Contemporary Problems* 71(1): 1–36.
Brandsma, G. (2010) *Backstage Europe: Comitology, Accountability and Democracy in the European Union*, unpublished PhD dissertation, Utrecht University, Utrecht.
Bryant, J. (2000) "France and NATO from 1966 to Kosovo: Coming Full Circle?" *European Security* 9(3): 21–37.
Burley, A. and W. Mattli (1993) "Europe before the Court: A Political Theory of Legal Integration," *International Organization* 47(1): 41–76.
Cameron, F. (2007) *An Introduction to European Foreign Policy*, London: Routledge.

Cascone, G. (2008) "ESDP Operations and NATO: Co-operation, Rivalry or Muddling-through?" in M. Merlingen and R. Ostrauskaite (eds), *The European Security and Defence Policy: An Implementation Perspective*, London: Routledge.

Charbonneau, B. (2009) "What Is So Special about the EU? EU–UN Cooperation in Crisis Management in Africa," *International Peacekeeping* 16(4): 546–561.

Charbonneau, B. (2010) "France," in D. Black and P. Williams (eds), *The International Politics of Mass Atrocities: The Case of Darfur*, London: Routledge.

Checkel, J. (2001) "Why Comply? Social Learning and European Identity Change," *International Organization* 55(3): 553–588.

Checkel, J. (2005) "Constructivism and EU Politics," in K. Jørgensen, M. Pollack, and B. Rosamond (eds), *Handbook of European Union Politics*, London: Sage.

Christiansen, T. (1997) "Tensions of European Governance: Politicized Bureaucracy and Multiple Accountability in the European Commission," *Journal of European Public Policy* 4(1): 73–90.

Christiansen, T. (2002) "Out of the Shadows: The General Secretariat of the Council of Ministers," *Journal of Legislative Studies* 8(4): 80–97.

Christiansen, T. and S. Vanhoonacker (2008) "At a Critical Juncture? Change and Continuity in the Institutional Development of the Council Secretariat," *West European Politics* 31(4): 751–770.

Commission (2005) *Information Note to the Council*, RELEX/A4 REG PA (05) D/508248, Brussels: European Commission.

Commission (2009) *Overview of the EC assistance in the Rule of Law Sector in Kosovo* [Online] available at: http://www.delprn.ec.europa.eu/ (last accessed: April 8, 2010).

Council (2001) *EU crisis management and conflict prevention: guidelines on fact-finding missions*, doc. 15048/01, Brussels: Council of the European Union.

Council (2003) *Suggestions for procedures for coherent, comprehensive EU crisis management*, doc. 11127/03, Brussels: Council of the European Union.

Council (2004) *Council conclusions*, 22 March, Brussels: Council of the European Union.

Council (2007) *Outcome of proceedings of the meeting of the Committee for Civilian Aspects of Crisis Management*, 6091/07, 31 January, Brussels: Council of the European Union.

Cross, M. (2010) "Cooperation by Committee: The EU Military Committee and the Committee for Civilian Crisis Management," *Occasional Paper* 82, Paris: EU Institute for Security Studies.

Cross, M. (2011) *Security Integration in Europe: How Knowledge-Based Networks Are Transforming the European Union*, Ann Arbor: The University of Michigan Press.

Crowe, B. (2003) "A Common European Foreign Policy after Iraq?" *International Affairs* 79(3): 533–546.

Curtin, D. (2009) *Executive Power of the European Union: Law, Practices, and the Living Constitution*, Oxford: Oxford University Press.

Dahl, R. (1957) "The Concept of Power," *Behavioral Science* 2: 201–215.

Dahl, R. ([1963] 2003) *Modern Political Analysis*, Upper Saddle River: Prentice-Hall.

Devuyst, Y. (1998) "Treaty Reform in the European Union: The Amsterdam Process," *Journal of European Public Policy* 5(4): 615–631.

Dijkstra, H. (2010a) "Explaining Variation in the Role of the EU Council Secretariat in First and Second Pillar Policy-Making," *Journal of European Public Policy* 17(4): 527–544.

Dijkstra, H. (2010b) "The Military Operation of the EU in Chad and the Central African Republic: Good Policy, Bad Politics," *International Peacekeeping* 17(3): 395–407.

Dijkstra, H. (2011) "Solana and his Civil Servants: An Overview of Political-Administrative Relations," in G. Mueller-Brandeck-Bocquet and C. Rueger (eds), *The High Representative for the EU Foreign and Security Policy: Review and Prospects*, Baden-Baden: Nomos.

Dijkstra, H. and S. Vanhoonacker (2011) "The Changing Politics of Information in European Foreign Policy," *Journal of European Integration* 33(5): 541–558.

Dinan, D. (1999) *Ever Closer Union: An Introduction to European Integration*, Basingstoke: Palgrave.

Dinan, D. (2004) *Europe Recast: A History of European Union*, Basingstoke: Palgrave Macmillan.

Duke, S. (2002a) "The Common Foreign and Security Policy: Significant but Modest Changes," in F. Laursen (ed.), *The Amsterdam Treaty: National Preference Formation, Interstate Bargaining and Outcome*, Odense: Odense University Press.

Duke, S. (2002b) *The EU and Crisis Management: Development and Prospects*, Maastricht: EIPA.

Duke, S. (2003) "A Foreign Minister for Europe: But Where's the Foreign Ministry?" *Discussion Papers in Diplomacy* 89, The Hague: Clingendael.

Duke, S. (2006) "The Commission and the CFSP," *EIPA Working Papers*, Maastricht: EIPA.

Duke, S. and S. Vanhoonacker (2006) "Administrative Governance in the CFSP: Development and Practice," *European Foreign Affairs Review* 11(2): 163–182.

Dür, A. (2008) "Measuring Interest Group Influence in the EU: A Note on Methodology," *European Union Politics* 9(4): 559–576.

Dyer, J. (1997) "Effective Interim Collaboration: How Firms Minimize Transaction Costs and Maximise Transaction Value," *Strategic Management Journal* 18(7): 533–556.

Edwards, G. and A. Pijpers (eds) (1997) *The Politics of European Treaty Reform: The 1996 Intergovernmental Conference and Beyond*, London: Pinter.

Elgie, R. (2002) "The Politics of the European Central Bank: Principal-Agent Theory and the Democratic Deficit," *Journal of European Public Policy* 9(2): 186–200.

Elgström, O. and M. Smith (2000) "Introduction: Negotiation and Policy-Making in the European Union: Processes, System and Order," *Journal of European Public Policy* 7(5): 673–683.

Elsig, M. and M. Pollack (2013) "Agents, Trustees, and International Courts: The Politics of Judicial Appointment at the World Trade Organization," *European Journal of International Relations*, published online, doi:10.1177/1354066112448201.

Epstein, D. and S. O'Halloran (1999) *Delegating Powers: A Transaction Cost Politics Approach to Policy Making under Separate Powers*, Cambridge: Cambridge University Press.

Epstein, D. and S. O'Halloran (2008) "Sovereignty and Delegation in International Organizations," *Law and Contemporary Problems* 71(1): 77–92.

Eriksson, J. and M. Rhinard (2009) "The Internal-External Security Nexus: Notes on an Emerging Research Agenda," *Cooperation and Conflict* 44(3): 243–267.

"EUFOR Tchad/RCA in Retrospect: Lessons Learned for Planning and Implementing CSDP Operations" (2010) Institute for European Studies of the Vrije Universiteit Brussel, 9 February.

EUObserver (2011a) *UK snubs Ashton over EU military headquarters*, 19 July.
EUObserver (2011b) *Group of five calls for EU military headquarters*, 9 September.
European Security Review (2003) *US blocks early EU takeover of SFOR* 18(9).
Feith, P. (2007) "The Aceh Peace Process: Nothing Less than a Success," *Special Report of the US Institute for Peace* 184.
Financial Times (2002) EU moves closer to taking over Nato's role in Bosnia, 17 December.
Financial Times (2003a) US puts off EU takeover of Bosnia mission, 4 June.
Financial Times (2003b) Bosnia role boosts EU military ambitions, 25 February.
Financial Times (2003c) EU closer to taking over Bosnia peace role, 10 October.
Financial Times (2004) Relief work may aid peace moves in conflict areas, 29 December.
Financial Times (2005a) Berlin links aid pledge to peace moves, 6 January.
Financial Times (2005b) Aceh peace talks agree August target date for deal, 24 February.
Financial Times (2006) Germany aims for Bosnia troop pull-out next year, 31 October.
Fiorina, M. (1977) "The Case of the Vanishing Marginals: The Bureaucracy Did It," *American Political Science Review* 71(1): 177–181.
Franchino, F. (2000a) "Statutory Discretion and Procedural Control of the European Commission's Executive Functions," *Journal of Legislative Studies* 6(3): 29–50.
Franchino, F. (2000b) "Control of the Commission's Executive Functions," *European Union Politics* 1(1): 63–92.
Franchino, F. (2000c) "The Commission's Executive Discretion, Information and Comitology," *Journal of Theoretical Politics* 12(2): 155–181.
Franchino, F. (2007) *The Powers of the Union: Delegation in the EU*, Cambridge: Cambridge University Press.
George, A. and A. Bennett (2005) *Case Studies and Theory Development in the Social Sciences*, Cambridge: MIT Press.
George, S. (1997) "Britain and the IGC," in G. Edwards and A. Pijpers (eds), *The Politics of European Treaty Reform: The 1996 Intergovernmental Conference and Beyond*, London: Pinter.
Giegerich, B. et al. (2006) "Towards a Strategic Partnership? The US and Russian Response to the European Security and Defence Policy," *Security Dialogue* 37(3): 385–407.
Goodin, R. (1996) "Institutions and their Design," in R. Goodin (ed.), *The Theory of Institutional Design*, Cambridge: Cambridge University Press.
Grevi, G. (2005) "The Aceh Monitoring Mission: Towards Integrated Crisis Management," in P. Braud and G. Grevi (eds), *The EU Mission in Aceh: Implementing Peace, Chaillot Paper* 61, Paris: EU Institute for Security Studies.
Grevi, G. (2009) "EULEX Kosovo: The EU Rule-of-Law Mission in Kosovo (EULEX Kosovo)," in G. Grevi, D. Helly and D. Keohane (eds), *European Security and Defence Policy: The First 10 Years (1999–2009)*, Paris: EU Institute for Security Studies.
Grevi, G., D. Helly, and D. Keohane (eds) (2009) *ESDP: The First 10 Years (1999–2009)*, Paris: EU Institute for Security Studies.
Grieco, J. (1988) "Anarchy and the Limits of Cooperation: A Realist Critique of the Newest Liberal Institutionalism," *International Organization* 42(3): 485–507.

Groenleer, M. (2009) *The Autonomy of European Union Agencies*, Delft: Eburon.
Gross, E. (2009a) *The Europeanization of National Foreign Policy: Continuity and Change in European Crisis Management*, Basingstoke: Palgrave Macmillan.
Gross, E. (2009b) "EU Military Operation in the Former Yugoslav Republic of Macedonia (Concordia)," in G. Grevi, D. Helly, and D. Keohane (eds), *European Security and Defence Policy: The First Ten Years (1999–2009)*, Paris: EU Institute for Security Studies.
Guardian (2002) Turkey relents to pave way for EU force, 16 December.
Guardian (2004) Setback for Kosovo as UN official resigns, 26 May.
Haas, E. (1958) *The Uniting of Europe*, Stanford: Stanford University Press.
Haas, E. (1964) *Beyond the Nation State: Functionalism and International Organization*, Stanford: Stanford University Press.
Haas, E. (1975) "The Obsolescence of Regional Integration Theory," *Working Paper* 25, Berkeley: Institute of International Studies.
Haas, E. (2001) "Does Constructivism Subsume Neo-Functionalism?" in T. Christiansen, K. Jørgensen, and A. Wiener (eds), *The Social Construction of Europe*, London: Sage.
Haas, E. (2004) *The Uniting of Europe: Politics, Social and Economic Forces, 1950–1957*, 3rd ed., Notre Dame: University of Notre Dame Press.
Haas, P. (1992) "Introduction: Epistemic Communities and International Policy Coordination," *International Organization* 46(1): 1–35.
Haftendorn, H., R. Keohane, and C. Wallender (eds) (1999) *Imperfect Unions: Security Institutions Over Time and Space*, Oxford: Oxford University Press.
Haine, J. (2003) "From Laeken to Copenhagen: European defence core documents," *Chaillot Paper* 57, Paris: EU Institute for Security Studies.
Hall, R. (1997) "Moral Authority as a Power Resource," *International Organization* 51(4): 591–622.
Hathway, O. (2008) "International Delegation and Domestic Sovereignty," *Law and Contemporary Problems* 71(1): 115–150.
Hawkins, D. et al. (eds) (2006) *Delegation and Agency in International Organizations*, Cambridge: Cambridge University Press.
Helsingin Sanomat (2006) *Finns stay on as Aceh peace process continues: For Juha Christensen, peace in Aceh began as a hobby, and turned into a job*, 12 December.
Helsingin Sanomat (2007) *Finnish government considering sending troops to Chad instead of Darfur* [translated by BBC World Monitoring], 14 August.
Herrberg, A. (2008) "The Brussels 'Backstage' of the Aceh Peace Process," in Aguswandi and J. Large (eds), *Reconfiguring Politics: The Indonesia – Aceh Peace Process* [online] available at: http://www.c-r.org/our-work/accord/aceh/backstage.php (last accessed: April 23, 2009).
Hill, C. (1982) "Changing Gear in Political Co-operation," *Political Quarterly* 53(1): 47–60.
Hix, S. (1998) *The Political System of the European Union*, Basingstoke: Palgrave Macmillan.
Hix, S. (2005) *The Political System of the European Union*, Basingstoke: Palgrave Macmillan.
Hoffmann, S. (1966) "Obstinate or Obsolete? The Fate of the Nation State and the Case of Western Europe," *Daedalus* 95(3): 862–915.
Howorth, J. (2000) "European Integration and Defence: The Ultimate Challenge?" *Chaillot Paper* 43, Paris: EU Institute for Security Studies.

Howorth, J. (2007) *Security and Defence Policy in the European Union*, Basingstoke: Palgrave Macmillan.

Howorth, J. (2010) "Strategy and the Importance of Defence Cooperation among EU Member States," *Egmont Security Policy Brief* 12, Brussels: Egmont Institute.

Huber, K. (2008) "Aceh's Arduous Journey to Peace," in Aguswandi and J. Large (eds), *Reconfiguring Politics: The Indonesia – Aceh Peace Process* [online] available at: http://www.c-r.org/our-work/accord/aceh/journey.php (last accessed: April 23, 2009).

International Crisis Group (2001) "No Early Exit: NATO's Continuing Challenge in Bosnia," *ICG Balkans Report* 110, Brussels: International Crisis Group.

International Crisis Group (2004) "EUFOR-IA: Changing Bosnia's Security Arrangements," *ICG Europe Briefing*, Brussels: International Crisis Group.

International Crisis Group (2005) "Aceh: A Chance for Peace," *Asia Briefing* 40, 15 August, Brussels: International Crisis Group.

International Crisis Group (2008) "Chad: A New Conflict Resolution Framework," *Africa Report* 144, Brussels: International Crisis Group.

International Herald Tribune (2005) Jakarta is upbeat on Aceh peace: Both sides maneuver around critical issue, 25 February.

International Herald Tribune (2006a) Merkel under fire over Congo mission; Left and right assail plan for Germany to lead 1,500 EU peacekeepers, 20 March.

International Herald Tribune (2006b) Germany planning a Bosnia withdrawal, 31 October.

Ioannides, I. (2006) "EU Police Mission Proxima: Testing the 'European' Approach to Peace Building," in A. Nowak (ed.), *Civilian Crisis Management: The EU way, Chaillot Paper* 90, Paris: EU Institute for Security Studies.

ISIS Europe (2011) *European Security Review – Althea*, October, Brussels: ISIS Europe.

Jervis, R. (1982) "Security Regimes," *International Organization* 36(2): 357–378.

Joerges, C. and J. Neyer (1997a) "Transforming Strategic Interaction into Deliberative Problem-Solving: European Comitology in the Foodstuffs Sector," *Journal of European Public Policy* 4(4): 609–625.

Joerges, C. and J. Neyer (1997b) "From Intergovernmental Bargaining to Deliberative Political Processes: The Constitutionalisation of Comitology," *European Law Journal* 3(3): 273–299.

Juncos, A. (2007) "Police Mission in Bosnia Herzegovina," in M. Emerson and E. Gross (eds), *Evaluating the EU's Crisis Missions in the Balkans*, Brussels: CEPS.

Kahler, M. (2001) *Leadership Selection in the Major Multilaterals*, Washington, D.C.: Institute for International Economics.

Kassim, H. et al. (eds) (2001) *The National Co-ordination of EU Policy: The European Level*, Oxford: Oxford University Press.

Kassim, H. and A. Menon (2003) "The Principal-Agent Approach and the Study of the European Union: Promise Unfulfilled?" *Journal of European Public Policy* 10(1): 121–139.

Keleman, D. (2002) "The Politics of 'Eurocratic' Structure and the New European Agencies," *West European Politics* 25(4): 93–118.

Keohane, R. (1984) *After Hegemony: Cooperation and Discord in the World Political Economy*, Princeton: Princeton University Press.

Ker-Lindsay, J. (2009) *Kosovo: The Path to Contested Statehood in the Balkans*, London: Tauris.

Kiewiet, D. and M. McCubbins (1991) *The Logic of Delegation: Congressional Parties and the Appropriations Process*, Chicago: Chicago University Press.
King, G., R. Keohane, and S. Verba (1994) *Designing Social Inquiry: Scientific Inference in Qualitative Research*, Princeton: Princeton University Press.
King, I. and W. Mason (2006) *Peace at Any Price: How the World Failed Kosovo*, London: Hurst and Company.
Kingdon, J. (1984) *Agendas, Alternatives, and Public Policies*, Boston: Little, Brown and Company.
Kingsbury, D. (2006) *Peace in Aceh: A Personal Account of the Helsinki Peace Process*, Jakarta: Equinox Publishing.
Kirwan, P. (2008) "From European to Global Security Actor: The Aceh Monitoring Mission in Indonesia," in M. Merlingen and R. Ostrauskaitė (eds), *European Security and Defence Policy: An Implementation Perspective*, London: Routledge.
Klein, N. (2010) *European Agents Out of Control: Delegation and Agency in the Civil-Military Crisis Management of the European Union (1999–2008)*, Baden Baden: Nomos.
Knight, J. (1992) *Institutions and Social Conflict*, Cambridge: Cambridge University Press.
Koeth, W. (2010) "State Building without a State: The EU's Dilemma in Defining Its Relations with Kosovo," *European Foreign Affairs Review* 15(2): 227–247.
Koremenos, B., C. Lipson, and D. Snidal (2001) "The Rational Design of International Institutions," *International Organization* 55(4): 761–799.
Koremenos, B. (2005) "Contracting around International Uncertainty," *American Political Science Review* 99(4): 549–565.
Kratochwil, F. (1989) *Rules, Norms and Decisions: On the Conditions of Practical and Legal Reasoning in International Relations and Domestic Affairs*, Cambridge: Cambridge University Press.
Kupferschmidt, F. (2006) "Putting Strategic Partnership to the Test: Cooperation between NATO and the EU in Operation Althea," *SWP Research Paper* 3, Berlin: SWP German Institute for International and Security Affairs.
Kurowska, X. (2008) "More than a Balkan Crisis Manager: The EUJUST Themis in Georgia," in M. Merlingen and R. Ostrauskaite (eds) *European Security and Defence Policy: An implementation perspective*, London: Routledge.
Lake, D. and M. McCubbins (2006) "The Logic of Delegation to International Organizations," in D. Hawkins et al. (eds), *Delegation and Agency in International Organizations*, Cambridge: Cambridge University Press.
Laursen, F. and S. Vanhoonacker (eds) (1992) *The Intergovernmental Conference on Political Union: Institutional Reforms, New Policies, and International Identity of the European Community*, Dordrecht: Martinus Nijhoff Publishers.
Lax, D. and J. Sebenius (1986) *Manager as Negotiator: Bargaining for Cooperation and Competitive Gain*, New York: The Free Press.
Leakey, D. (2006) "ESDP and Civil/Military Cooperation: Bosnia and Herzegovina, 2005," in A. Deighton and V. Maurer (eds), *Securing Europe? Implementing the European Security Strategy*, Zürich: Swiss Federal Institute for Technology.
Lewis, J. (1998) "Is the 'Hard Bargaining' Image of the Council Misleading? The Committee of Permanent Representatives and the Local Elections Directive," *Journal of Common Market Studies* 36(4): 479–504.
Lewis, J. (2005) "The Janus Face of Brussels: Socialization and Everyday Decision Making in the European Union," *International Organization* 59(4): 937–971.

Liberation (2007) *Darfur is Kouchner's first "guest" at Quai d'Orsay* [translated by BBC World Monitoring], 21 May.
Liesinen, K. and S. Lahdensuo (2008) "Negotiating Decommissioning and Reintegration in Aceh, Indonesia," in Cate Buchanan (ed.), *Reflections on Guns, Fighters and Armed Violence in Peace Processes*, Geneva: Centre for Humanitarian Dialogue.
Lindberg, L. (1963) *The Political Dynamics of European Economic Integration*, Stanford: Stanford University Press.
Lipson, C. (1984) "International Cooperation in Economic and Security Affairs," *World Politics* 37(1): 1–23.
Lowenfeld, A. (1994) "Remedies Along with Rights: Institutional Reform in the New GATT," *American Journal of International Law* 88(3): 477–488.
Luce, R. and H. Raiffa (1957) *Games and Decisions: Introduction and Critical Survey*, New York: Wiley.
Lukes, S. (1974) *Power: A Radical View*, London: Macmillan.
Mace, C. (2004) "Operation Concordia: Developing a 'European' Approach to Crisis Management?" *International Peacekeeping* 11(3): 474–490.
Majone, G. (ed.) (1996) *Regulating Europe*, London: Routledge.
Majone, G. (2001) "Two Logics of Delegation: Agency and Fiduciary Relations in EU Governance," *European Union Politics* 2(1): 103–122.
Major, C. (2009) "EUFOR DR Congo," in G. Grevi, D. Helly, and D. Keohane (eds), *ESDP: The First 10 Years (1999–2009)*, Paris: EU Institute for Security Studies.
March, J. and J. Olsen (1984) "The New Institutionalism: Organizational Factors in Political Life," *American Political Science Review* 78(3): 734–749.
March, J. and J. Olsen (1998) "The Institutional Dynamics of International Political Orders," *International Organization* 52(4): 943–969.
Matlary, J. (2009) *EU Security Dynamics: In the National Interest*, Palgrave Macmillan.
Mattelaer, A. (2008) "The Strategic Planning of EU Military Operations – The Case of EUFOR Tchad/RCA," *IES Working Papers* 5, Brussels: Institute for European Studies.
Mattelaer, A. (2010) "The CSDP Mission Planning Process of the European Union: Innovations and Shortfalls," *European Integration Online Papers* 14 [online] available at: http://eiop.or.at/eiop/index.php/eiop/article/view/2010_009a (last accessed: May 5, 2013).
McColl, J. (2009) "EUFOR ALTHEA: Successful Contribution to Stability," *Impetus: Bulletin of the EU Military Staff* 7: 21–23.
McNamara, K. (2002) "Rational Fictions: Central Bank Independence and the Social Logic of Delegation," *West European Politics* 25(1): 47–76.
Mérand, F. (2008) *European Defence Policy: Beyond the Nation State*, Oxford: Oxford University Press.
Mérand, F., S. Hofmann, and B. Irondelle (2010) "Transgovernmental Networks in the European Security and Defense Policy," *European Integration Online Papers* 14 [online] available at: http://eiop.or.at/eiop/index.php/eiop/article/view/2010_005a (last accessed: May 5, 2013).
Mérand, F., S. Hofmann, and B. Irondelle (2011) "Governance and State Power: A Network Analysis of European Security," *Journal of Common Market Studies* 49(1): 121–147.

Merikallio, K. (2008) *Making Peace: Ahtisaari and Aceh*, Helsinki: WSOY.
Merlingen, M. (2009) "EU Police Mission," in G. Grevi, D. Helly, and D. Keohane (eds), *ESDP: The First 10 Years (1999–2009)*, Paris: EU Institute for Security Studies.
Merlingen, M. and R. Ostrauskaitė (eds) (2008) *European Security and Defence Policy: An Implementation Perspective*, London: Routledge.
Meunier, S. and K. Nicolaïdes (1999) "Who Speaks for Europe? The Delegation of Trade Authority in the EU," *Journal of Common Market Studies* 37(3): 477–501.
Miller, G. (2005) "The Political Evolution of Principal–Agent Models," *Annual Review of Political Science* 8: 203–225.
Milner, H. and A. Moravcsik (eds) (2009) *Power, Interdependence, and Nonstate Actors in World Politics*, Princeton: Princeton University Press.
Milward, A. (1984) *The Reconstruction of Western Europe, 1945–51*, London: Routledge.
Milward, A. (1992) *The European Rescue of the Nation-State*, London: Routledge.
Miskimmon, A. (2007) *Germany and EU Foreign Policy: Between Europeanization and National Adaptation*, Basingstoke: Palgrave Macmillan.
Missiroli, A. (2003) "From Copenhagen to Brussels: European Defence Core Documents," *Chaillot Paper* 67, Paris: EU Institute for Security Studies.
Moe, T. (1984) "The New Economics of Organization," *American Journal of Political Science* 28(4): 739–777.
Moe, T. (1990) "Political Institutions: The Neglected Side of the Story," *Journal of Law, Economics and Organization* 6: 213–253.
Moravcsik, A. (1991) "Negotiating the Single European Act: National Interests and Conventional Statecraft in the European Community," *International Organization* 45(1): 19–56.
Moravcsik, A. (1993) "Preferences and Power in the European Community: A Liberal Intergovernmentalist Approach," *Journal of Common Market Studies* 31(4): 473–524.
Moravcsik, A. (1998) *The Choice for Europe: Social Purpose and State Power from Messina to Maastricht*, Ithaca: Cornell University Press.
Moravcsik, A. (1999) "A New Statecraft? Supranational Entrepreneurs and International Cooperation," *International Organization* 53(2): 267–306.
Moravcsik, A. (2005) "The European Constitutional Compromise and the Neo-functionalist Legacy," *Journal of European Public Policy* 12(2): 349–386.
Moravcsik, A. and K. Nicolaides (1999) "Explaining the Amsterdam Treaty: Interests, Infuence, Institutions," *Journal of Common Market Studies* 37(1): 59–85.
Müller, W. and K. Strøm (1999) *Policy, Office, or Votes?: How Political Parties in Western Europe Make Hard Decisions*, Cambridge: Cambridge University Press.
Myint-U, T. and A. Scott (2007) *The UN Secretariat: A Brief History (1945–2006)*, New York: International Peace Academy.
NATO (2003) *Final Communiqué of Meeting of the North Atlantic Council in Defence Ministers Session*, 1 December, Brussels: NATO.
NATO (2008) *EU Operations Headquarters (OHQ) at SHAPE, Mons/Belgium* [Online] available at: http://www.nato.int/shape/issues/shape_eu/shape.htm (last accessed: November 26, 2009).
Nielsen, D. and M. Tierney (2003) "Delegation to International Organizations: Agency Theory and World Bank Environmental Reform," *International Organization* 57(2): 241–276.

Niemann, A. (2006) *Explaining Decisions in the European Union*, Cambridge: Cambridge University Press.

Niksanen, W. (1968) "The Peculiar Economics of Bureaucracy," *American Economic Review* 58(2): 293–305.

Nur Djuli, M. and N. Abdul Rahman (2008) "The Helsinki Negotiations: A Perspective from Free Aceh Movement Negotiators," in Aguswandi and J. Large (eds), *Reconfiguring Politics: The Indonesia – Aceh Peace Process* [online] available at: http://www.c-r.org/our-work/accord/aceh/helsinki-negotiations.php (last accessed: April 23, 2009).

Nuttall, S. (1992) *European Political Cooperation*, Oxford: Clarendon Press.

Nuttall, S. (1997) "The Commission and Foreign Policy-Making," in G. Edwards and D. Spence (eds), *The European Commission*, London: Cartermill International.

Nuttall, S. (2000) *European Foreign Policy*, Oxford: Oxford University Press.

Oestreich, J. (ed.) (2012) *International Organizations as Self-Directed Actors: A Framework for Analysis*, London: Routledge.

Offe, C. (2006) "Political Institutions and Social Power: Conceptual Explorations," In I. Shapiro, S. Skowronek, and D. Galvin (eds), *Rethinking Political Institutions: The Art of the State*, New York: New York University Press.

Olsen, J. (2010) *Governing through Institution Building: Institutional Theory and Recent European Experiments in Democratic Organization*, Oxford: Oxford University Press.

Oxfam (2008) "Mission Incomplete: Why Civilians Remain at Risk in Eastern Chad," *Briefing Paper* 119, Oxford: Oxfam.

Panke, D. (2010) "Developing Good Instructions in No Time – An Impossibility? Comparing Domestic Coordination Practices for EU Policies of 19 Small States," *West European Politics*, 33(4): 769–789.

Parsons, C. (2002) Showing Ideas as Causes: The Origins of the European Union, *International Organization* 56(1): 47–84.

Patten, C. (2005) *Not Quite the Diplomat: Home Truths about World Affairs*, London: Allen Lane.

Perritt, H. (2010) *The Road to Independence for Kosovo: A Chronicle of the Ahtisaari Plan*, Cambridge: Cambridge University Press.

Peters, D. (2010) *Constrained Balancing: The EU's Security Policy*, Basingstoke: Palgrave Macmillan.

Peters, G. (1992) "Bureaucratic politics and the institutions of the European Community," in A. Sbragia (ed.), *Euro-Politics: Institutions and Policymaking in the New European Community*, Washington, D.C.: Brookings Institution.

Peters, G. (2001) "Agenda-setting in the European Union," in J. Richardson (ed.), *European Union: Power and Policy-Making*, London: Routledge.

Peterson, J. (1995) "Decision-Making in the European Union: Toward a Framework for Analysis," *Journal of European Public Policy* 2(1): 69–93.

Pierson, P. (1996) "The Path to European Integration: A Historical Institutionalist Analysis," *Comparative Political Studies* 29(2): 123–163.

Pierson, P. (2004) *Politics in Time: History, Institutions and Social Analysis*, Princeton: Princeton University Press.

Pohl, B. (2009) "Why ALTHEA?" Paper presented during the Conference of the Netherlands Institute of Government, Leiden, The Netherlands, 12–13 December.

Pollack, M. (1997) "Delegation, Agency, and Agenda-Setting in the European Community," *International Organization* 51(1): 99–134.

Pollack, M. (2003) *The Engines of European Integration: Agency, Delegation, and Agenda Setting in the EU*, Oxford: Oxford University Press.
Pollack, M. (2005) "Rational Choice and EU Politics," in K. Jørgensen, M. Pollack, and B. Rosamond (eds), *Handbook of European Union Politics*, London: Sage.
Pond, E. (2008) "The EU's Test in Kosovo," *The Washington Quarterly* 31(4): 97–112.
Pratt, J. and R. Zeckhauser (eds) (1985) *Principals and Agents: The Structure of Business*, Cambridge: Harvard Business School Press.
Presidency Conclusions (2003) *Conclusions on the General Affairs and External Relations Council*, 24 February, Brussels: Council of the European Union.
Presidency Conclusions (2004) *Conclusions on the General Affairs and External Relations Council*, 23 February, Brussels: Council of the European Union.
Princen, S. (2007) "Agenda-Setting in the European Union: A Theoretical Exploration and Agenda for Research," *Journal of European Public Policy* 14(1): 21–38.
Princen, S. and M. Rhinard (2006) "Crashing and Creeping: Agenda-Setting Dynamics in the European Union," *Journal of European Public Policy* 13(7): 1119–1132.
Regelsberger, E. (2011) "The High Representative for the Common Foreign and Security Policy – Treaty Provisions in Theory and Practice 1999–2009," in G. Mueller-Brandeck-Bocquet and C. Rueger (eds), *The High Representative for the EU Foreign and Security Policy: Review and Prospects*, Baden-Baden: Nomos.
Reichard, M. (2006) *The EU-NATO Relationship: A Legal and Political Perspective*, Aldershot: Ashgate.
Reuters (2009) *Kosovo Serb policemen return to work*, 30 June [online] available at: http://uk.reuters.com/article/2009/06/30/idUKBYT059184 (last accessed: May 5, 2013).
Rhodes, R., I. Bache, and S. George (1996) "Policy networks and policy-making in the European Union: A critical appraisal," in L. Hooghe (ed.), *Cohesion Policy and European Integration: Building Multi-Level Governance*, Oxford: Clarendon Press.
Riker, W. (1980) "Implications from the Disequilibrium of Majority Rule in the Study of Institutions," *American Political Science Review* 74(2): 432–446.
Risse, T. (2000) "Let's Argue!": Communicative Action in World Politics', *International Organization* 54(1): 1–39.
Rittberger, B. (2003) "The Creation and Empowerment of the European Parliament," *Journal of Common Market Studies* 41(2): 203–225.
Robertson, G., G. Papandreou, and J. Solana (2003) *"Press Conference Following the NATO-EU Meeting in Madrid,"* 3 June [online] available at: http://www.nato.int/docu/speech/2003/s030603i.htm (last accessed: October 26, 2009).
Rosamond, B. (2005) "The Uniting of Europe and the Foundation of EU Studies: Revisiting the Neofunctionalism of Ernst B. Haas," *Journal of European Public Policy* 12(2): 237–254.
Rosenau, J. (1997) *Along the Domestic-Foreign Frontier: Exploring Governance in a Turbulent World*, Cambridge: Cambridge University Press.
Ross, G. (1995) *Jacques Delors and European Integration*, Oxford: Oxford University Press.
Ruggie, J. (1992) "Multilateralism: The Anatomy of an Institution," *International Organization* 46(3): 561–598.

Rutten, M. (2001) "From St-Malo to Nice: European Defence Core Documents," *Chaillot Paper* 47, Paris: EU Institute for Security Studies.
Rutten, M. (2002) "From Nice to Laeken: European Defence Core Documents," *Chaillot Paper* 51, Paris: EU Institute for Security Studies.
Sandford, R. (1996) "International Environmental Treaty Secretariats: A Case of Neglected Potential?" *Environmental Impact Assessment Review* 16(1): 3–12.
Sandholtz, W. and J. Zysman (1989) "1992: Recasting the European Bargain," *World Politics* 42(1): 95–128.
Scharpf, F. (1988) "The Joint-Decision Trap: Lessons from German Federalism and European Integration," *Public Administration* 66(3): 239–278.
Schmitter, P. (2004) "Neo-neofunctionalism," in A. Wiener and T. Diez (eds), *European Integration Theory*, Oxford: Oxford University Press.
Schimmelfennig, F. (2001) "The Community Trap: Liberal Norms, Rhetorical Action, and the Eastern Enlargement of the European Union," *International Organization* 55(1): 57–80.
Schout, A. and S. Vanhoonacker (2006) "Evaluating Presidencies of the Council of the EU: Revisiting Nice," *Journal of Common Market Studies* 44(5): 1051–1077.
Schulze, K. (2007) "Mission Not So Impossible: The AMM and the Transition from Conflict to Peace in Aceh (2005–2006)," *RSIS Working Papers* 131, Singapore: S. Rajaratnam School of International Studies.
Seibert, B. (2007) "African Adventure? Assessing the European Union's Military Intervention in Chad and the Central African Republic," *MIT Security Studies Programme Working Paper*, Cambridge: M.I.T. Security Studies Program.
Seibert, B. (2010) "Operation EUFOR Tchad/RCA and the European Union's Common Security and Defence Policy," *Strategic Studies Institute Monograph*, Carlisle: US Army War College.
Shepsle, K. and B. Weingast (1984) "Uncovered Sets and Sophisticated Voting Outcomes with Implications for Agenda Institutions," *American Journal of Political Science* 28(1): 49–74.
Shepsle, K. and B. Weingast (1995) *Positive Theories of Congressional Institutions*, Ann Arbor: University of Michigan Press.
Simon, H. (1987) "Bounded Rationality," in J. Eatwell, M. Milgate, and P. Newman (eds), The New Palgrave, New York: W.W. Norton.
Simon, L. and A. Mattelaer (2011) "EUnity of Command: The Planning and Conduct of CSDP Operations," *Egmont Paper* 41, Brussels: Egmont Institute.
Smith, M.E. (2004) *Europe's Foreign and Security Policy: The Institutionalization of Cooperation*, Cambridge: Cambridge University Press.
Solana, J. (2004a) *Summary of the Report by Javier Solana, EU High Representative for CFSP, on a Possible EU Deployment in BiH Presented to the EU Council of Foreign Ministers*, 23 February [online] available at: http://www.ohr.int/other-doc/eu-stmnt/default.asp?content_id=31930 (last accessed: October 27, 2009).
Solana, J. (2004b) *Summary of remarks by Javier SOLANA, EU High Representative for the CFSP, during his visit to Sarajevo, Bosnia and Herzegovina*, 15 July.
Solana, J. and O. Rehn (2005) *Summary note on the joint report on the future EU role and contribution in Kosovo*, 9 December.
Spence, M. and R. Zeckhauser (1971) "Insurance, Information, and Individual Action," *American Economic Review* 61(2): 380–387.
Spence, D. (2006a) "The Commission's External Service," in D. Spence and G. Edwards (eds), *The European Commission*, London: John Harper.

Spence, D. (2006b) "The Commission and the Common Foreign and Security Policy," in D. Spence and G. Edwards (eds), *The European Commission*, London: John Harper.

Stetter, S. (2004) "Cross-Pillar Politics: Functional Unity and Institutional Fragmentation of EU Foreign Policies," *Journal of European Public Policy* 11(4): 720–739.

Stone, R. (2009) "Institutions, Power, and Interdependence," in Milner, H. and A. Moravcsik (eds), *Power, Interdependence, and Nonstate Actors in World Politics*, Princeton: Princeton University Press.

Strøm, K. (1990) "A Behavioral Theory of Competitive Political Parties," *American Journal of Political Science* 34(2): 565–598.

Tallberg, J. (2000) "The Anatomy of Autonomy: An Institutional Account of Variation in Supranational Influence," *Journal of Common Market Studies* 38(5): 843–64.

Tallberg, J. (2002a) "Delegation to Supranational Institutions: Why, How, and with What Consequences?" *West European Politics* 25(1): 23–46.

Tallberg, J. (2002b) "Paths to Compliance: Enforcement, Management, and the European Union," *International Organization* 56(3): 609–643.

Tallberg, J. (2003) "The Agenda-Shaping Powers of the EU Council Presidency," *Journal of European Public Policy* 10(1): 1–19.

Tallberg, J. (2004) "The Power of the Presidency: Brokerage, Efficiency and Distribution in EU Negotiations," *Journal of Common Market Studies* 42(5): 999–1022.

Tallberg, J. (2006) *Leadership and Negotiation in the European Union*, Cambridge: Cambridge University Press.

Taylor, P. (1990) "Regionalism and Functionalism Reconsidered," in P. Taylor and A. Groom (eds), *Frameworks for International Cooperation*, London: Pinder.

Thatcher, M. (1993) *The Downing Street Years*, London: Harper Collins Publishers.

Thatcher, M. and A. Stone Sweet (2002) "Theory and Practice of Delegation to Non-Majoritarian Institutions," *West European Politics* 25(1): 1–22.

The Independent (2008) Chad President under siege as fighting rages, 4 February.

Tranholm-Mikkelsen, J. (1991) "Neo-functionalism: Obstinate or Obsolete? A Reappraisal in the Light of the New Dynamism of the EC," *Millennium* 20(1): 1–22.

Trondal, J. (2006) "Governing at the Frontier of the European Commission. The Case of Seconded National Experts," *West European Politics* 29(1): 147–160.

Trondal, J. (2007) "Is the European Commission a 'Hothouse' for Supranationalism? Exploring Actor-Level Supranationalism," *Journal of Common Market Studies* 45(5): 1111–1133.

Trondal, J. (2008) "The Anatomy of Autonomy: Reassessing the Autonomy of the European Commission," *European Journal of Political Research* 47(4): 467–488.

Tsebelis, G. (1995) "Decision Making in Political Systems: Veto Players in Presidentialism, Parliamentarism, Multicameralism and Multipartyism," *British Journal of Political Science* 25(3): 289–325.

Tsebelis, G. (2002) *Veto Players: How Political Institutions Work*, Princeton: Princeton University Press.

United Nations (2004) *Report of the Secretary-General on the United Nations Interim Administration Mission in Kosovo*, S/2004/348, 29 April.

United Nations (2007a) *Report of the Secretary-General on Chad and the Central African Republic*, S/2007/488, 10 August.
United Nations (2007b) *Report of the Secretary-General on Chad and the Central African Republic*, S/2007/739, 17 December.
United Nations (2008a) *Report of the Secretary-General on Chad and the Central African Republic*, S/2008/760, 4 December.
United Nations (2008b) *Report of the Secretary-General on Chad and the Central African Republic*, S/2008/601, 12 September.
United Nations (2008c) *Transcript of 6042nd Meeting of the UN Security Council*, 12 December.
United Nations (2008d) *Report of the Secretary-General on the United Nations Interim Administration Mission in Kosovo*, S/2008/354, 12 June.
United Nations (2009) *Report of the Secretary-General on Chad and the Central African Republic*, S/2009/199, 14 April.
UNOSEK (2006) *Press Briefing by UN Deputy Special Envoy for the Future Status Process for Kosovo Albert Rohan in Pristina*, 16 May.
Van den Bos, B. (2008) *Mirakel en Debacle: De Nederlandse besluitvorming over de Politieke Unie in het Verdrag van Maastricht*, Assen: Van Gorcum.
Vanhoonacker, S. and A. Jacobs (2010) "ESDP and Institutional Change: The Case of Belgium," *Security Dialogue* 41(5): 559–581.
Wagner, W. (2003) "Why the EU's Common Foreign and Security Policy Will Remain Intergovernmental: A Rationalist Institutionalist Choice Analysis of European Crisis Management Policy," *Journal of European Public Policy* 10(4): 576–595.
Wall, J. and A. Lynn (1993) "Mediation: A Current Review," *Journal of Conflict Resolution* 37(1): 160–194.
Wall, S. (2008) *A Stranger in Europe: Britain and the EU from Thatcher to Blair*, Oxford: Oxford University Press.
Waltz, K. (1979) *Theory of International Politics*, New York: McGraw-Hill.
Waterman, R. and K. Meier (1998) "Principal-Agent Models: An Expansion?" *Journal of Public Administration Research and Theory* 8(2): 173–202.
Weiss, M. (2011) *Transaction Costs and Security Institutions: Unravelling the ESDP*, Basingstoke: Palgrave Macmillan.
Weller, M. (2008) "Negotiating the Final Status of Kosovo," *Chaillot Paper* 114, Paris: EU Institute for Security Studies.
Williamson, O. (1985) *The Economic Institutions of Capitalism: Firms, Markets, Relations, Contracting*, New York: The Free Press.
Woodbridge, J. (2002) "Ready and Willing to Take Charge in the Balkans?" *European Security Review* 14: 3–4.
Young, O. (1986) "International Regimes: Towards a New Theory of Institutions," *World Politics* 39(1): 104–122.

Index

Aceh 124–44
  Law on the Governing of Aceh 140
  Memorandum of Understanding 1, 125, 131, 134–7
  negotiations 126–31
  tsunami 125–6
Aceh Monitoring Mission 1, 92, 97, 124–44
  agenda-setting 125–31
  Commission on Security Arrangements 137, 141
  Concept of Operations 133
  Crisis Management Concept 131
  implementation 133–41
  Interim Monitoring Presence 131, 133–5
  Joint Action 133
advance planning 80
Afghanistan
  Soviet invasion 48–9
  police mission 12, 70, 92, 177
  NATO operation, *see* NATO
agency 34–45, 195–9
  hidden action 45
  opportunities 43–5
agenda-setting 43–4, 191, 197
CSDP 78–82, 98
agent preferences, *see* goal conflict
agent selection 11, 33, 42, 55, 56–7, 59, 73–6, 195
Ahtisaari, Martti 124–30, 132, 138, 142, 168, 170, 173, 178, 187
Albright, Madelaine 64
alternative explanations 5–9, 76–7, 191, 199–202
Annan, Kofi 168
Ashdown, Paddy 101, 115
Ashton, Catherine 66
Association of Southeast Asian Nations (ASEAN) 127, 135–6, 138
Athena mechanism 154

Ban Ki-moon 163, 180
Barroso, José Manuel 126
Belgium 48, 65, 103
Bildt, Carl 156
Blair, Tony 57, 65
Bosnia-Herzegovina 95, 100–23
  Dayton agreement 105, 108, 113–14, 118
  war criminals 93, 109
bounded rationality 21–3, 26
Bout de Marnhac, Xavier 93
bureaucratic politics 36, 56–7, 59, 83

CFSP budget 70, 132–3, 177–8, 180
China 146–7
Chirac, Jacques 57, 61–2, 65
Civilian Planning and Conduct Capability (CPCC) 2, 70–1, 85–6, 91–2, 175, 184–5
Cold War, end of 51–2, 77
command and control 30, 63–7, 109, 184–5
Common Foreign and Security Policy (CFSP) 53
Committee for the Civilian Aspect of Crisis Management (CIVCOM) 12–13, 67–8, 83–4, 86, 94, 175–6, 184–5, 198–9
comprehensive approach 106, 151–2
Concept of Operations (CONOPS) 87, 89–91
Congo, Democratic Republic of 85, 95
  Operation Artemis 103
  EUFOR 66, 97
control mechanisms 40–3
  re-contracting 11, 21–2, 41, 73–4
  sanctions 41
  shadow bureaucracies 39, 42
constructivism 8–9, 76, 191, 199–202
COREPER 53, 67, 87, 155
Correspondance européenne (COREU) 48, 126, 147

Council of Ministers 85–6, 131, 147, 150, 152, 154–5, 158, 169
 Council Decision 86–7, 89, 91, 96
 Council Secretariat 2, 58–9, 62, 71, 79, 108, 151, 153
   CFSP unit 54
   Directorate for Defense Issues 63–4, 67, 147
   Directorate for Civilian Crisis Management 68, 85, 173
   Directorate-General for External Relations 59
   Policy Unit 56–7, 58–9
credible commitments 28–9, 30–1, 192, 195
Crisis Management Concept 83–5
Crisis Management Initiative 125–9
Crisis Management Planning Directorate (CMPD) 2, 80, 82–3, 85
Crisis Management Procedures 98
Crisis Response Coordination Team (CRCT) 108, 151
crisis response planning 82
Cyprus 88, 207

Darfur 145–50
Déby, Idriss 146–8, 159, 162
decision-making 44
   Aceh Monitoring Mission 131–3
   CSDP 82–7, 98
   EUFOR Tchad/RCA 150–5
   EULEX Kosovo 172–9
   Operation Althea 104–12
de Hoop Scheffer, Jaap 112
de Kermabon, Yves 93, 175
delegation 20–33, 74–6, 191–5
   non-delegation 11, 32–3, 55, 66–7, 74–6, 191–2, 194–5
   process 10, 21–2, 194
Delors, Jacques 51–2
Disarmament, Demobilization, and Reintegration 136–7
doctrine 12, 84, 198
Dooge Report 50

efficiency gains 10–11, 74–6, 191–2, 194
enablers 89, 157–8, 160

enlargement 52, 59
European Commission 49–52, 53–5, 59, 68, 71, 73–4, 79–80, 83, 92, 95
   Aceh Monitoring Mission 131–2, 138, 141–2
   Commissioner for External Relations 54, 73
   Directorate-General for Development and Cooperation 73, 80
   Directorate-General for Enlargement 80, 178, 187
   Directorate-General for External Relations 54, 127, 138
   EUFOR Tchad/RCA 151–2, 158, 161
   EULEX Kosovo 177–8, 181, 185–7
   EuropeAid 138
   Foreign Policy Instruments 87
   Humanitarian Aid and Civil Protection (ECHO) 80
   Operation Althea 107–8
   Rapid Reaction Mechanism 127
European Council 65, 102, 179
   Cologne 60
   Göteborg 69
   Hampton Court 70, 133, 170, 177
   Helsinki 61–2
   London 49
   Milan 50–1
   Nice 64, 68
   Rome 52–3
   Thessaloniki 101, 170
   Vienna 60
European Defence Community 47
European External Action Service 2, 71–4, 80–2, 94, 96–7
   Corporate Board 80
   Crisis Platform 83
   Organizational chart 81
   Regional Directorates 80
   Union Delegation 71, 95
European Parliament 9, 50, 132, 177, 200
European Political Cooperation
   EPC Secretariat 51
   Copenhagen Report 48
   London Report 49
   Luxembourg Report 47–8
   Troika Secretariat 49

European Union Force Tchad/RCA
  89–90, 145–66
 agenda-setting 146–50
 Concept of Operations 157–8
 Crisis Management Concept 148, 152, 154
 implementation 155–64
 Joint Action 154–5
 joint options paper 148
 Mid-Mandate Review 153, 161–2
 Operations Plan 148, 158
 Strategic Military Options 154–5, 157
European Union Military Committee (EUMC) 12–13, 62–4, 83–4, 86, 89, 94, 161, 198
European Union Military Staff (EUMS) 2, 62–7, 85–6, 88–91, 154–5
European Union Rule of Law Mission in Kosovo (EULEX) 12, 67, 70, 92–3, 96, 167–89
 agenda-setting 168–72
 Concept of Operations 175, 179
 Crisis Management Concept 175
 implementation 179–87
 Joint Action 172, 175, 179
 Operations Plan 175, 179
 Planning Team 92, 172–4, 177–80
 status neutral 172
 Strategic Options 174–5
European Union Police Mission (EUPM) 2, 69, 95, 101, 117
European Union Special Representative (EUSR) 58, 59, 95, 101, 107–8, 117
expert bureaucracy 25–6, 30, 33, 35, 56–7

fact-finding mission 82–3
 Aceh 130, 134
 Bosnia-Herzegovina 90
 composition 82–3
 EUFOR Tchad/RCA 152
 EULEX Kosovo 172
feedback loops 21
Feith, Pieter 93, 111, 124, 129–30, 133–4, 137–8, 140, 142–4, 176–7, 179
Ferrero-Waldner, Benita 59, 127

Finland 126, 129, 132–3, 135
Fischer, Joschka 126
Force Commander 86, 90–4, 161
Force Headquarters 90–1, 93, 157, 159, 175
force generation 89–90, 113, 156
Fouchet Plans 47–8
France 48, 50–1, 60, 65–6, 102, 110, 118, 133, 147, 150, 153–4, 156, 164–5
Free Aceh Movement (GAM) 1, 125–30, 133–7, 142
Full Operational Capability (FOC) 91, 161, 182

Ganascia, Jean Philippe 93, 152, 160
Gerakan Aceh Merdeka (GAM), *see* Free Aceh Movement
Germany 65–6, 97, 118, 150
 reunification 51
Georgia 69
 monitoring mission 12, 92
goal conflict 34–6
 competence-maximizing 34–6
 policy-seeking 35–6

Head of Mission 87, 91–3, 132, 184–5
High Representative for the CFSP 57–8, 79–80
High Representative of the Union for Foreign and Security Policy 71–3, 78–80
historical institutionalism 9
Horn of Africa 66, 89

implementation 29–31
 CSDP 92–9
incomplete contracting 28–9
Indonesia 1, 97, 125–30, 136–7, 139–40
influence, definition 14–15
information
 hidden information 44–5
 information asymmetry 39–40, 44–5
 information-gathering 27, 39
 information-processing 27, 39–40
Initial Operational Capability (IOC) 91, 182

Initiating Military Directive (IMD)   89
Intelligence Centre (INTCEN)   2
intergovernmentalism   6–7
Intergovernmental Conference   51, 52, 55–8
international bureaucracies   4
International Criminal Tribunal for former Yugoslavia (ICTY)   109, 115
Iraq, intervention in   65

Jessen-Petersen, Søren   169, 187
Joint Action   86
Joint Operations Centre (SITCEN)   63

Kohl, Helmut   51, 52
Kosovo   105, 167–89
  2004 riots   168–9
  Declaration of Independence   178
  International Civilian Representative   137, 178
  standards before status   168
  war   58, 60, 168
Kouchner, Bernard   146–8, 162

Laeken Declaration   65, 71, 194
Leakey, David   93, 112–17, 122, 152, 158
learning   8–9
Lehne, Stefan   169, 187
Le Touquet summit   103, 106
legitimacy   8
logic of appropriateness   8, 201

Macedonia
  Operation Concordia   102
  Police Mission   69
Major, John   57
methodology   13–16, 46–7
  case studies   14–16
  interviews   14, 15
  process-tracing   13–14
Michel, Louis   126
Mitterrand, François   50, 52

Nash, Pat   93–4, 156–7, 161
North Atlantic Treaty Organization (NATO)   60–1, 64–6, 85, 100–2, 105–6, 111, 120, 200–1

Afghanistan operation (ISAF)   117–18, 150
Allied Forces Southern Europe   110–11
Berlin Plus agreement   88, 100–2, 109
EU-NATO relations in Bosnia-Herzegovina   108–11, 120
Deputy Supreme Allied Commander Europe (DSACEUR)   88, 93, 110
Implementation Force (IFOR)   100–1
Kosovo Force (KFOR)   110, 168–9, 183
over the horizon forces   110, 118
Stabilization Force (SFOR)   100–1, 103, 105–6, 112–14, 121–2
Supreme Headquarters Allied Powers Europe (SHAPE)   88, 93, 112–13
neofunctionalism   5–6
non-compliance   28

Office of the High Representative   101, 105–6
  Bonn-powers   105
  closure   119
  Mission Implementation Plan   106–8, 114–15
Peace Implementation Council   101
Oksanen, Jaakko   129–30, 133
Operation Althea   95, 97, 100–23, 151
  agenda-setting   101–3
  Concept of Operations   118–19
  Crisis Management Concept   107–8
  fight against organized crime   107–8, 115–16
  implementation   112–20
  Joint Action   107–8, 111–12
  Liaison and Observation Teams   114, 118, 120
  Operation Plan   114, 118
  Operations Commander   63–4, 86, 89–90, 93–4, 96–8, 110, 118, 155–7, 161
  Civilian Operations Commander   86, 93, 175–6, 184–5

Operations Headquarters (OHQ) 63–7, 85–91, 93–4, 97, 103, 155, 158, 175
  chocolate summit 65, 103
  civil-military cell 65–6, 131
  Operations Centre 66–7, 85, 88–9
Operations Plan (OPLAN) 90–1
Organization for Security and Cooperation in Europe (OSCE) 96, 133, 168–9, 178

Patten, Chris 59
Poland 66
Political Advisor (POLAD) 89–90, 94
Political Committee 48, 62
Political and Security Committee (PSC) 62, 82, 84, 86, 94, 130–2, 140–1, 147, 155, 158, 161, 177, 185
Political-Military Group (PMG) 83, 198
Presidency, rotating 3, 48
  Ireland 57
  Italy 50–1
  Finland 61
  France 64, 68
  Germany 60–1, 148
  Luxembourg 53
  Portugal 67, 148
  Sweden 68–9
  The Netherlands 53
  United Kingdom 131
principal-agent model 7–8, 9–13, 20–45, 191
  multiple principals 21–2, 32, 192
problem-solving 9
Provisional Statement of Requirements (PSOR) 89–90, 157

rational choice institutionalism 7–8, 9–13, 20–45
Rehn, Olli 80, 170–1, 173, 187–8
Reinhartshausen 61
RELEX Counselors 87, 154–5
representation, external 30, 59
research question 3–5, 190–1

resources, bureaucratic 11–13, 36–40
  content expertise 12–13, 39–40, 191, 197–8
  continuity 37
  formal competences 11
  institutional memory 37
  networks 38–9
  position in policy-making 11–12, 38, 44, 191, 197
  process expertise 38
  time 12, 40
Robertson, George 103
rules of engagement 90
Russia 119, 178, 181

sanctions, economic 50
Sarkozy, Nicolas 146–7, 159
Security Sector Reform 16, 80, 92, 125
Serbia 178
Single European Act 49–52
Solana, Javier 58, 79–80, 101–3, 106–8, 111–13, 120–3, 127, 129, 132, 140–4, 162, 169–71, 173, 187–9, 200
Solemn Declaration 49–50
sovereignty 3–4
sovereignty costs 10–11, 31–3, 54–5, 74–6, 191–2, 194
  definition 31
  excessive 32, 198–9
Spinelli, Altiero 50
St Malo summit 2, 60
Stabilisation and Association Process 108, 186–7
Status of Forces Agreement (SOFA) 91, 97, 164, 179
standard operating procedures 42, 84, 198
Strategic Options 85–7, 89
  Civilian/Police Strategic Options 85–6
  Military Strategic Options 85
Sudan 146, 148
Sweden 133, 135, 156

Thatcher, Margaret 52
The Netherlands 48, 133

transaction costs 22–3, 55, 74–6, 192
  administrative costs 24–5
  agenda management 23–4, 35
  brokerage 24, 35, 44
  coordination costs 26–7
  ex ante 23–7
  ex post 28–31
  implementation costs 29–30
  information costs 24–6, 59
  negotiation costs 23–5
Treaty of Amsterdam 55–9, 79
  Reflection Group 56–7
Treaty of Lisbon 71–4, 78–9
  Constitutional Treaty 72–3
  Convention 71–2
Treaty of Maastricht 52–5
  Commission proposal 52, 53
Turkey 88

uncertainty 11, 21, 32, 191
unintended consequences 11, 21, 192
United Kingdom 50–1, 60, 102, 117–18, 150, 154
United Nations (UN) 97, 145, 152, 162–4
  AU-UN Mission in Darfur (UNAMID) 146
  chapter VII 106, 109, 120
  Department of Peacekeeping Operations (DPKO) 146, 163, 178
  Mission in Bosnia-Herzegovina (UNMIBH) 101
  Mission in the Central African Republic and Chad (MINURCAT) 145–6, 151–4, 156, 160–4
  Mission in Kosovo (UNMIK) 168–9, 179–82, 188
  Secretary-General 178, 180
  Security Council 147–8, 153, 162, 168, 170, 178, 180, 182
  Special Representative of the Secretary-General (SRSG) 168–9
  Protection Force (UNPROFOR) 102, 105
  UNSCR 1244 168, 173, 179
  UNSCR 1551 106, 111
  UNSCR 1575 113
  UNSCR 1778 152–3, 163
  UNSCR 1834 162
  UNSCR 1861 163
United States 61, 77, 101–6, 109, 118

van den Broek, Hans 102
Verhofstadt, Guy 64–5

Western Balkans 85, 95, 101, 170
  Contact Group 169, 178–9
  Quint 169
  war 53, 55–6
Western European Union 64

Yugoslavia, former, *see* Western Balkans

Printed and bound by CPI Group (UK) Ltd, Croydon, CR0 4YY